16.95

Business Decision Making
with Multiplan

A Multiplan Business User's Guide

Business Decision Making
with Multiplan

William R. Osgood ▪ James F. Molloy, Jr.

Multiplan adaptation by Michel Selva

Curtin & London, Inc.   Somerville, Massachusetts

Van Nostrand Reinhold Company   New York Cincinnati Toronto Melbourne

Printed in the United States of America

Published in 1984 by Curtin & London, Inc.
and Van Nostrand Reinhold Company
135 West 50th Street, New York, NY 10020, U.S.A.

Macmillan of Canada
Division of Gage Publishing Limited
164 Commander Boulevard
Agincourt, Ontario M1S 3C7, Canada

52788

Van Nostrand Reinhold Pty. Ltd.
480 Latrobe Street
Melbourne, Victoria 3000, Australia

Multiplan is a trademark of Microsoft Corporation, Bellevue, Washington

Concept development: Dennis P. Curtin
Editor: Katherine Carlone
Managing editor: Nancy Benjamin
Production editor: Geoffrey Mandel

Interior design and cover design: Susan Marsh
Illustrations: Elisa Tanaka
Composition: York Graphic Services
Printing and binding: Halliday Lithograph

10 9 8 7 6 5 4 3 2 1

Library of Congress Cataloging in Publication Data

Osgood, William R.
  Business decision making for higher profits.

  Includes index.
  1. Multiplan (Computer program) 2. Business—Data processing.
I. Molloy, James F. II. Selva, Michel. III. Title.
HF5548.4.M74O84 1984 658.4'03'0285425 84-9425
ISBN 0-930764-90-0

Disclaimer

This Multiplan Business User's Guide and accompanying magnetic disk are designed to help you improve your business judgment. However, the authors (and publishers) assume no responsibility whatsoever for the uses made of this material or for decisions based on its use, and make no warranties, either express or implied, regarding the contents of this book or any accompanying magnetic disks, its merchantability, or its fitness for any particular purpose.

Neither the publishers nor anyone else who has been involved in the creation, production, or delivery of this product shall be liable for any direct, incidental or consequential damages, such as, but not limited to, loss of anticipated profits or benefits resulting from its use or from any breach of any warranty. Some states do not allow the exclusion or limitation of direct, incidental or consequential damages, so the above limitation may not apply to you.

Contents

Tips

Preface

Making effective decisions within any business is difficult under even the best of circumstances. Unfortunately, all too often the actual conditions are less than the best, and so the problem is further compounded. Of course, the other side of this dilemma is that business success is directly correlated with effective decision making. Accordingly, the path to business success is paved with good decisions and almost any business operation can be improved, often substantially, by improving the quality of the decision-making process.

Good decision making, in large part, requires the consideration of fairly large amounts of data and the evaluation of a range of alternatives. Managing this quantity of data seems to be such a complex task that all too often it is not performed. Also, for any problem, there is generally more than one solution. It is important to inspect each of these alternative strategies and try to anticipate the impact of each on future operations. This is a difficult feat as well, typically involving tedious and complicated iterations and forecasts. Very simply, the great majority of business decision makers, particularly in smaller ventures, have neither the skills nor the time needed for these activities.

On the more positive side, there is a methodology you can use to improve the effectiveness of the decisions you must make in running your own business. It is our purpose in this book to show you this methodology in a step-by-step process that you can apply to your own operation. We are (and you can be) aided greatly in this task by the microcomputer and a software program, such as the Multiplan program from Microsoft Corporation. A personal business computer can plow through the complicated and time-consuming analytical activities quickly and easily. In fact, with the help of the computer, we can inspect a wide range of alternatives and the implications of large amounts of data almost instantaneously. By exploring these "What Ifs," we can predict the impact of various choices without having to go through the actual activities.

Here again is another barrier. Computer user manuals are designed to explain how computers work and how programs function. However, most business decision makers do not want to know how their computer works or how to write a program; instead, they want to use their computers as the problem-solving tools they really are. In this book, we deal directly with this problem. Rather than teach you about computer programming, we will show you the exact activities you need to perform to get the best possible use from the Multiplan program's powerful spreadsheet features and the other tools available for your computer.

For most individuals, decisions are made in response to problems. Also, most businesses encounter similar problems. Accordingly, we have organized our book by major business problem areas, and we show how to go about developing solutions in response to each. If you have a problem with pricing, for example, you could turn to the chapter on pricing (Chapter 7). There you will find a discussion of pricing in general, various approaches to pricing, and pricing problems. We then show you the effects of various pricing strategies, and finally, we show you the actual keys you need to punch to enter our pricing example into the computer and arrive at the same answer. You will then be able to plug your own data into the computer and reach a useful and effective conclusion for implementation in your own business.

Remember, computers do not make decisions; good managers do. However, the computer can make your decisions better and your life easier if used in the careful analytical way that we will show you in this book. Good luck.

About the Authors

Dr. William R. Osgood is a business consultant working with new ventures as well as problem and high growth potential situations, and maintains his own consulting operation in East Kingston, New Hampshire. Dr. Osgood has written several books on business planning and management.

Dr. James F. Molloy is a transportation specialist and consults with smaller firms on a variety of issues. His consulting business, TRAMCO, is located in Cambridge, Massachusetts.

Both Osgood and Molloy teach undergraduate and graduate courses in new venture creation and small business management, and give seminars on these and other business topics.

Michel Selva develops and teaches courses on a wide variety of computer applications.

1 Business decision making

Introduction

Good decisions in your business can be a fortunate consequence of a lucky fluke or the result of a carefully reasoned, methodical process. While luck is always desirable, it is undependable, so the second approach is most often wiser and more successful. It is our purpose here to describe a methodology for decision making that will be effective in a small firm and that you can apply yourself to improve your own operation with a minimum of outside assistance.

Our hypothesis here is simple: *Good decisions will improve the profitability of any business.* Our objective is equally simple. We want to outline a basic approach to profit-oriented decision making and to describe the tools and techniques needed for its implementation. The primary tool we will be working with is your computer. The techniques we will describe are standard approaches to business analysis, which you can use yourself as a means of improving your own business.

What is good decision making all about?

Good decision making is based on an evaluation of information about the issue in question. More information is better than less. However, the information itself must be relevant to the issue at hand. Bad (meaning incorrect, wrong, or inappropriate) information is generally worse than no information at all. At least in the absence of information you know that you don't have any, and so are more cautious with your assumptions. With some information, be it good or bad, there is something to work with, and so often the illusion is created that if adequate sophistication is applied, accuracy may result. The computer industry has a slogan for this problem: "Garbage in equals garbage out."

Good decision making is problem solving. Problems are upsetting to a great many people. However, problems should not be frightening; they should simply be solved. The solving process itself need not be a difficult matter either. In fact, the first step to good problem solving is making sure you know what problem you need to solve. As foolish as this may sound, defining the problem is often an important limitation on effective problem solving in a great many organizations. The more specifically the problem can be defined, the more focused your analysis can be, and the more direct your solutions will be. Once the problem has been brought squarely into focus, the information we have just talked about can be applied to its solution. Good information, to be effective, must be focused on the issues at hand. This is true with other tools described here as well. They are good tools, but they must be properly applied.

Another aspect of good decision making is timing. Decisions are often made after the fact or in response to emergencies that crop up in day-to-day operation. Some individuals are very skilled at this type of decision making. In fact, it is almost a definition of the American entrepreneur. A problem crops up, and he or she quickly makes a decision. There are two problems with this approach. First, there is not very much time to gather and analyze information, and so the decision that is made may well be based on incomplete data. More information and further analysis could possibly lead to additional insights into the nature of the problem and perhaps produce a more effective solution. A second limitation is that the decision maker may be dealing with symptoms and not with the underlying problem. This is known as "villain finding." The temptation is to identify quickly what is wrong with the situation and then fix it. The difficulty here is that you may be dealing with a symptom and not a cause, and so by treating the symptom, you may well still be stuck with the problem. An additional problem with this approach is that you have not only wasted time and resources in treating symptoms of problems, but the process may also cause you to believe that you have cured the problem and so lead you to still further erroneous decisions.

Perhaps the most important limitation to the villain-finding approach is that you may be wasting your time solving a problem that might have been avoided altogether. The point is, why waste your time and energy solving problems you may not have to encounter? The alternative problem-solving approach has a name as well. It is *proaction*, as opposed to the more traditional *reaction* or problem solving after the fact. Through proaction, a careful analysis is made of situations and possible problems are identified. It is, of course, likely that not all problems can be avoided, and this possibility is not even being suggested here. On the other hand, certainly some problems can be avoided, and when they are anticipated, courses of action can be developed that will avoid them to the greatest extent possible. Where problems are unavoidable, at least they will be expected, and so their arrival will not be a surprise. In fact, it may be possible to have solutions already developed in anticipation of the arrival of such problems, and so, when they occur, a decision-making process is already in place for their resolution.

Another aspect of proactive decision making is that not only does it lead to problem avoidance, but it may also be possible to identify future opportunities, and so structure actions in the present to take maximum advantage of those opportunities. This aspect of decision making is called *futurity*. Futurity is an analysis of the impact of present decisions and actions on the future. The notion of futurity leads to more effective decision making because it makes clear the fact that actions have more than temporary consequences. In business decision making, it is especially important to consider the longer-term consequences of all decisions that are made. One of the very important benefits that will result from the use of your computer as a decision-aiding tool is that this aspect of futurity is instantly revealed as you analyze the consequences of different alternatives.

There is a final warning or limitation that should be mentioned here. It may be possible to overanalyze situations. There are plenty of people around who are good analyzers and poor decision makers. This malaise also has a name, *analysis paralysis*, which results when there is too much information available and too much opportunity for its consideration. Under these conditions, no conclusions are drawn and the information is hashed over and over again until the time for action has passed. Consequently, no actual decision is made, which is in effect a decision by default.

Once we have clarified our problem and secured the information necessary to understand the decision-making framework, it is important for us to consider the impact of the various alternatives that may be available to the business. In analysis paralysis, we make no decision; that is, we allow a situation to continue without taking any action. No action is as much an alternative as any other, so good decision making requires us to evaluate the impact of this as well as all the other alternatives available to the business operation. Decisions, good or bad, have impact, good or bad, and so it is far wiser to anticipate this impact rather than wait for experience to show us whether we made a good or bad decision.

One of the difficulties in making business decisions is that there are frequently a great number of alternatives that may represent possible courses of action for the firm. The hard part is deciding which one is best. The answer to this dilemma is relatively simple. Using our computer as an analytical tool, we can quite specifically forecast the impact of each of the alternatives under consideration. This is an activity where our computer is perhaps most valuable. By using the computer, it is possible to inspect instantly the consequences of each of these alternatives, and bring into play the notion of futurity, of examining the impact of our present decisions on the future.

The greatest challenge of decision making is not in the analysis — that is quite straightforward — but rather in investing creative energies in seeking alternatives. As in the case of villain finding, all too often we are anxious to implement the first alternative that comes to mind. This may be as dangerous as allowing ourselves to go with the no-choice of decision making by default resulting from analysis paralysis. Let us instead try to identify creatively as many alternatives as possible. This is a skill that can be acquired and is improved by practice.

The most useful way of looking at this decision-making, problem-solving process is to change the perspective about 180 degrees from the usual. Most people see problems as limitations on their activities, and so engage in problem solving in a defensive manner. The attitude and the approach that we want to take here is quite different. Rather than seeing problems as limitations, we look at problems as opportunities waiting to be taken advantage of. This is a positive approach. This is the proactive approach. This is the difference between playing a winning game and a game that you try not to lose. Reactive problem solving is a limitation, a defensive game, and defensive strategies are not focused on winning; they are focused on trying not to lose. This difference in approach may seem slight and subtle, but the impact can be substantial. Each of the techniques we will be describing is a tool you can use to help yourself, not just to keep your business out of trouble, but to enable it to move forward into a positive and profitable future.

What are the major problem areas?

We have divided the problem-solving tool kit presented here into several functional categories. Rather than looking at the types of problems you may find yourself needing to solve, we will look instead at the major areas of a business operation where you may experience problems. One of the limitations we frequently see with discussions on problem-solving techniques is that although they may describe quite clearly how the various problem-solving tools work, they do not describe how to apply them within a business context. Consequently, individuals trying to run their own operations frequently experience difficulty in determining which tool they should use and when, and so may not use any. We attempt to deal with this limitation in two ways. First, by taking a functional approach to the problem-solving process, we will examine each of the major areas of business to show how our problem-solving techniques can work. Second, we use a case example to illustrate the application of these tools in an actual business situation.

Each of the functional areas we will be concerned with are summarized here and will be treated in depth later.

Cost control There are basically three ways to improve profitability in a business. The first two, selling more and improving your margin, are generally understood. The third is spending less, which is all too frequently an option not considered. We will look at fixed and variable costs and consider a special problem in both categories, that of semivariable costs. In other words, certain costs do not behave in a linear fashion. The question is, "What happens to the operation and its profitability as we begin to adjust these costs?" Our computer can help us immediately understand some of the consequences.

Market development The most popular strategy for improving operational profitability is to sell more. However, in order to sell more, you must know to whom, in what quantity, and at what price. You must also consider the costs of reaching different customer target segments.

Forecasting demand One of the proactive techniques we can use is deciding in advance how much we think we can sell and then determining the optimum levels of supply, orders, and inventory. Having a forecast also allows us to anticipate our manpower needs, space needs, and virtually all other questionable areas of the operation. By taking this proactive approach, we can avoid bad surprises and use our resources to their best capabilities. There is, of course, a methodical and systematic approach to developing forecasts that have the potential to be as accurate as possible, and our computer plays an important role in the process.

Cash flow Probably the single greatest concern for a new or growing firm is its cash flow. This refers to the flow of cash into and out of the firm. The problem with a new or growing operation is that the cash is likely to flow out of the firm faster than it flows in. Cash flow planning and monitoring can help to ensure that the firm does not run out of this most critical asset. This is such an important concept that we will be looking at the impact of each of the decision-making tools on the cash flow of the operation.

Breakeven The notion of breakeven is critical to a great many decision options available to the firm. Breakeven very simply refers to that point in the operation where the firm neither makes a profit nor experiences a loss. Breakeven also helps us to determine, for example, the additional sales that are needed to support an increase in expense categories. Breakeven helps us to determine the additional sales needed if we reduce our price, thereby reducing our margin. The concept of breakeven is another critical decision-making tool. In fact, cash flow and breakeven are the two major benchmarks against which we will be evaluating the impact of all of our other decision-making tools.

Budgets Most people are aware of the concept of budgets. Some may even use them, but most are not aware of the methodology of establishing rational budgets that can be realistic guides to the future. We will outline this methodology and show how the computer can help evaluate historical trends to provide the best guidance for what may occur. Once we have this vision of the future, it can become the basis for realistic budgeting.

Budget deviation analysis Even those few who understand the methodologies of establishing budgets and their purposes may not be familiar with the control and monitoring technique that the budget represents. When actual deviations from the budget are studied, the budget becomes the foundation for controlling the entire operation. Actually, budget deviation analysis is quite a straightforward task, but one that is generally tedious to perform. A computer is a tremendous help in this process, as it eliminates the tedium by making an analysis available at a glance and instantly pinpointing the problem areas.

Risk analysis There is a whole science or discipline associated with evaluating risk and the various techniques available to deal with risks such as hedging. One of the best means for dealing with risk is to be fully aware of the consequences if everything does not work out quite as you hoped. This is known as evaluating the down-side risk. Once you have evaluated the down-side, it is possible to determine whether or not you can afford the exposure to these chances and also what you will do if this less desirable outcome actually occurs. Using the computer allows us to play "what if" games and thus allows us to model these various potential occurrences without having to actually experience them and learn about down-side risk the hard way.

Developing a decision-making model

Before we begin to consider the techniques of decision making, it is important to have a solid understanding of the methodology. A general approach to decision making has already been outlined: define the problem, get the information, look at the alternatives. Now we would like to expand on that general approach by presenting a six-step decision-making model that should be used as the framework for all of the techniques that follow. It is essential to know what you are trying to do before you proceed. Using the six simple steps outlined here will help you develop an accurate sense of direction and keep you from wasting your time and computer power and, more importantly, keep you from making bad decisions with good information.

The six-step approach can be used under any circumstances to significantly improve the quality of decision making. The model works, not because of its complexity and sophistication, but because of its simplicity. The secret is to break the situation down into simple components, proceed with a thorough analysis of each part, and then integrate the results into a final decision. The six steps of the decision-making model are:

STEP ONE: Clarify the problem(s)
STEP TWO: Identify alternatives
STEP THREE: Evaluate pros and cons of each alternative
STEP FOUR: Select the best alternative
STEP FIVE: Develop an action plan
STEP SIX: Monitor progress

STEP ONE: Clarify the problem(s)

Again, before you can do anything, you must know what the problem is. As foolish as this may sound, all too often people proceed blindly without a clear understanding of what they are trying to accomplish. Consequently, their efforts are more frequently focused on symptoms than on underlying causes. The result is that, while they may eliminate the symptom, they do not solve the problem. As we noted earlier, another frequently encountered problem-solving deficiency is villain finding. The impulse is to identify what is wrong as quickly as possible and immediately fix it. Unfortunately, the consequence again may be treatment of symptoms and not causes. Time spent at this stage of the analysis pays dividends by making the rest of the task much easier. The more specific you can be here, the easier your overall task will be.

STEP TWO: Identify alternatives

Following the advice not to rush quickly into finding solutions, spending time in identifying and considering alternatives can yield the big dividends of improved decisions and, ultimately, time saved. This is an opportunity for creativity, for actively thinking of all possible alternatives and listing them, even if some appear at first glance to be foolish or inappropriate. Do not worry about the evaluation of alternatives at this stage. Concentrate instead on listing the largest number of possible alternatives that you can dream up. This step is also a good place to break away from old patterns and habits of always treating the same problem in the same way. Use your imagination and creativity to the greatest extent possible.

STEP THREE: Evaluate pros and cons of each alternative

Once the alternatives have been identified, it is necessary to look at both the good and bad points that may be associated with each. Practically speaking, for nearly every alternative available in most situations, there are likely to be both advantages and disadvantages associated with its use. Frequently the difficulty is one of setting aside our own biases about a given choice in order to take an objective view of that course of action. If we know we have a built-in bias toward a given alternative, then it is that much more important to make sure that we do a fair job of looking at the other side of that particular issue.

STEP FOUR: Select the best alternative

If a thorough job has been done in steps two and three, then step four is obvious and easy. When there is still some close similarity between the two best alternatives, a matter of personal preference can help make the choice. In evaluating all alternatives, it is important to keep in mind the matter of your own personal involvement in the situation. A good alternative for one individual may not work for another. So make sure that such personal differences are taken into consideration in making the analysis and the final choice.

STEP FIVE: Develop an action plan

Selecting the best alternative is only part of the answer. The rest of the answer is in its implementation. Here it is important to be specific and detailed, to lay out a complete course of action for the full implementation of the selected plan. If only one individual is involved, then show the series of activities that person must perform to implement the chosen alternative. If more than one individual is involved, show the responsibilities of each.

STEP SIX: Monitor progress

With any activity in your business organization, it is important to know how closely performance is matching the plan. If reality is not matching your expectations, it is critical to know this as soon as possible so that corrective action can be taken. For activities that are reasonably quantifiable, your computer will become an extremely valuable control tool. For other types of activities, it is possible to set up simple manual systems to track activity and compare it with the plan.

The case example

In order to illustrate the workings and effects of the different tools and techniques we will be describing, we have developed a case study of a typical retail business, which we will use as our example throughout the text. The case we have selected is that of the Acme Hardware Company, which is presently owned and operated by its founder, Mr. Adams. The firm was started sixteen years ago and has provided a satisfactory income to its owner throughout that period. Recently, however, Mr. Adams has been experiencing more and more small and seemingly unrelated problems and has generally been finding that cash seems tight within the operation, although sales seem to be strong and the business continues to show a small increase in sales each operating period. Mr. Adams has been increasingly concerned about this situation and has just purchased a microcomputer, hoping that it will help him develop a better understanding of where he may be experiencing problems and what he might do about them. We will go through the series of steps and activities Mr. Adams tries in order to find solutions for some of his problems and show exactly how, in a step-by-step fashion, you can use these same techniques to diagnose your own business operation.

The next chapter will describe what you need to know about your microcomputer in order to start using it as a problem-solving tool in your own business. Chapter 3 will show you the actual series of steps you will need to follow to enter the example into your computer. In each of the rest of the chapters, we will first explain a key management concept. Next, by example, we will show how that concept or approach is useful to Mr. Adams in evaluating the Acme Hardware operation. We will conclude each of these discussions with "What If" examples and worksheets, and show you how to enter and analyze your own data.

These are good tools we will describe for your use. The methodology is proven and effective. Its value, however, will only appear through your own time and effort in applying the concepts to your own situation.

A special Business User's Guide disk to accompany **Business Decision Making** is available from the publishers. The disk is not essential but it will save you much time, since it contains the income statement, balance sheet, and worksheet (used to break down major line items on the income statement and also to calculate breakeven, cash flow, and financial ratios). If you did not purchase the Disk Edition of this book, and you want to order the disk, use the Order Form on page 144.

2 The computer system you need

Introduction

Computers don't make decisions — managers do. Computers (so far, at least) don't have feelings or form opinions, and so consequently we are not suggesting that they will solve your business problems for you. On the other hand, computers are remarkably effective as support tools for the decision-making process because of their extraordinary ability to process information. Computers can store, sort, summarize, manipulate, and print out information with speed and accuracy never before possible. Microcomputers, the newest actors on the computing scene, can perform these tasks for even the smallest firm at a price it can afford, in an extremely cost-efficient manner.

Our entire concern here is with microcomputers as business decision-aiding tools, so we will not be considering the uses of larger-scale computers. Nor will we be considering unique or customized applications of the systems we will describe. We will describe standard applications for standard equipment that can be used effectively in any business organization, large or small. In our discussion we will first cover the equipment and processing systems you will need. We will give you some tips to improve your operating efficiency, provide a general example to show how the system will be used, and offer some suggestions for the care and maintenance of the equipment and accessories.

Contrary to popular opinion, you do not need to become a computer programmer to benefit from the use of these tools. If you carefully follow the step-by-step "cookbook" approach that we describe here, you will be able to overcome computer anxiety and use your computer to the fullest extent possible.

The computer you need

The computer, as a general-purpose machine, can handle information in a variety of ways. Its specific capabilities are a function of the particular configuration of the system you possess. The system configuration is a combination of hardware (the specific pieces of equipment) and software (the instructions that tell the computer's hardware system what to do).

Hardware is generally seen as a pretty straightforward topic. There are specific pieces of equipment that we can see and touch, and turn on and off. Software, on the other hand, is all too often seen as something incomprehensibly mysterious and much better ignored or at best used under the careful supervision of a highly trained specialist. In fact, it is the mystery of software that so often creates computer anxiety, which paralyzes otherwise rational and responsible individuals and creates a state of complete inability to operate the equip-

ment we are discussing. This does not have to be so, and it is an important objective of our discussion here to help dispel this anxiety. In fact, an important premise behind this whole book is that it is not necessary to know why the software works; it is instead important that you know exactly what to do in order to make the software produce the results that you desire.

In essence, software is a set of directions, the program, which tells the computer what to do through specially coded instructions. If you want a computer to perform business functions, you can use prepackaged business software, such as Multiplan, which will be one of the primary computer tools discussed here. This software converts a personal computer into a business computer, quickly and completely. One of the real benefits of Multiplan and of other similar software is that you do not have to know very much about computers or anything about programming languages to be able to use these tools effectively. Instead, you just need to follow the step-by-step instructions that we will outline for you here.

Of course, software is only part of the complete computer system you will need. To be effective, a system must be composed of interacting and interdependent parts that work together to form a whole, such as in a stereo system or an accounting system. In a computer system it is important that each part function both on its own *and* in conjunction with the other component parts. If this does not occur, the system will be nonoperational. With the rapid growth of computer technology, there are a variety of competing and sometimes incompatible products on the market. These products do not necessarily all work together and, even when they should, there are relatively few people who can explain how to make them do so. Where such possible incompatibilities exist, we have what is known as a compatibility problem.

If you have a computer system, you may have already encountered the compatibility problem. For instance, a computer company representative can tell you everything you want to know about the computer; the software company spokesperson can explain all about the software; and the person at the printer company can give advice about its printers. Unfortunately, there are not enough people around who can tell you whether or not the software running on your computer will work with your printer. Obviously, you cannot resolve a compatibility problem on your own. The best solution is to avoid the problem altogether.

The way to do this is to select and use brand name products with proven customer support. Unless you are an experimenter or a hobbyist with a great deal of time to spare, the best advice is to follow the crowd in choosing equipment and software. Let others do the testing, and then only buy products that have passed the threshold of acceptance. For these reasons, it is also important to always work with a reliable dealer. Even though the computer field is growing much too rapidly for anyone to understand it completely, a knowledgeable dealer will give you useful and practiced guidance in selecting the equipment and technology most appropriate to your particular needs and situation.

The computer system that we will describe here and that you will need in order to use the methodologies and routines we will present is composed of reliable products that have passed the consumer tests and will work together. We have selected the essentials, the bare minimum you will need to form a functioning system. We have also suggested some accessories that expand the capabilities of a system, but they are optional. For further advice, consult your dealer on these and other accessories.

There are five essential parts to the computer system you need (see the illustration on the opposite page). Each part is briefly discussed here, and major parts are covered in more detail later in this chapter.

1 A personal computer: There are hundreds of personal computers on the market today that can be used to run Multiplan. At a minimum, the computer you use should have the following:

■ Two floppy disk drives or one floppy disk drive and one "Winchester" or hard disk unit. (Although Multiplan will run on a machine with only one floppy disk drive, your data storage capability will be severely limited.)

■ A monitor with an 80-column screen display. A black-and-white monitor is sufficient for following the exercises in this book. A green or amber monitor is easier on your eyes and generally is not much more expensive than a black-and-white one. A color (RGB) monitor will permit you to use Multiplan's more exotic features, such as multicolored window displays, but the extra cost — as much as a thousand dollars more than a basic machine with a monochrome display — is hardly justified for this use alone.

■ Enough memory (random access memory, or RAM) to hold Multiplan plus the largest worksheet you expect to use.

2 Multiplan: The Multiplan program comes in the form of a program disk accompanied by an instruction manual. Some special versions of Multiplan, such as the IBM PC version, also come with a separate tutorial disk.

When purchasing a copy of Multiplan, be sure to specify the exact model of the computer you are using; the disk size and data storage format of the Multiplan program disk must match the characteristics of your computer exactly.

3 Floppy disks: A floppy disk is a round, flat, rotating sheet of plastic coated with a magnetic surface that records and stores information. You need two blank disks, one for saving the example that we will be working on throughout the book, and another to use for a backup copy of the information.

4 Printer: A printer is a typewriter-like machine that prints out reports just as they appear on the Multiplan screen. Although a printer isn't absolutely necessary, it is extremely helpful for sharing information with others or troubleshooting potential problems. It can print out an entire Multiplan worksheet, while the screen may display only a part of the worksheet at any one time.

Printers come in two standard forms: 80 or 132 characters wide. The 80-character model uses standard 8½-inch-wide paper. The 132-character model is more popular for business purposes and is sometimes called the standard business printer. You can use either an 80- or 132-character printer with this book. Many newer dot matrix printers (Epson MX and FX, Star Gemini, and Okidata) are capable of printing in *compressed mode,* 18 characters per inch. Using compressed mode, a Multiplan worksheet up to 132 characters wide can be printed on paper 8½ inches wide. Since none of the worksheets used in this book exceed 132 characters in width, a dot matrix printer using compressed mode will allow you to print the worksheets on standard letter-size paper without breaking up the columns.

Many high-quality printers are available at a cost of a few hundred to a few thousand dollars. We suggest that you discuss these options with a dealer and actually take your computer in to have the dealer install the printer to make sure it works with your system.

5 Reference books: Although books aren't a part of a computer system per se, they are so helpful in setting up and operating a system that we have included them here. In fact, we assume that you have already gone through your computer user's guide and the Multiplan manual. It is impossible to duplicate in this book all the instructional material found in these manuals. However, throughout this book, we have presented those procedures that you really need to know and use as you progress through the steps.

The parts of the computer system you need

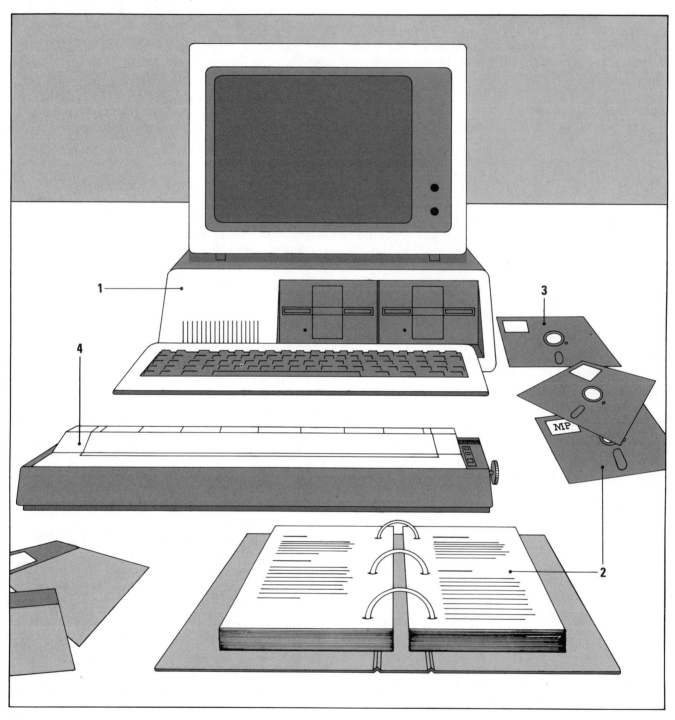

1 A computer

2 The Multiplan program and manual

3 Floppy disks and disk drives

4 A printer

Personal computers

A variety of personal computers suitable for use in a business environment are available. When choosing your first computer or upgrading to a more sophisticated model, you should seriously consider certain key features before making your choice. The most important features to consider are those that affect memory and storage, data input, and screen display.

Memory and storage

Memory capacity (called RAM for random access memory) determines how much data the computer can actively work with at one time. RAM is measured by the number of *bytes*. A byte is the amount of storage space taken up by a single character or number value. In computer product literature, RAM is expressed in *kilobytes* (thousands of bytes), which is symbolized by the letter *K*. For example, a storage capacity of 64K means 64,000 bytes.

When you use Multiplan, the program itself is stored in the RAM. The computer's operating system (discussed later) also takes up some room in memory. The remaining unused memory capacity is available for the data you will enter into your Multiplan worksheet. Since Multiplan and the operating system take up a fixed amount of memory, more RAM means you can store more data.

RAM is also referred to as *volatile memory* because its contents are wiped out whenever the power is shut off or the computer is reset. In order to save data from one work session to the next, a more permanent storage medium is needed.

Disk storage capacity, like the computer's internal memory, is also measured in kilobytes. The larger the number of Ks available per disk, the more files can be stored. Having a large disk capacity is helpful for a number of reasons: It reduces the number of individual disks you will need; it makes it easier to keep track of disks; and it reduces the chances of encountering Disk full messages when you try to save a worksheet. (See TIPS on "How to overcome a Disk full message" on page 41.)

The operating system is generally "invisible" to the user of Multiplan. Whether your computer runs under CP/M-80, CP/M-86, MS-DOS, Apple-DOS, or another operating system, Multiplan looks and acts the same way. As a Multiplan user, the only operating system characteristics you should concern yourself with are the procedures for formatting disks, naming disk files, designating different disk drives on your machine, and making backup copies of your important disks.

Data input

Numeric keypads are separated from the regular keyboard and can speed the entry of numbers into worksheets. Organized much like a calculator keypad, they put all the digits from 0 to 9 in close proximity so that you don't have to enter numbers with the row of numeric keys at the top of the keyboard.

Function keys can be "programmed" so they will perform functions that you find repetitive. Once programmed, they will execute a series of keystrokes when pressed in conjunction with the control key.

Arrow keys are used to move the cell pointer around on the screen. Most computers have four separate arrow keys that move the cell pointer up, down, left, or right. If you do not have arrow keys, you can use the control-key "diamond" (CTRL-S, CTRL-D, CTRL-E, and CTRL-X) to move the cell pointer.

Multiplan: Your electronic worksheet

The Multiplan program, an electronic worksheet, takes the work out of working with numbers. Using its automatic calculation feature, you can instantly see the results of changing a number. You don't have to sit down with pen and paper or a calculator to figure out possible results; the Multiplan program does it for you. That shortens the time between "cause" and "effect"; with your electronic worksheet you can analyze the financial effect of decisions before you make them. Put the Multiplan program to work for you, and its capabilities expand your capabilities. You can work faster, more efficiently, more effectively.

Multiplan is designed to perform a variety of business functions for business people, most of whom don't have the time, desire, or skill to write their own computer programs. And because of Multiplan, they don't have to.

Multiplan can store and manipulate a lot of information in its 63 columns and 255 rows. The number of rows and columns you can actually use depends upon the amount of memory your computer has. In this book, you'll use up to 7 columns and 160 rows.

As you work at the computer, a Multiplan screen like the one illustrated opposite will appear on the computer monitor.

The Multiplan screen display

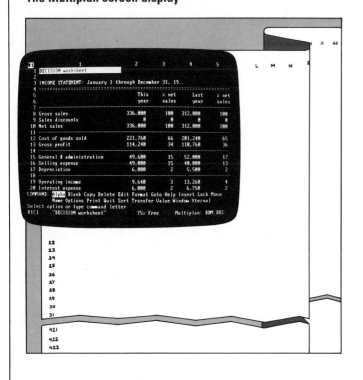

The screen provides a "window" on your worksheet by constantly displaying the information you have entered on the computer. However, the screen only displays part of your electronic worksheet at a time. To reveal the rest of the worksheet, you have to "scroll" it by using the arrow keys or the Goto command.

Photos of Multiplan screens or printouts throughout the book show you what your worksheet should look like at each step. Screen photos and printouts provide constant visual checks that help you see whether you are correctly entering the data.

If you have a printer, you can get a copy of your worksheet at any point. See your Multiplan manual for detailed instructions on how to print a worksheet.

The Multiplan screen display in detail

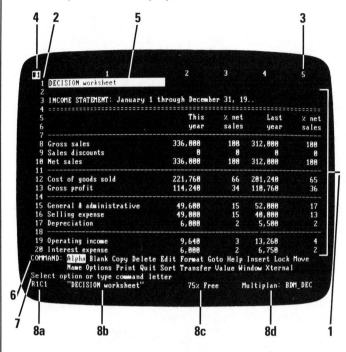

The Multiplan screen display that appears when you load the program is packed with information. Here is a brief review of what appears on the screen and an explanation of how this information is used throughout this book.

1 Worksheet window: The standard computer video display shows 25 lines of information between the top and bottom of the screen. In the Multiplan display, the first line is taken up by the column numbers, while the last four lines display commands, messages, and status information. The remaining 20 lines are a "window" into the spreadsheet.

Since the row numbers take up 4 characters starting at the left edge of the screen, there is room for 75 characters. Only full columns are displayed, and so seven columns will be visible at a time if all columns are ten characters in width.

2 Row numbers: Numbers from 1 to 255 appear along the left margin of the screen, indicating the rows.

3 Column numbers: Numbers from 1 to 63 appear along the top of the screen, indicating the columns.

4 Window number: This appears at the top left corner of the worksheet window. Since only one window is currently open in this example, the window is numbered #1.

5 Cell highlight: This shows the current location of the cell pointer. If your video monitor does not allow reverse video, the current cell will be indicated by brackets [ ].

6 The command line: This actually takes up two lines of the video display. The command line lists the potential actions you can take to affect or add to your spreadsheet.

7 Message line: This prompts you with hints or asks for confirmation before Multiplan executes "dangerous" commands such as deleting a disk file or clearing the worksheet.

8 The status line: This is the bottom line of the screen. It gives the following information:

(a) Current cell coordinates: All cell coordinates in Multiplan are given in row-column order.

(b) Current cell contents: If the current cell contains over 20 characters, only the first 20 will be visible here.

(c) Available RAM storage: This tells you how much room you have left for your data in your computer's memory. In effect, this tells you how big and complex the current worksheet can be.

(d) Worksheet name: If you loaded a worksheet into Multiplan from a disk file, the file name will appear here. Otherwise, the default file name **TEMP** will be displayed.

The Multiplan worksheet

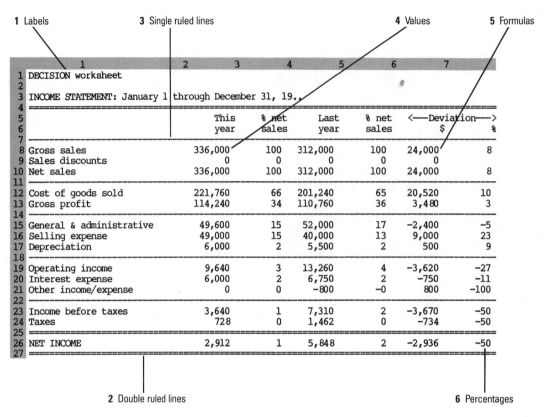

1 Labels   **3** Single ruled lines   **4** Values   **5** Formulas

	1	2	3	4	5	6	7
1	DECISION worksheet						
2							
3	INCOME STATEMENT: January 1 through December 31, 19..						
4	===						
5		This	% net	Last	% net	<——Deviation——>	
6		year	sales	year	sales	$	%
7	---						
8	Gross sales	336,000	100	312,000	100	24,000	8
9	Sales discounts	0	0	0	0	0	
10	Net sales	336,000	100	312,000	100	24,000	8
11							
12	Cost of goods sold	221,760	66	201,240	65	20,520	10
13	Gross profit	114,240	34	110,760	36	3,480	3
14	---						
15	General & administrative	49,600	15	52,000	17	-2,400	-5
16	Selling expense	49,000	15	40,000	13	9,000	23
17	Depreciation	6,000	2	5,500	2	500	9
18	---						
19	Operating income	9,640	3	13,260	4	-3,620	-27
20	Interest expense	6,000	2	6,750	2	-750	-11
21	Other income/expense	0	0	-800	-0	800	-100
22							
23	Income before taxes	3,640	1	7,310	2	-3,670	-50
24	Taxes	728	0	1,462	0	-734	-50
25	===						
26	NET INCOME	2,912	1	5,848	2	-2,936	-50
27	===						

2 Double ruled lines   **6** Percentages

As you build the worksheet, you will encounter the following expressions:

1 Labels: Labels identify the worksheet and individual parts of it.

2 Double ruled lines: These divide worksheets into major sections to make them easier to read. The lines are made by using the equal (=) sign.

3 Single ruled lines: These also separate major sections of the worksheet. They are entered using the hyphen (-).

4 Values: Values are numbers typed in directly from the keyboard.

5 Formulas: Formulas can either be self-contained or can calculate values based on the contents of other cells. For example, R10C2-R11C2.

6 Percentages: Percentages are arrived at by dividing one value by another and using the % function in the formula to display the result as a whole number.

How the DECISION worksheet will work

	1	2	3	4	5	6	7
1	DECISION worksheet						
3	INCOME STATEMENT: January 1 through December 31, 19..						
5		This year	% net sales	Last year	% net sales	<—Deviation—> $	%
8	Gross sales	336,000	100	312,000	100	24,000	8
9	Sales discounts	0	0	0	0	0	
10	Net sales	336,000	100	312,000	100	24,000	8
12	Cost of goods sold	221,760	66	201,240	65	20,520	10
13	Gross profit	114,240	34	110,760	36	3,480	3
15	General & administrative	49,600	15	52,000	17	-2,400	-5
16	Selling expense	49,000	15	40,000	13	9,000	23
17	Depreciation	6,000	2	5,500	2	500	9
19	Operating income	9,640	3	13,260	4	-3,620	-27
20	Interest expense	6,000	2	6,750	2	-750	-11
21	Other income/expense	0	0	-800	-0	800	-100
23	Income before taxes	3,640	1	7,310	2	-3,670	-50
24	Taxes	728	0	1,462	0	-734	-50
26	NET INCOME	2,912	1	5,848	2	-2,936	-50
28	BALANCE SHEET: December 31, 19..						
30		This year		Last year			
33	ASSETS:						
35	<Current assets>						
36	Cash	1,335		4,750			
37	Accounts receivable	17,777		16,000			
38	Inventory	83,292		70,000			
39	Prepaid expenses	3,400		3,400			
41	Total current assets	105,804		94,150			
43	<Fixed assets>						
44	Buildings & equipment	33,000		38,950			
45	Less accumulated depreciation	-13,000		-7,000			
46	Land	0		0			
48	Total fixed assets	20,000		31,950			

	1	2	3	4
77	Analysis section			
79	G&A EXPENSE BREAKDOWN	Fixed	Variable	Total
81	Rent	12,000	0	12,000
82	Officer salaries	20,000	0	20,000
83	Clerical expense	4,000	1,000	5,000
84	Insurance	3,600	0	3,600
85	Utilities	2,000	400	2,400
86	Office supplies	800	400	1,200
87	Legal & accounting	3,000	0	3,000
88	Miscellaneous	1,200	1,200	2,400
90	Total G&A expenses	46,600	3,000	49,600
92	SELLING EXPENSE BREAKDOWN	Fixed	Variable	Total
94	Wages	20,000	10,000	30,000
95	Delivery	0	1,800	1,800
96	Operating supplies	4,000	800	4,800
97	Advertising	4,000	2,000	6,000
98	Travel & entertainment	800	400	1,200
99	Miscellaneous	800	400	1,200
100	Credit card	0	4,000	4,000
102	Total selling expenses	29,600	19,400	49,000
104	COST OF GOODS ANALYSIS			
106	Beginning inventory			70,000
107	Inventory purchases			235,052
108	Less purchase discounts of	0 percent		0
109	Total goods available			305,052
110	Less ending inventory			83,292
112	Cost of goods sold			221,760
114	BREAKEVEN ANALYSIS			
116	Sales revenue needed to break even			322,683
118	Sales revenue needed to cover cash expenses			300,732
120	Sales revenue needed to cover cash expenses			314,963
121	and debt service			
123	CASH FLOW ANALYSIS			
125	Net cash th... ff f... the i...me st...ent			12

The DECISION worksheet you will build in the following chapters contains four major sections: an income statement, a balance sheet, an analysis section, and a ratio section. As you enter each section into the computer, you will learn what business terms such as depreciation, current assets, and fixed and variable costs really mean and how they are calculated. When each section of the worksheet is completed, you will then be guided through a series of "What If" questions to demonstrate how changes in one or more items change others. With Multiplan, the results of any change can be seen immediately.

Here is how the finished DECISION worksheet will work:

1 You enter a change, for instance, an increase in general and administrative (overhead) costs.

2 Formulas in the income statement automatically recalculate all line items affected by the change that was made; in this case, operating income, income before taxes, taxes, and net income would all go down. This ability to enter a change and immediately see the results is one of the reasons personal computers are so widely used in financial decision making. Some of the areas we'll explore using the DECISION worksheet are:

- Determining breakeven points
- Controlling overhead
- Marketing
- Pricing
- Inventory control
- Operating management
- Cash flow

3 Formulas in the balance sheet work just like those in the income statement. For instance, a change in the income statement that causes a change in net income will instantly show the change in cash on the balance sheet.

4 The finished worksheet will have more than the income statement and balance sheet. Formulas will automatically calculate all line items on the income statement showing each as a percentage of net sales. Other sections will explain and show you how to calculate detailed general and administrative, selling, and cost of goods expense breakdowns. You'll also see how to use deviation analysis to compare your progress with previous periods in your own firm or with other firms in the same industry. Finally, you'll see how to use financial ratios to analyze your financial statements.

Disks: Anatomy and care

Disk anatomy

Although a disk can perform amazing functions, its anatomy is quite simple. Since reference is made in this book to parts of a disk, a brief review of disk anatomy is included here.

1 Storage envelope: This envelope protects the disk from scratches, dust, and fingerprints. With better disks, the envelope is also treated to eliminate the static buildup that attracts abrasive grit. Always store a diskette in its storage envelope.

2 Outer cover: The black plastic outer cover protects the disk while allowing it to spin smoothly. The cover is permanently sealed for safety, and contains lubricants and cleaning agents that prolong the life of the disk. Always grasp a disk only by this outer cover.

3 Labels: A disk comes with a manufacturer's label on it. A user's label can be added to identify and number the disk for easy reference.

4 The oval opening: This is a space where an operating disk drive head picks up and records information on the disk. There is an oval opening on both the top and bottom sides.

5 The top side: On a single-sided disk, the top side is the one with the manufacturer's label on it. A disk is inserted into the machine top-side-up, with the oval opening directed toward the machine.

6 The actual disk: The round, flexible plastic disk has a magnetic surface that stores information in a manner somewhat analogous to that of a tape recorder. This actual, or inner, disk can be seen through three openings in the disk's outer cover.

7 Alignment notches: These two notches align the disk squarely over the disk drive head when the disk is inserted into the machine.

8 The central hole: The disk drive unit fits into the central hole to engage and rotate the disk.

9 The hub ring: This plastic protective ring, normally not on a disk, can be glued on to the rim of a disk's central hole to prevent the hole from deteriorating as the drive unit repeatedly rotates the disk.

10 The write-protect notch: This notch cues the disk drive whether or not to store a file on the disk. When the notch is left open, the disk drive "senses" this and will store a file (on command) on the disk. If you cover the notch with tape, the disk drive will not accept new files on the disk until the tape is removed. That protects — or write-protects — the disk.

11 The recording and reading head: This area is used by the disk drive head to locate disk sectors on which information is stored.

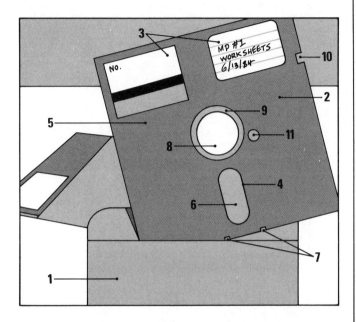

COMPUTER TIPS Cleaning the disk drive

This is one those "housekeeping chores" it is easy to overlook. But you shouldn't overlook it forever or disk errors can occur. The disk drive head operates like a tape recorder head. It picks up signals from the magnetic recording material in the disk, and in the process it also picks up debris. If this debris isn't removed, it can begin to reduce the sensitivity of the head as well as its accuracy in recording and picking up data. The easiest way to clean the head is with a special cleaning disk. When it is inserted into the drive just like a regular disk, it cleans the head as it spins.

Disk care and handling

Disks are relatively durable under ordinary conditions and have a useful life of about 40 hours' spinning time. That life, however, can be shortened or abruptly ended by improper handling, while proper care assures that disks will accurately store and play back the data you need. Here are some useful tips on how to care for disks and assure them a useful, productive life.

Disk do's and don'ts

DO . . . Keep disks in their protective storage envelopes. The envelope reduces static buildup, which can attract dust that can scratch the disk.

DO . . . Keep disks dry, away from sneezes, coffee, or anything wet. A wet disk is a ruined disk.

DO . . . Prevent disks from getting too hot or too cold. They should be stored at temperatures of 10–52° C (50–125° F). Temperature extremes can destroy a disk's sensitivity, so treat them the same way you treat photographic film, i.e., keep them out of direct sunlight, don't leave them in a car exposed to temperature extremes, and so forth.

DO . . . Keep disks away from magnets. The magnets found in radio or stereo speakers, televisions, electric motors, air conditioners, novelty items, or even some cabinet latches can ruin disks' sensitivity. How far is "away"? A safe distance is at least two feet.

DO . . . Always make backup copies of important disks and store them a safe distance from your working area, ideally off the premises. Make sure that the same accident can't happen to both the disk and its copy. Often the information on the disk is worth much more than the disk itself.

DO . . . Load the disk into the drive unit gently. Otherwise, it may bend, center improperly, or rotate in an elliptical orbit that misses data.

DON'T . . . Touch a disk's recording surface. Handle it only by its protective cover.

DON'T . . . Use a hard pen to write on a disk label. Use only a felt-tip pen and light pressure.

DON'T . . . Leave a disk in a nonoperating disk drive for more than an hour. Open the drive door and lift the drive head from the surface of the disk.

DON'T . . . Insert or remove a disk when the disk drive is running (when the red light is on).

DON'T . . . Bend, fold, or crimp disks.

One more note: Even with the best of care, disks can only last so long. Close to the end of their expected functional life, they show their own form of senility by losing information or giving invalid commands. These are indications that it's time to replace the disk, which, ideally, you've already copied.

Housekeeping

When you first begin to use a personal computer, keeping track of your disks isn't a problem because you have so few of them. After a very short period, however, they can begin to overrun your desk, and you need a method for filing and storing them. Here are some tips for organizing your files so that you can find what you want . . . when you want it.

1 Label each disk with the same volume number, for instance, MP #1, MP #2, etc., for Multiplan disks.

2 Periodically print out the directory, or list of files on each disk, and save the printout with the disk. Some filing systems such as binders have a place for the directory to be kept. You can easily keep things straight by matching the number on the disk label with a label on each printout. To avoid confusion, print out directories of the disks one at a time, in sequential order, then number the printed-out directory listings to match the disks.

3 Financial statements

Introduction

The best way to illustrate the actual use of Multiplan is through an application. As an example, we will show how Mr. Adams applies Multiplan to his business and will present the steps you (and Mr. Adams) must follow to accomplish the desired result. Once you have followed Mr. Adams through an analysis of the Acme Hardware Company, it is our hope and expectation that you will be able to substitute your own data into the worksheets. In this way, you can begin to use your computer to produce the same type of analysis for your own business.

Mr. Adams has purchased two personal computers, a printer, and software, giving him an effectively integrated system. In the process of purchasing this system, getting it home, and hooking it up, he asked his reputable microcomputer dealer 4,000 questions and listened carefully to the answers. Once all of the gear was at his home and connected, Mr. Adams sat down and read the operating instructions. As outrageous as this suggestion sounds, reading the instructions can frequently be helpful. However, once he had finished reading the instructions, he was still confused on two points. First, he was unsure of how to actually proceed with using the system; and second, he was somewhat confused about the business management implications of using the various analytical tools available. We were called in at this point and provided Mr. Adams with some management counseling to help him with the second part of his problem. We also developed with him a step-by-step method to follow, dealing with the first part of the problem. Our explanation and advice are given in this book to help you proceed with an analysis of your own operation.

The income statement and balance sheet

To start using his new tool, the first thing Mr. Adams needed to do was to enter his income statement and balance sheet information. Later in this chapter we develop formats for these financial statements. It is important to note that these formats have great flexibility. Income and expense categories can easily be expanded to accommodate other types of business situations as well as those similar to Mr. Adams's. Before Mr. Adams could proceed further, he needed his income statement and balance sheet. Fortunately, he had available fairly current statements from his accountant. You'll need your income statement and balance sheet as well in order to apply the analysis format to your own situation. If you do not have fairly current financial statements, you're in trouble and need help beyond the scope of this book.

The income or profit-and-loss statement shows the performance of the business over a period of time. The balance sheet, on the other hand, is a "photograph" of the condition of the business at a specific moment. In Mr. Adams's case, the income statement covers one year (a conventional time period), and the balance sheet is dated the end of his fiscal year (another conventional time period). Of course, many other time units can be used without compromising the analysis.

The income or profit-and-loss statement essentially consists of three sections. These are sales, variable costs (the costs typically associated with sales), and the fixed or overhead costs of maintaining the organizational unit. Strictly speaking, the variable costs would not exist if there were no sales. Strictly speaking again, you generally expect the variable costs to change in direct proportion to sales. Consequently, these variable costs (in this case, the cost of goods sold) can be expressed as a percentage of sales. Thus, if sales increase, the cost of goods sold would increase in direct proportion to the percentage increase in sales.

Overhead, or fixed expenses, will continue whether the business has sales or not. These costs typically include such standard items as office personnel salaries, insurance, utilities, and other costs that are not related to changes in the operational level. Of course, an economist would be quick to point out that all costs are variable costs in the long run and that changes can be made in any of the cost categories. However, practically speaking, most of the costs that we would classify as fixed costs are not subject to a great deal of immediate change; and so they are locked in over short to intermediate periods of time. For small firms this may be true even of such typically variable costs as direct labor. (Each of these categories will be discussed more fully later on.)

Values on the income statement are important indicators of the financial well-being of a business. Net sales, minus the cost of goods sold, will equal the gross profit. This is an important number because it shows us the net revenues available from operations. Once the direct costs of supplying the goods and services have been deducted, yielding gross profit, the overhead costs are subtracted to yield net income (profit or loss).

The balance sheet is similarly divided into three major categories: assets, liabilities, and owner equity. Assets are those things a business owns, liabilities are those things a business owes, and the difference between the two is owner equity or the actual ownership of the operation. These sections are further subdivided and will be described later in the chapter, but this general distinction is adequate for our purposes here. The relationships between the balance sheet accounts can have a critical significance, and so an understanding of these relationships can improve decision making. In the next section, we will show you the income statement and balance sheet for Mr. Adams's business, along with the step-by-step process by which he entered his information into the computer and the results. You can then begin to apply the same step-by-step process to enter your own information as a first step in the analytical process.

Most income statements and balance sheets contain the same general categories; they can be expanded beyond these general categories to handle whatever level of detail and sophistication is appropriate to a set of specific circumstances. For our purposes here and for the benefit of analyzing Mr. Adams's hardware store, which is a relatively simple operation, we will use the general format that is outlined in the following section. As we show you how to build the DECISION worksheet, brief definitions are provided for each term to assist you both in understanding the worksheet and in transferring the analysis to your own operation.

Notation used in this book

Before you start to enter the worksheet, take a moment to review the notation system used throughout this book. To simplify instructions describing keystrokes used with Multiplan, we use the following symbols:

R23C1   Individual cells on the worksheet are indicated by row and column coordinates. A cell is the space where a row and a column intersect. For example, **R23C1** is the cell located at the intersection of row 23 and column 1.

R23C1: R27C5   A range of cells is indicated by two cell references separated by a colon. For example, R23C1:R27C5 refers to a rectangular block of cells whose upper-left corner is cell R23C1 and whose lower-right corner is R27C5. If a range is only one row or one column wide, a shorthand form of range reference is used. For example, R19C1:5 refers to a range of five adjacent cells in row 19.

Goto   Whenever the instructions ask you to Goto a specific cell, you can either use Multiplan's GOTO command and specify the coordinates, or else you can move the cell pointer to the desired location using the arrow keys (↑) (↓) (→) (←).

Select   Multiplan commands are selected by typing 1, 2, or 3 letters. The actual command is shown in parentheses, but you need only type the letters shown in **boldface**.

Type   Whenever you see the word Type in the step-by-step instructions, you should type all items appearing in **boldface** exactly as they appear in the text, including spaces and punctuation. Depending on which command preceded the Type instruction, you might be performing one of the following tasks:

- Entering text (to identify a column or a line item) in a cell

- Entering a value

- Entering a formula

- Supplying a parameter in a command field (For example, the FORMAT DEFAULT CELLS command has three fields: "alignment," "format code," and "# of decimals.")

(→) (←)
(↑)
(↓)   The arrow keys are used extensively in Multiplan. In this book, we will use these special graphic symbols to indicate the up, down, left, and right direction keys.

(RET)
(TAB)
(SP)   These are the standard computer keyboard keys used in Multiplan. In this book, we use these three symbols to represent the carriage return, tab, and space bar.

Recalculate   Throughout this book, we work with the automatic recalculation feature turned off. This necessitates doing a manual recalculation from time to time. On most computers, recalculation is accomplished by typing the **!** (exclamation point). Some machines use a special function key (such as **F4** on the IBM PC) to do recalculation. Please check the manual that came with the Multiplan package you purchased for your computer.

Getting ready

First, let's get your computer ready to build the DECISION worksheet. Be sure to follow the steps and instructions carefully, since skipping a step could cause problems later. (*Note*: If you are using the publisher's data disk described on page 144, format only one blank disk for a backup copy in Step 1, then follow Steps 2–6.) Materials you need:

1 Multiplan program disk

2 One or two blank disks (not used until you save data on page 31)

3 Adhesive disk labels

Reminder: If you stop work and turn the computer off, all data will be erased from the computer's memory. Your worksheet will be lost unless you have saved the data on a disk. Since saving your work is not described or recommended until you have partially entered the worksheet on the computer (Step Eleven under "Entering the income statement," page 31), leave your computer on as you proceed through the steps in the "Getting Ready" and "Entering the income statement" sections.

STEP 1 **Label and format two blank disks.** This is a quick but necessary step. Labeling helps you keep track of your disks, and formatting is required before you can store information on the disks.

Begin by labeling the disks. Write an identifying code on an adhesive label; then peel the label off the backing and attach it to the top side of the disk. We suggest that you code the disks using the software package and a number, such as MP #1, MP #2, and so forth, for the disks containing Multiplan worksheets. You could also use a more descriptive title, such as "DECISION worksheets."

See your computer manual for the actual procedure for formatting the disks.

STEP 2 **Load Multiplan** into the computer. A copy of the Multiplan disk should be inserted into the primary disk drive only when the drive isn't working (when it isn't humming and the helpful red light is off).

Start by turning the computer on, and follow these steps:

1 Touching only the protective cover, hold the Multiplan program disk with its label facing up toward you (if the disk is in your right hand and your thumb is on the label, you are holding it correctly). Point the end of the disk with the oblong opening toward disk drive A, and insert the disk into the drive door (see the illustration). Gently push the disk forward until you feel resistance. (Never push hard because the disk will buckle if it gets caught on an obstruction.) Carefully jiggle the disk to make sure it is fully inserted.

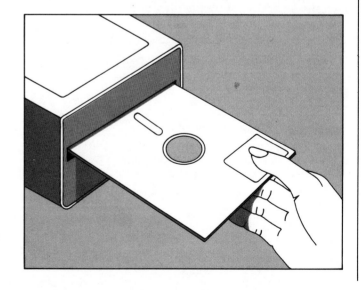

2 Gently close the drive door. As you slowly lower the door, make sure that the two metal fingers just clear the front end of the disk. If they hit the top of the disk, it isn't inserted far enough into the drive.

3 The disk drive will start and the red light will come on. When the drive stops, the program is loaded into memory and the characteristic Multiplan display — with column numbers across the top and row numbers down the side — should appear on the screen. (See the illustration opposite.)

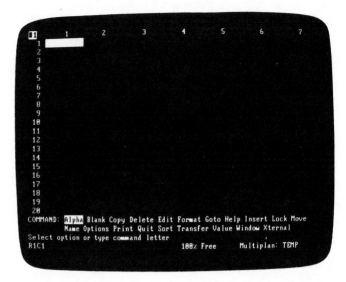

STEP 3 **Clear the screen.** Data, labels, formulas, or formats could be on the Multiplan worksheet and not appear on the screen display. To be sure the computer's memory and the spreadsheet are clear of data before you begin work, always clear the screen.

Result If the screen was already clear, you won't see any change. Whenever you start a new worksheet, however, it is wise to use this command to be sure the screen is clear of all previously entered data, some of which might be on the spreadsheet but not on the area covered by the screen.

To enter
a command to clear the screen

Select TC (for Transfer Clear)
Type **Y** (for Yes) to confirm

STEP 4 **Set column widths.** Column widths on the worksheet must be wide enough to hold the largest numbers and labels. We need a column width of 30 characters for the labels in column 1; the other columns can be left at their default setting of 10 characters.

To change column widths
from the default setting of 10 characters

Goto any cell in column 1

Select FW (for Format Width)
Type **30** in the "in chars or d(efault)" field (RET)

Result There should now be five columns visible on the screen. Column 1 should be three times wider than each of the other columns.

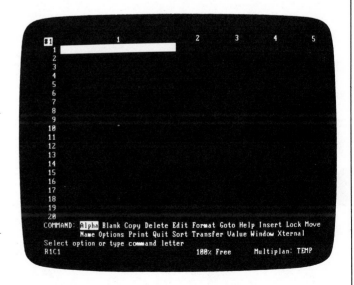

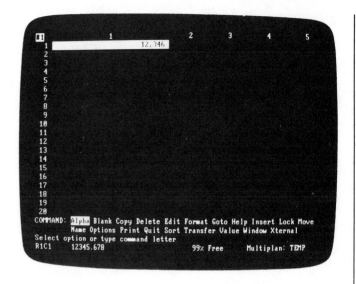

Format the screen display for better readability. Multiplan allows for a variety of options in the appearance of the screen display. In this worksheet, we'd like to show most numbers as integers (whole numbers), since there's no need to keep track of pennies. Also, the figures will be easier to read if there are commas to separate hundreds from thousands.

To enter

a command to simplify the screen display

Select FDC (for Format Default Cells)
Type (TAB)
Type **I** in the "format code" field (RET)

Select FO (for Format Options)
Type **Y** in the "commas" field (RET)

Result No change is apparent on the screen. If you wish to verify the result, follow this procedure: Goto R1C1 and type **12345.678** (RET) The rounded-off figure of **12,346** should appear on the screen.

Enter a command to speed up data entry. Normally, Multiplan automatically recalculates the value of every cell in the worksheet each time an entry is made. As a worksheet increases in size and complexity, this automatic recalculation takes more and more time, and can slow down data entry considerably. To speed up data entry, you can turn off automatic recalculation.

To enter

a command to turn off automatic recalculation

Select O (for Options)
Type **N** in the "recalc" field (RET)

Result Although no change appears on the screen, the recalculation feature should now work only at your command. This means that you can enter data rapidly, without waiting for the entire sheet to recalculate after each entry. If you need to recalculate at any point, just type **!** (the exclamation point, SHIFT and 1 on most keyboards) or press the specified function key (**F4** on the IBM PC).

MULTIPLAN TIPS Variable column widths

Using Multiplan's variable column width feature will allow you a great deal of flexibility in designing your worksheets. A worksheet is easier to read if you use wide columns for descriptive labels and narrower columns for the data that will be generated in other columns.

When you first start up Multiplan on your computer, the columns are all the same width, the default width of 10 characters. Since computer screens are generally set up to display 80 characters across, there will be 7 columns visible on the screen.

Use the Format Width command to change the width of a column.

Entering the DECISION worksheet

You are now ready to begin building the DECISION worksheet on the computer. Before you actually begin putting information into the computer, take a few minutes to read below how the steps are organized and described in the instructions. The same organization is used in other sections where worksheets are entered in the later chapters.

Each step has a number and title, such as "Step One — Enter headings and ruled lines," or "Step Eleven — Save your work." Under each step, you'll be entering data or using computer procedures to transform or save data as you build the worksheet. Follow the steps in sequence, unless you are using the data disk from the publisher (see page 144). In that case, see the special instructions that come with the disk.

Each step is broken down into smaller units, or substeps. For most of the steps, the smaller units are row-by-row instructions that follow this outline:

Row number: For example, "Rows 1 and 3."

Row title: For example, "Enter headings."

Row description: Explanation of the label or term to be entered. All business terms used, such as *gross sales*, are explained.

Result: This describes what should happen if you have entered the data correctly. Occasionally, photos of the screen display appear to illustrate the result. Except in the earliest sections, results are not given for entering labels or values into entry spaces on a row, since the expected result is so obvious. You should, however, always check the Results section after entering a formula.

Illustrations, such as the one below, show what data you'll be entering as you follow the instructions beginning on page 22. Note that the illustration has shaded areas. The *unshaded* area shows what you will be entering. For example, this illustration tells you that you'd be entering all data in the white space from row 8, Gross sales, down to row 26, Net income.

```
        1             2       3      4      5      6        7
 1 DECISION worksheet
 2
 3 INCOME STATEMENT: January 1 through December 31, 19..
 4
 5                        This  % net  Last  % net  <----Deviation---->
 6                        year  sales  year  sales       $          %
 7
 8 Gross sales          336,000
 9 Sales discounts            0
10 Net sales            336,000
11
12 Cost of goods sold   221,760
13 Gross profit         114,240
14
15 General & administrative 49,600
16 Selling expenses      49,000
17 Depreciation           6,000
18
19 Operating income       9,640
20 Interest expense       6,000
21 Other income/expense       0
22
23 Income before taxes    3,640
24 Taxes                    728
25
26 NET INCOME             2,912
27
```

MULTIPLAN TIPS Entering data: A shortcut

Although the (RET) key is often the final keystroke when you enter information, it isn't the only one you can use. When making entries across a row or down a column, you can save time by using the (→) (←) (↑) (↓) keys. In one stroke, this will enter the label, value, or formula you just typed and move the cell pointer to the next cell. The command line will read **ALPHA/VALUE**, signifying that Multiplan expects you to type either a label or a value into the current cell. If your first keystroke is either a number or a math symbol, i.e. **0 1 2 3 4 5 6 7 8 9 + − . (=**, then Multiplan will "read" this entry as a value or formula, and the command line will immediately change to **VALUE**. On the other hand, if your first keystroke in the new cell pointer location is one of the following: **ABCDEFGHIJKLMNOPQRSTUVW XYZ ! @ # $ % ^ & * { } [ ] : ; ' < > ? /**, then Multiplan anticipates a label entry, and the command line changes to **ALPHA**.

MULTIPLAN TIPS Speeding entries by avoiding continual recalculations

When you build a worksheet, every time you enter a new formula or a new value the entire worksheet is automatically recalculated. The message line will tell you that Multiplan is "crunching numbers" and show how many cells remain to be recalculated. While this activity is taking place, Multiplan takes over control of the screen and keyboard, and you must wait for the recalculation to end before resuming your keyboard entries.

The larger the model you are building, the longer this takes. Initially this isn't a problem, but when you find yourself waiting longer and longer, you'll want a quicker way. Use the Options command to change to manual recalculation mode. In manual mode, the screen display will change only when you press the recalc control key; recalculation also will take place automatically when the Transfer Save command is used.

To turn off automatic recalculation:
Select **O** (for Options)
The command line reads
OPTIONS recalc: Yes No
Type **N** (RET)

You can switch back to automatic recalcution with the same Options command; just type **Y** (RET).

Entering the income statement

Step One

Enter headings and ruled lines

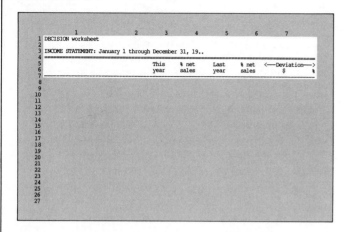

```
                 1          2      3      4      5      6      7
1  DECISION worksheet
2
3  INCOME STATEMENT: January 1 through December 31, 19..
4
5                             This   % net  Last   % net  <—Deviation—>
6                             year   sales  year   sales    $        %
7
8
...
```

ROWS 1 and 3   **Enter headings** to identify the DECISION worksheet, the income statement section, and the period covered.

To enter
  headings for the worksheet and the income statement

  Select FC (for Format Cells)
    Type **R3C1:4** in the "cells" field (TAB) (TAB)
    Type **C** (for Continuous) in the "format code" field (RET)

  Goto R1C1

  Select A (for Alpha)
    Type **DECISION worksheet** (↓) (↓)
    Type **INCOME STATEMENT: January 1 through December 31, 19..** (RET)

. . . .

ROWS 4 and 7   **Enter ruled lines** across columns 1 through 7. Ruled lines will be used throughout our worksheet to separate major sections of the financial statements, making the screen display and printouts easier to read. The continuous format allows us to stretch repeating equal signs and hyphens across all seven columns, even though the REPT formulas only appear in column 1.

We will also assign names to these ruled lines. The name *line2* will refer to the double ruled line, and the name *line1* will refer to the single ruled line. Later on, when we want to enter more lines, we will be able to refer to them by name.

To enter
  ruled lines in the worksheet (and then name them)

  Select FC (for Format Cells)
    Type **R4C1:7,R7C1:7** in the "cells" field (TAB) (TAB)
    Type **C** (for Continuous) in the "format code" field (RET)

  Goto R4C1

  Select V (for Value)
    Type **REPT("=",90)** (RET)

  Select N (for Name)
    Type **line2** in the "define name" field (TAB)
    Type **R4C1:7** in the "to refer to" field (RET)

  Goto R7C1

  Select V (for Value)
    Type **REPT("-",90)** (RET)

  Select N (for Name)
    Type **line1** in the "define name" field (TAB)
    Type **R7C1:7** in the "to refer to" field (RET)

. . . .

ROWS 5 and 6   **Enter column headings** for "this year," "last year," and "deviation." Once this period's income statement has been entered, we can enter that of the preceding period and compare the two. As we look at the two operating periods, if we see any changes, we should make a careful investigation to determine their causes. If we see positive deviations, of course, we would want to do more of whatever it was that produced the positive result. However, if we see negative deviations, we want to quickly identify the causes so that we will be able to avoid them in the future.

To enter
  column headings for the worksheet

  Select FC (for Format Cells)
    Type **R5C2:R6C5,R6C6:7** in the "cells" field (TAB)
    Type **R** (for Right) in the "alignment" field (RET)

  Select FC (for Format Cells)
    Type **R5C6:7** in the "cells" field (TAB) (TAB)
    Type **C** (for Continuous) in the "format code" field (RET)

  Goto R5C2

  Select A (for Alpha)
    Type **This** (↓)
    Type **year** (→) (↑)

Type **% net** ⬇
Type **sales** ➡ ⬆
Type **Last** ⬇
Type **year** ➡ ⬆
Type **% net** ⬇
Type **sales** ➡ ⬆
Type (SP) (SP) (SP) **<---Deviation--->** ⬇
Type **$** ➡
Type **%** (RET)

Step Two

Enter line items, values, and formulas for "this year"

R O W
8
Gross sales include revenues from all the firm's activities. These could be further broken down on supplemental schedules to show the source of income, such as retail, wholesale, or international, if doing so aids your business analysis.

```
             1           2     3     4     5     6        7
 1 DECISION worksheet
 2
 3 INCOME STATEMENT: January 1 through December 31, 19..
 4
 5                       This  % net  Last  % net  <---Deviation--->
 6                       year  sales  year  sales     $        %
 7
 8 Gross sales          336,000
 9 Sales discounts            0
10 Net sales            336,000
11
12 Cost of goods sold   221,760
13 Gross profit         114,240
14
15 General & administrative 49,600
16 Selling expenses      49,000
17 Depreciation           6,000
18
19 Operating income       9,640
20 Interest expense       6,000
21 Other income/expense       0
22
23 Income before taxes    3,640
24 Taxes                    728
25
26 NET INCOME             2,912
27
```

MULTIPLAN TIPS Entering formulas or values

At the main command level, a number or symbol from the following list will trigger Multiplan's Value command, just as if you had selected **V** from the main command menu:

0 1 2 3 4 5 6 7 8 9 = + − . " (

The number or character you typed becomes the first character of the formula, unless it was an equal sign (=).

If the formula you wish to enter begins with a letter (such as **SUM** or **IF**), you must select **V** or type = before entering the formula.

To enter
a label to identify this as the gross sales row
a value of $336,000 in cell R8C2

Goto R8C1

Select A (for Alpha)
Type **Gross sales** ➡
Type **336000** (RET)

....

R O W
9
Sales discounts, along with sales returns and allowances, which are normally entered on this row, are subtracted from the gross sales figure so that we can see the actual value of the adjustments made to reduce the gross sales figure.

To enter
a label to identify this as the sales discounts row
a value of 0 in cell R9C2 for sales discounts

Goto R9C1

Select A (for Alpha)
Type **Sales discounts** ➡
Type **0** (RET)

....

R O W
10
Net sales are the actual operating revenues available to the firm once the discounts and other adjustments have been subtracted from the gross sales. This figure is critical because it shows us what is actually available to the firm and helps us to determine how the firm is actually doing relative to its other activities.

MULTIPLAN TIPS Entering labels

At the main command level, any letter you type will be interpreted as a command (except **J K R U Y** or **Z**, which will cause the computer to beep in displeasure and return you to the main command menu for another try). A label entry must therefore be preceded by selecting **A** (for Alpha) or by pressing the (↵) key.

If you forget to do this and simply attempt to type in a label, Multiplan will take a cue from the first letter you type in and display the command menu for that particular command. For example, if you try to enter the label **SALES** into a cell without first selecting **Alpha**, Multiplan assumes that you want to use the Sort command. The only way out of this situation is to use the Cancel command (the ESC key or CTRL-C on most computers) and start over at the main command level.

Entering the income statement Continued

To enter
> *a label* to identify this row as net sales
> *a formula* in cell R10C2 that will subtract sales discounts from gross sales

Goto R10C1

Select A (for Alpha)
> Type **Net sales** →
> Type **= R8C2-R9C2** (RET)

Result Since sales discounts are zero, net sales should be the same as gross sales ($336,000).

....

ROW 12 **Cost of goods sold** represents the total variable costs of the operation. These are the costs that result from having a product available for sale, whether it is purchased from outside vendors or is manufactured within the organization. If all goods are purchased, this is a relatively simple line item; if goods are manufactured, it can be quite a detailed series of costs, which would normally be calculated by you or your accountant on a separate worksheet.

To enter
> *a label* to identify this row as cost of goods sold
> *a value* in cell R12C2 of $221,760

Goto R12C1

Select A (for Alpha)
> Type **Cost of goods sold** →
> Type **221760** (RET)

....

ROW 13 **Gross profit** represents the amount that is left over once we have subtracted all the variable costs or the cost of goods sold. As long as we price all of our sales above our cost of goods sold, we will have some gross profit. Gross profit is also known as *contribution*, or the amount of contribution sales are making to the organization's activities. The terms *gross profit*, *margin*, and *contribution* are all applied to essentially the same set of figures, and all mean basically the same thing. Later on it will be seen that gross profit is a critical component of breakeven.

To enter
> *a label* to identify this line as gross profit
> *a formula* in cell R13C2 that will subtract cost of goods sold from net sales to give gross profit

Goto R13C1

Select A (for Alpha)
> Type **Gross profit** →
> Type **= R10C2-R12C2** (RET)

Result Gross profit will be $114,240.

....

ROW 15 **General and administrative (G&A) expenses** are also known as overhead. These costs are relatively fixed in most organizations and include such things as officers' salaries, rent, insurance, and other such regular costs, which are not particularly affected by changes in the sales level. These costs are discussed in more detail in the section on overhead.

To enter
> *a label* to identify this as the general and administrative expenses row
> *a value* of $49,600 in cell R15C2

Goto R15C1

Select A (for Alpha)
> Type **General & administrative** →
> Type **49600** (RET)

....

ROW 16 **Selling expenses** is one category of the G&A costs that we generally want to highlight. Included here would be sales commissions, sales travel costs, samples, advertising, and any other direct marketing or selling costs. As will be seen in our later discussion on overhead, these costs often tend to be more semivariable relative to sales than actually fixed or completely variable.

To enter
> *a label* to identify this as the selling expense row
> *a value* of $49,000 in cell R16C2

Goto R16C1

Select A (for Alpha)
> Type **Selling expenses** →
> Type **49000** (RET)

....

ROW 17 **Depreciation** represents the gradual expensing over time of costly capital assets. There are various methods of depreciation, such as straight-line versus accelerated, which are important to consider and

Multiplan offers several options that can improve the way dollar amounts are displayed on a worksheet.

All values over 1000 can be displayed with a comma at the thousand position, million position, and so on. For example, a value entered as **1000000** can be displayed as **1,000,000**.

To display values over 1000 with commas:

Select **FO** (for Format Options)
The command line reads
FORMAT OPTIONS commas: Yes No
Type **Y** (RET)

There is a "dollar" format, which displays values with a leading dollar sign, a decimal point, and two decimal places. For example, a value entered as **1250.2** into a cell with dollar format would be displayed as **$1250.20**.

In this book we have not used this format, since all of our monetary figures are whole dollars, and the .00 appearing after each number makes the screen display look a little crowded. However, if you wish to use values accurate to the nearest penny in your own worksheets, the dollar format will be helpful.

To display values with dollar signs:

Select **FDC** (for Format Default Cells)
Type (TAB) **$** (RET)

The above command will display all numerical values entered in the worksheet in the dollar format, except in cells where the format has been set to another format code.

The Format Cells command can also be used to select the dollar format in a specified cell or group of cells.

The simplest way to move the cell pointer short distances on the electronic worksheet is to use the arrow keys (↑) (↓) (→) (←). Press an arrow key once to move the cell pointer to the next cell, or hold the key down to move the pointer across several cells.

A faster way to move around the worksheet, especially when the distances involved are large, is to use the Goto command. For example, if the cell pointer is located at R1C1 (this cell is also called the home position), and we wish to move it to cell R100C5, we would proceed as follows:

Select **G** (for Goto)
The command line reads
GOTO: Name Row-Col Window
Type **R**
The command line changes to
GOTO row: column:
Type **100** (TAB) **5** (RET)

Even if you don't know the exact row-column coordinates of the cell you want to go to, enter a rough approximation of the coordinates and make your final movement with the arrow keys. You'll still save time. If you've named a cell (using the Name command), the procedure is just as simple: select **GN** (for Goto Name), type in the name of the cell, and then press (RET).

A third way to move around the worksheet is available on certain computers, including the IBM PC, the Compaq, and other machines whose keyboards include Page up, Page down, Home, and End keys. The Page keys will move you up or down one "page" or screenful of the worksheet at a time; the Home key will take you to R1C1 or to the upper-left corner of your screen (depending on your computer); and End will take you to the last nonblank cell in the worksheet (i.e., the cell with the largest row and column coordinates that contains a value).

discuss with your accountant for tax purposes but are not relevant to our discussion. Here, depreciation represents the gradual expensing of the capital assets that will be listed on the balance sheet.

To enter
a label to identify this as the depreciation row
a value of $6,000 in cell R17C2

Goto R17C1

Select A (for Alpha)
Type **Depreciation** (→)
Type **6000** (RET)

ROW 19 **Operating income** is what we have left over once we subtract from the gross profits all of the costs that are directly related to the operation of the firm. This line tells us how we are doing as far as the operation itself is concerned.

To enter
a label to identify this as the operating income line of the income statement

a formula in cell R19C2 that will subtract G&A, selling, and depreciation expenses from gross profit

Goto R19C1

Select A (for Alpha)
Type **Operating income** $\rightarrow$
Type **=R13C2-SUM(R14:18C2)** RET

Result Operating income is $9,640.

. . . .

R O W 20 **Interest expense** is separated from the other operating costs because we want to inspect the condition of the operation excluding whatever methods we have used to finance its activity. However, interest expense is a real cost to the firm, so we must subtract it in order to determine how we are actually doing.

To enter
a label to identify this as the interest expense line of the income statement
a value of $6,000 in cell R20C2

Goto R20C1

Select A (for Alpha)
Type **Interest expense** $\rightarrow$
Type **6000** RET

. . . .

R O W 21 **Other income and expense** would include items that are not directly related to the operation of the business itself. We may have excess plant capacity that we sublet to another business organization; if that were the case, the rent we receive for that space would be included here.

To enter
a label to identify this as the other income and expense line of the income statement
a value of 0 in cell R21C2

Goto R21C1

Select A (for Alpha)
Type **Other income/expense** $\rightarrow$
Type **0** RET

R O W 23 **Income before taxes** is the result of all of our operating activities for the total business venture before we worry about tax considerations. This is another important subtotal because it helps us to compare activities from one period to the next without adjusting for differences in the tax laws or changes in our personal situation that might affect our actual tax rate.

To enter
a label to identify this as the income before taxes line of the income statement
a formula in cell R23C2 that will subtract interest and other income and expense entries from operating income

Goto R23C1

Select A (for Alpha)
Type **Income before taxes** $\rightarrow$
Type **=R19C2-R20C2-R21C2** RET

Result The formula should calculate $3,640 for this line item.

. . . .

R O W 24 **Taxes** are a fact of life and must be paid by most business organizations that make a profit, so they must be deducted from the residual income as a further expense. We have arbitrarily used a tax rate of 20 percent for Mr. Adams and the Acme Hardware Company merely to illustrate the potential impact of taxes on net operations. The actual rate can only be determined once the tax forms are completed for the operation and for Mr. Adams's personal situation.

To enter
a label to identify this as the tax line of the income statement
a formula in cell R24C2 that will calculate taxes at a rate of 20 percent of income before taxes (row 23) if income before taxes is greater than zero. If income before taxes is zero or less, taxes will be zero. The formula to be entered reads "If income before taxes in cell R23C2 is greater than zero then multiply it by 20 percent; otherwise make taxes zero."

Goto R24C1

Select A (for Alpha)
Type **Taxes** $\rightarrow$
Type **=IF(R23C2>0,0.2*R23C2,0)** RET

Result The calculated taxes should be $728.

ROW 26 **Net income** represents the true "bottom line" of all operational activities. This figure is also important because it will be transferred in the worksheet to the retained earnings line of the balance sheet.

To enter
> *a label* to identify this as the net income line of the income statement
>
> *a formula* in cell R26C2 that will subtract taxes from income before taxes

Goto R26C1

Select A (for Alpha)
> Type **NET INCOME** $\rightarrow$
> Type **= R23C2-R24C2** (RET)

Result Net income should be $2,912.

Step Three

Assign names to columns 2 and 4

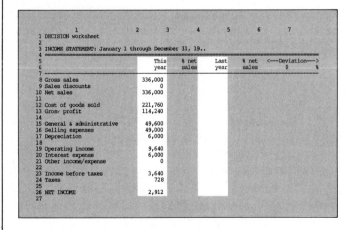

COLUMNS 2 and 4 The formulas in columns 3, 5, 6, and 7 will all make reference to the "this year" and "last year" columns by name.

Select N (for Name)
> Type **thisyear** in the "define name" field (TAB)
> Type **C2** in the "to refer to" field (RET)

Select N (for Name)
> Type **lastyear** in the "define name" field (TAB)
> Type **C4** in the "to refer to" field (RET)

Step Four

Enter operating ratios

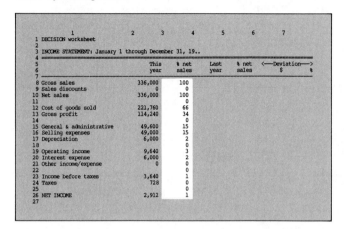

COLUMN 3 **Operating ratios** are calculated for the worksheet. We want to look at all of the expenses on the income statement as percentages as well as actual dollar amounts. Using percentages facilitates comparisons from one operating period to another when levels of activity are significantly different, between different business entities, and between one business and industry averages. The percentages we are interested in, also referred to as operating ratios, are the relationships between each of the expense categories and the actual sales. We calculate this relationship as a percentage quite simply by dividing each expense category by the net sales.

To enter
> *formulas* in column 3 that will calculate operating ratio percentages by dividing each dollar amount in column 2 by net sales. The result of this division is multiplied by 100 to display the calculated percentages as whole numbers, that is, 25% rather than .25.

Goto R8C3

Select V (for Value)
> Type **thisyear/R10C2%** (RET)

Select CD (for Copy Down)
> Type **18** in the "number of cells" field (RET)

Recalculate the worksheet by pressing !, **F4**, or the specified function key.

Entering the income statement Continued

Result When recalculation is complete, the figures in column 3 on your screen should match those in the illustration on page 27. Note that there are "extra" formulas that yield a value of zero in rows 11, 14, 18, 22, and 25. These extra formulas will disappear when we enter ruled lines across these rows in a later step.

The percentages calculated by the formulas are rounded off to the nearest whole number, so in some cases they may appear to be off by 1 percent. For instance, if you add up the percentage figures displayed in this example, the total is 101 percent:

Cost of goods sold	66%
General & admin.	15%
Selling expense	15%
Depreciation	2%
Interest expense	2%
Net income	1%
	101%

Step Five

Enter comparison figures for "last year"

```
             1              2     3      4      5     6      7
 1 DECISION worksheet
 2
 3 INCOME STATEMENT: January 1 through December 31, 19..
 4
 5                             This   % net   Last   % net  <----Deviation---->
 6                             year   sales   year   sales     $          %
 7
 8 Gross sales               336,000   100   312,000
 9 Sales discounts                 0     0         0
10 Net sales                 336,000   100   312,000
11                                       0
12 Cost of goods sold        221,760    66   201,240
13 Gross profit              114,240    34   110,760
14                                       0
15 General & administrative   49,600    15    52,000
16 Selling expenses           49,000    15    40,000
17 Depreciation                6,000     2     5,500
18                                       0
19 Operating income            9,640     3    13,260
20 Interest expense            6,000     2     6,750
21 Other income/expense            0     0      -800
22                                       0
23 Income before taxes         3,640     1     7,310
24 Taxes                         728     0     1,462
25                                       0
26 NET INCOME                  2,912     1     5,848
27
```

COLUMN 4 **Last year's income statement figures** will be entered into column 4, so that you can compare them with "this year's" figures in the deviation columns.

To enter

values on all the rows in the "last year" columns

Goto R8C4

Type **312000** ↓
Type **0** ↓
Type **312000** ↓ ↓
Type **201240** ↓
Type **110760** ↓ ↓
Type **52000** ↓
Type **40000** ↓
Type **5500** ↓ ↓
Type **13260** ↓
Type **6750** ↓
Type **-800** ↓ ↓
Type **7310** ↓
Type **1462** ↓ ↓
Type **5848** RET

Step Six

Enter operating ratios for "last year"

```
             1              2     3      4      5     6      7
 1 DECISION worksheet
 2
 3 INCOME STATEMENT: January 1 through December 31, 19..
 4
 5                             This   % net   Last   % net  <----Deviation---->
 6                             year   sales   year   sales     $          %
 7
 8 Gross sales               336,000   100   312,000   100
 9 Sales discounts                 0     0         0     0
10 Net sales                 336,000   100   312,000   100
11                                       0                0
12 Cost of goods sold        221,760    66   201,240    65
13 Gross profit              114,240    34   110,760    36
14                                       0                0
15 General & administrative   49,600    15    52,000    17
16 Selling expenses           49,000    15    40,000    13
17 Depreciation                6,000     2     5,500     2
18                                       0                0
19 Operating income            9,640     3    13,260     4
20 Interest expense            6,000     2     6,750     2
21 Other income/expense            0     0      -800    -0
22                                       0                0
23 Income before taxes         3,640     1     7,310     2
24 Taxes                         728     0     1,462     0
25                                       0                0
26 NET INCOME                  2,912     1     5,848     2
27
```

COLUMN 5 **Enter formulas to calculate last year's figures** in terms of last year's net sales. These figures will provide a comparison for the deviation columns to be entered next.

To enter

formulas to calculate operating ratios (the results are multiplied by 100 to display the calculated percentages as whole numbers)

Goto R8C5

Select V (for Value)
Type **lastyear/R10C4%** RET

There are two ways to calculate percentages:

1 The percent symbol, when incorporated into a formula, will multiply a value by 100. For example, the formula **R5C2/R12C2%** will effectively yield the same result as **(R5C2/R12C2)*100**. The percent symbol itself is *not* displayed.

2 The percent format, when selected with either the Format Default Cells or Format Cells command, will display values as a percentage followed by the percent symbol.

Select CD (for Copy Down)
Type **18** in the "number of cells" field (RET)

Recalculate the worksheet

Result When recalculation is complete, your results should match those in the illustration. Again, note that the extra formulas that yield a value of zero (rows 11, 14, 18, 22, and 25) will be wiped out by ruled lines in a later step.

Step Seven

Enter formulas into the dollar amount deviation column

```
          1                2      3       4      5       6          7
 1 DECISION worksheet
 2
 3 INCOME STATEMENT: January 1 through December 31, 19..
 4
 5                           This   % net   Last   % net  <---Deviation--->
 6                           year   sales   year   sales       $         %
 7
 8 Gross sales             336,000   100  312,000   100     24,000
 9 Sales discounts               0     0        0     0          0
10 Net sales               336,000   100  312,000   100     24,000
11                               0                   0          0
12 Cost of goods sold      221,760    66  201,240    65     20,520
13 Gross profit            114,240    34  110,760    36      3,480
14                               0                   0          0
15 General & administrative 49,600    15   52,000    17     -2,400
16 Selling expenses         49,000    15   40,000    13      9,000
17 Depreciation              6,000     2    5,500     2        500
18                               0                   0          0
19 Operating income          9,640     3   13,260     4     -3,620
20 Interest expense          6,000     2    6,750     2       -750
21 Other income/expense          0     0     -800    -0        800
22                               0                   0          0
23 Income before taxes       3,640     1    7,310     2     -3,670
24 Taxes                       728     0    1,462     0       -734
25                               0                   0          0
26 NET INCOME                2,912     1    5,848     2     -2,936
27
```

‾C‾O‾L‾U‾M‾N‾ **Deviation** in this case means formulas used to
6 ‾‾‾‾‾‾ calculate the dollar increase or decrease in each line item from last year to this year.

To enter
formulas in column 6 that will subtract last year's results (column 4) from this year's results (column 2) to show the change from year to year in dollars

Goto R8C6

Select V (for Value)
Type **thisyear-lastyear** (RET)

Select CD (for Copy Down)
Type **18** in the "number of cells" field (RET)

Recalculate the worksheet

Result Your results in column 6 should match those in the illustration.

Step Eight

Enter formulas into the percentage deviation column

```
          1                2      3       4      5       6          7
 1 DECISION worksheet
 2
 3 INCOME STATEMENT: January 1 through December 31, 19..
 4
 5                           This   % net   Last   % net  <---Deviation--->
 6                           year   sales   year   sales       $         %
 7
 8 Gross sales             336,000   100  312,000   100     24,000      8
 9 Sales discounts               0     0        0     0          0
10 Net sales               336,000   100  312,000   100     24,000      8
11                               0                   0          0
12 Cost of goods sold      221,760    66  201,240    65     20,520     10
13 Gross profit            114,240    34  110,760    36      3,480      3
14                               0                   0          0
15 General & administrative 49,600    15   52,000    17     -2,400     -5
16 Selling expenses         49,000    15   40,000    13      9,000     23
17 Depreciation              6,000     2    5,500     2        500      9
18                               0                   0          0
19 Operating income          9,640     3   13,260     4     -3,620    -27
20 Interest expense          6,000     2    6,750     2       -750    -11
21 Other income/expense          0     0     -800    -0        800   -100
22                               0                   0          0
23 Income before taxes       3,640     1    7,310     2     -3,670    -50
24 Taxes                       728     0    1,462     0       -734    -50
25                               0                   0          0
26 NET INCOME                2,912     1    5,848     2     -2,936    -50
27
```

‾C‾O‾L‾U‾M‾N‾ **Deviation** calculations continue in this col-
7 ‾‾‾‾‾‾ umn. Here, formulas to calculate the percentage increase or decrease in each line item from last year to this year will be entered.

To enter
formulas in column 7 that will calculate the percentage change from last year to this year for each line item of the income statement. The formula divides the increase or decrease from last year to this year in column 6 on each line by last year's dollar results in column 4. The results are multiplied by 100 to display the percentage change as

a whole number rather than as a decimal. The formulas are embedded in an IF statement so that the calculated result won't be an ERROR message if the divisor (column 4) is zero. The formula reads, "If last year's dollar figure in column 4 is less than or greater than zero, then divide the dollar deviation (this year's figure minus last year's figure) by last year's figure. If the figure in column 4 is zero, then leave the cell blank." (See page 42.)

Goto R8C7

Select V (for Value)
Type **IF(lastyear<>0,(thisyear-lastyear)/ lastyear%,"")** (RET)

Select CD (for Copy Down)
Type **18** in the "number of cells" field (RET)

Recalculate the worksheet

Result Your results in column 7 should match those in the illustration on page 29.

ANALYSIS We must be careful in our analysis at this point and not rely more heavily on either the dollar differences or percentage differences; both are important. A large percentage difference, which would automatically attract attention, may not be particularly significant on an overall basis if the expense category is actually only a small portion of our total activity. For example, we might budget $100 per month for maintenance and find that our actual cost was $200 (a 100 percent deviation) and, according to our analytical logic, an important problem. However, when we look at this cost within the context of our overall operation, where our aggregate expenses total $8,716, we see that the $100 deviation is actually quite insignificant. On the other hand, we might have a very small percentage deviation on a large expense item and have that obscure what is actually a large dollar difference. For example, a 20 percent deviation on a $3,000 expense category means a $600 difference. Consequently, we should be aware of both the percentage and the dollar difference to keep the problem in proper perspective.

Step Nine

```
                 1           2       3        4       5       6        7
 1 DECISION worksheet
 2
 3 INCOME STATEMENT: January 1 through December 31, 19..
 4
 5                         This    % net   Last    % net   <——Deviation——>
 6                         year    sales   year    sales        $        %
 7
 8 Gross sales           336,000    100   312,000   100    24,000        8
 9 Sales discounts             0      0         0     0         0
10 Net sales             336,000    100   312,000   100    24,000        8
11
12 Cost of goods sold    221,760     66   201,240    65    20,520       10
13 Gross profit          114,240     34   110,760    36     3,480        3
14
15 General & administrative 49,600   15    52,000    17    -2,400       -5
16 Selling expenses       49,000     15    40,000    13     9,000       23
17 Depreciation            6,000      2     5,500     2       500        9
18
19 Operating income        9,640      3    13,260     4    -3,620      -27
20 Interest expense        6,000      2     6,750     2      -750      -11
21 Other income/expense        0      0      -800    -0       800     -100
22
23 Income before taxes     3,640      1     7,310     2    -3,670      -50
24 Taxes                     728      0     1,462     0      -734      -50
25
26 NET INCOME              2,912      1     5,848     2    -2,936      -50
27
```

Copy ruled lines across the income statement. In a previous step, we defined the names *line2* and *line1* to refer to the double and single ruled lines, respectively. Here we make use of Multiplan's COPY FROM command to reproduce these lines elsewhere. Note that the Continuous cell format is copied to each new location, along with the REPT formula that generates the repeated characters.

To enter
the ruled lines throughout the worksheet as needed

Select CF (for Copy From)
Type **line2** in the "cells" field (TAB)
Type **R25C1,R27C1** in the "to cells" field (RET)

Select CF (for Copy From)
Type **line1** in the "cells" field (TAB)
Type **R11C1,R14C1,R18C1,R22C1** in the "to cells" field (RET)

Result Double and single ruled lines should now be visible on the screen, matching those in the illustration. Note that the ruled lines wiped out the extra formulas in columns 3, 5, 6, and 7.

Step Ten

Lock cells containing unchanging data, formulas, and text. In exercises appearing later in this book, we will be substituting test values for some cells in column 2. The remainder of the income statement should remain unchanged. In order to prevent inadvertent changes or deletions of the permanent data, formulas, and text, we will use the LOCK CELLS and LOCK FORMULAS commands.

To lock
> *values, formulas, and text* in the income statement section of the worksheet

> **Select LC** (for Lock Cells)
>> Type **R8:26C4** in the "cells" field (TAB)
>> Type **L** (for Locked) in the "status" field (RET)

> **Select LF** (for Lock Formulas)
>> Type **Y** (to confirm)

Step Eleven

Save your work. You will often want to save a Multiplan worksheet even when it isn't complete. This protects your work when you want to take a break and prevents its loss if a mistake is made or if something goes wrong. Saving a file is simple and doesn't affect either the data in the computer's memory or the display on the screen. After taking a few seconds to save the file, you can return to the problem exactly where you left it.

When you've inserted a blank disk in disk drive B, you will use the Transfer Options command to make disk drive B your "current" disk drive. This means that your worksheets will be saved on the disk in drive B, instead of the Multiplan program disk in drive A. (*Note:* some computers use disk drive designations other than "A" and "B." Enter your own disk drive designation when using the Transfer Options command.)

To save
> *your worksheet*

> **Insert** a labeled, formatted disk into the data disk drive of your computer (drive B on most machines)

> **Select TO** (for Transfer Options)
>> Type (TAB)
>> Type **B:** in the "setup" field (RET)

> **Select TS** (for Transfer Save)
>> Type **DECISION** in the "filename" field (RET)

Result Before it is saved, the worksheet will automatically recalculate. Then the disk drive will spin, the red light will come on, and the disk will record the worksheet so that it can be reloaded when needed. The display on the screen is unchanged, as is the data in memory. At this point, you can choose to continue or to turn the computer off. Everything that was in memory is now safely stored on the disk, from which it can easily be reloaded back into memory. You can now remove the data disk from drive B and store it until you want to save again. To be even safer, make a backup copy of the disk so that you have two of them. Store them separately so the same accident can't happen to both.

MULTIPLAN TIPS Using the SUM command

> When using the **SUM** command, it is usually a good idea to establish the range of the formula between two ruled lines rather than two cells that contain values. This allows you to add or delete rows, and as long as you do this between the ruled lines, the formula will continue to work. If you delete one of the ruled lines, Multiplan will display an error message.

Entering the balance sheet

Now we move on to the balance sheet. As noted earlier, the balance sheet contains three major categories: assets, liabilities, and owner equity. The balance sheet is called a balance sheet because a balance must exist between the assets on the one side and the liabilities plus owner equity on the other. Making this distinction helps us to see who owns how much of the business. The assets are all of the things of value within the business operation. Liabilities represent what the business owes, and if there is any difference after subtracting the total liabilities from the total assets, that is what the owners of the business own.

Step One

Enter headings and ruled lines for the assets section of the balance sheet

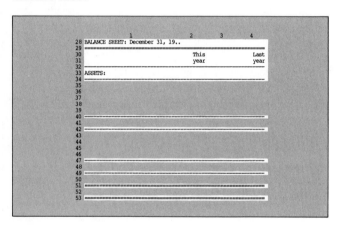

ROW 28   **Enter a heading** to identify the balance sheet section. Unlike the income statement, which covers a period of time, the balance sheet reflects the condition of business at a particular moment in time: generally, the last day of an accounting period. Thus, the date on a balance sheet might be the last day of a month, a quarter, or a fiscal year.

To enter
labels to identify the balance sheet section and the date it represents

Select FC (for Format Cells)
Type **R28C1:2** in the "cells" field (TAB) (TAB)
Type **C** (for Continuous) in the "format code" field (RET)

Goto R28C1

Select A (for Alpha)
Type **BALANCE SHEET: December 31, 19..** (RET)

....

ROWS 29–53   **Enter and name ruled lines** across columns 1 through 4. The lines we used in the income statement section are too long for this new section, so we must use a slightly different REPT formula. We'll differentiate these shorter lines by naming them *shortline2* (for the double line) and *shortline1* (for the single line).

Once the shorter lines have been installed in rows 29 and 32, they can be reproduced in the first part of the balance sheet section.

To enter
ruled lines

Select FC (for Format Cells)
Type **R29C1:4,R32C1:4** in the "cells" field (TAB) (TAB)
Type **C** (for Continuous) in the "format code" field (RET)

Goto R29C1

Select V (for Value)
Type **REPT("=",60)** (RET)

Select N (for Name)
Type **shortline2** in the "define name" field (TAB)
Type **R29C1:4** in the "to refer to" field (RET)

Select CF (for Copy From)
Type **shortline2** in the "cells" field (TAB)
Type **R51C1,R53C1** in the "to cells" field (RET)

Goto R32C1

Select V (for Value)
Type **REPT("-",60)** (RET)

Select N (for Name)
Type **shortline1** in the "define name" field (TAB)
Type **R32C1:4** in the "to refer to" field (RET)

Select CF (for Copy From)
Type **shortline1** in the "cells" field (TAB)
Type **R34C1,R40C1,R42C1,R47C1,R49C1** in the "to cells" field (RET)

Result Single and double ruled lines, stretching across the first four columns only, should appear in rows 29, 32, 34, 40, 42, 47, 49, 51, and 53.

Enter column headings to identify this year and last year, and a heading to identify this as the assets section of the balance sheet

To enter

> *labels* for the column heads and the assets section of the balance sheet

Select FC (for Format Cells)
> Type **R30C2:R31C4** in the "cells" field (TAB)
> Type **R** (for Right) in the "alignment" field (RET)

Goto R30C2

Select A (for Alpha)
> Type **This** (↓)
> Type **year** (→) (→) (↑)
> Type **Last** (↓)
> Type **year** (RET)

Goto R33C1

Select A (for Alpha)
> Type **ASSETS:** (RET)

Step Two

Enter labels, formulas, and values in columns 1 and 2

```
              1              2        3        4
28 BALANCE SHEET: December 31, 19..
29
30                         This              Last
31                         year              year
32
33 ASSETS:
34
35 <Current assets>
36 Cash                   1,335
37 Accounts receivable   17,777
38 Inventory             83,292
39 Prepaid expenses       3,400
40
41 Total current assets 105,804
42
43 <Fixed assets>
44 Buildings & equipment 33,000
45 Less accumulated depreciation -13,000      -7,000
46 Land                       0
47
48 Total fixed assets    20,000
49
50 Other assets           3,700
51
52 TOTAL ASSETS         129,504
53
```

Enter line item headings, formulas, and values in the first half of the balance sheet, which is concerned with assets. Since one of the formulas (for accumulated depreciation) depends in part upon last year's figure, we will enter this one value in column 4 now. The remainder of the last year figures will be entered in a separate step.

Current assets are those things the business owns that are or will become cash in one year or less. They include cash, accounts receivable, and inventory in our example.

To enter

> *a label* to identify this as the current assets section of the balance sheet

Goto R35C1

Select A (for Alpha)
> Type **<Current assets>** (RET)

....

Cash is cash within the business, in bank accounts, or wherever it may reside.

To enter

> *a label* to identify this as the cash line of the balance sheet
> *a value* in cell R36C2 for cash of $1,335

Goto R36C1

Select A (for Alpha)
> Type **Cash** (→)
> Type **1335** (RET)

....

Accounts receivable include money owed to the business, generally by customers.

To enter

> *a label* to identify this as the accounts receivable line of the balance sheet
> *a value* of $17,777 in cell R37C2

Goto R37C1

Select A (for Alpha)
> Type **Accounts receivable** (→)
> Type **17777** (RET)

....

Inventory represents goods that the business has purchased or manufactured and has available for sale.

Entering the balance sheet Continued

To enter
> *a label* to identify this as the inventory line of the balance sheet
> *a value* of $83,292 in cell R38C2

Goto R38C1

Select A (for Alpha)
> Type **Inventory** ⊖
> Type **83292** ⦅RET⦆

....

ROW 39 **Prepaid expenses** are those expenses the business has paid for but not yet used. For example, they could include an insurance premium that is paid at the beginning of the operating period but that has not yet been fully used up.

To enter
> *a label* to identify this as the prepaid expenses line of the balance sheet
> *a value* of $3,400 in cell R39C2

Goto R39C1

Select A (for Alpha)
> Type **Prepaid expenses** ⊖
> Type **3400** ⦅RET⦆

....

ROW 41 **Total current assets** are the sum of all current assets. It is helpful to separate the current assets from the other assets because in financial analysis the distinction helps us to better understand the financial relationships within the organization.

To enter
> *a label* to identify this as the total current assets line of the balance sheet
> *a formula* in cell R41C2 that will add individual current asset line items

Goto R41C1

Select A (for Alpha)
> Type **Total current assets** ⊖
> Type **= SUM(R34:40C2)** ⦅RET⦆

Result Total current assets should be $105,804.

ROW 43 **Fixed assets** are those assets such as buildings and equipment that will not be used in the course of ordinary events and that consequently have a useful life of more than one year. These are the long-term production assets that, along with the human resources, represent the productive capacity of the firm.

To enter
> *a label* to identify this as the fixed assets section of the balance sheet

Goto R43C1

Select A (for Alpha)
> Type <**Fixed assets**> ⦅RET⦆

....

ROW 44 **Buildings and equipment** are key fixed asset accounts often representing substantial value within the organization. (Of course if the business rents its building instead of owning it, the building value does not appear here on the balance sheet.)

To enter
> *a label* to identify this as the buildings and equipment line of the balance sheet
> *a value* of $33,000 in cell R44C2

Goto R44C1

Select A (for Alpha)
> Type **Buildings & equipment** ⊖
> Type **33000** ⦅RET⦆

....

ROW 45 **Accumulated depreciation** represents the gradual expensing of the depreciable fixed assets. Depreciation is an artificial expense in that it is a somewhat arbitrary assignment of the erosion of value over time. Although it is an intangible expense, it is nevertheless real in that most capital assets do in fact lose their value over time. The amount of the depreciation expense is transferred from the income statement and added to the accumulated depreciation account at the end of each operating period. This is then subtracted from the value of buildings and equipment. The present rate of depreciation for Acme Hardware in our worksheet is $6,000. This represents approximately 18 percent of the total capital depreciable assets and suggests a depreciable life of five years. The income statement has the depreciation charge for the year's operation. On the balance sheet, which is addressed here, the depreciation is the accumulation of these charges for this year and prior years.

To enter
> *a label* to identify this as the accumulated depreciation line of the balance sheet
> *a formula* in cell R45C2 that will subtract this year's depreciation from last year's accumulated depreciation
> *a value* of −$7,000 in cell R45C4

Goto R45C1

Select A (for Alpha)
> Type **Less accumulated depreciation** →
> Type **= R45C4-R17C2** → →
> Type **-7000** (RET)

Recalculate the worksheet

Result Since the value of accumulated depreciation for this year depends on the corresponding value for last year, we need to place a value in column 4 in order for the formula in R45C2 to work properly. When recalculation is complete, the value -13000 should appear in cell R45C2.

....

R O W 46 **Land,** while it is a capital asset, is not depreciable; so it is properly shown in a category by itself.

To enter
> *a label* to identify this as the land line of the balance sheet
> *a value* of 0 in cell R46C2

Goto R46C1

Select A (for Alpha)
> Type **Land** →
> Type **0** (RET)

....

R O W 48 **Total fixed assets** are the total of land, plus the net of buildings and equipment, minus the accumulated depreciation. Total fixed assets is another category that is helpful to us in analyzing financial statements to determine how well the business is using the resources available to it.

To enter
> *a label* to identify this as the total fixed assets line of the balance sheet
> *a formula* in cell R48C2 that will add all entries in the fixed assets section of the balance sheet

Goto R48C1

Select A (for Alpha)
> Type **Total fixed assets** →
> Type **= SUM(R42:47C2)** (RET)

Result You should get a result of $20,000 for total fixed assets.

....

R O W 50 **Other assets** would include anything that is not properly assigned to the first two asset categories. Items that might appear here could be goodwill, organizational costs, and the residual values of patents and other such intangibles that the business may own.

To enter
> *a label* to identify this as the other assets line of the balance sheet
> *a value* of $3,700 in cell R50C2

Goto R50C1

Select A (for Alpha)
> Type **Other assets** →
> Type **3700** (RET)

....

R O W 52 **Total assets** are the sum of the above major categories.

To enter
> *a label* to identify this as the total assets line of the balance sheet
> *a formula* in cell R52C2 that will add total current assets, total fixed assets, and other assets

Goto R52C1

Select A (for Alpha)
> Type **TOTAL ASSETS** →
> Type **= R41C2 + R48C2 + R50C2** (RET)

Result Total assets should be $129,504.

Entering the balance sheet Continued

Step Three

Enter figures for "last year"

```
               1          2      3       4
28 BALANCE SHEET: December 31, 19..
29 ==================================================
30                              This          Last
31                              year          year
32 ---------------------------------------------------
33 ASSETS:
34 ==================================================
35 <Current assets>
36 Cash                        1,335         4,750
37 Accounts receivable        17,777        16,000
38 Inventory                  83,292        70,000
39 Prepaid expenses            3,400         3,400
40 -----------------------------------------------
41 Total current assets      105,804        94,150
42
43 <Fixed assets>
44 Buildings & equipment      33,000        38,950
45 Less accumulated depreciation -13,000    -7,000
46 Land                            0             0
47 -----------------------------------------------
48 Total fixed assets         20,000        31,950
49
50 Other assets                3,700         2,545
51 -----------------------------------------------
52 TOTAL ASSETS              129,504       128,645
53 ==================================================
```

__COLUMN 4__ **Enter comparison figures** for "last year." As in the income statement these figures will not change once we've entered them. They are simply displayed to provide a basis for comparison with the changing values for "this year."

To enter

values on all the rows in the "last year" column

Goto R36C4

    Type **4750** ⟨↓⟩

    Type **16000** ⟨↓⟩

    Type **70000** ⟨↓⟩

    Type **3400** ⟨↓⟩ ⟨↓⟩

    Type **94150** ⟨↓⟩ ⟨↓⟩ ⟨↓⟩

    Type **38950** ⟨↓⟩ ⟨↓⟩

    Type **0** ⟨↓⟩ ⟨↓⟩

    Type **31950** ⟨↓⟩ ⟨↓⟩

    Type **2545** ⟨↓⟩ ⟨↓⟩

    Type **128645** ⟨RET⟩

Step Four

Enter ruled lines and a heading for the liabilities section of the balance sheet

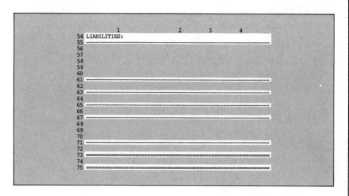

__ROWS 54–75__ **Enter ruled lines** to define the second half of the balance sheet, dealing with liabilities and equity.

To copy

single and double ruled lines entered and named earlier

Select CF (for Copy From)
    Type **shortline2** in the "cells" field ⟨TAB⟩
    Type **R73C1,R75C1** in the "to cells" field ⟨RET⟩

Select CF (for Copy From)
    Type **shortline1** in the "cells" field ⟨TAB⟩
    Type **R55C1,R61C1,R63C1,R65C1,R67C1,R71C1** in the "to cells" field ⟨RET⟩

....

__ROW 54__ **A heading** for the liabilities section is entered. Liabilities are essentially the debts of the organization, and are divided into two categories: current liabilities and long-term debt.

To enter

a heading for the liabilities section

Goto R54C1

Select A (for Alpha)
    Type **LIABILITIES:** ⟨RET⟩

Step Five

Enter labels and values in columns 1 and 2

```
         1              2      3      4
54 LIABILITIES:
55
56 <Current liabilities>
57 Accounts payable           18,480
58 Accrued wages & taxes       6,357
59 Notes payable (current)     3,890
60 Other current liabilities   5,900
61
62 Total current liabilities  34,627
63
64 Long-term debt             44,110
65
66 Total liabilities          78,737
67
68 <Owner equity>
69 Common stock               37,000
70 Retained earnings          13,767        10,855
71
72 Total owner equity         50,767
73
74 TOTAL LIABILITIES & EQUITY 129,504
75
```

ROW 56
Current liabilities are those obligations that must be paid in one year or less.

To enter
> *a label* to identify this as the current liabilities section of the balance sheet

Goto R56C1

Select A (for Alpha)
> Type **<Current liabilities>** (RET)

· ·

ROW 57
Accounts payable, a major category for most businesses, represents the use of trade credit for goods and/or services that have been purchased from vendors with the understanding that they will be paid for at some later period in time. Thus accounts payable is typically a very important source of financing for many business operations.

To enter
> *a label* to identify this as the accounts payable line of the balance sheet
> *a value* of $18,480 in cell R57C2

Goto R57C1

Select A (for Alpha)
> Type **Accounts payable** (→)
> Type **18480** (RET)

ROW 58
Accrued wages and taxes result when an accounting period occurs in the middle of a payroll and/or tax period. In this case, the wages that have been earned but not paid, or taxes due, will be expensed on the income statement and show up on the balance sheet as payables.

To enter
> *a label* to identify this as the accrued wages and taxes line of the balance sheet
> *a value* of $6,357 in cell R58C2

Goto R58C1

Select A (for Alpha)
> Type **Accrued wages & taxes** (→)
> Type **6357** (RET)

· ·

ROW 59
Notes payable (current) are the portion of the long-term debt that will be paid within this annual period.

To enter
> *a label* to identify this as the notes payable (current) line of the balance sheet
> *a value* of $3,890 in cell R59C2

Goto R59C1

Select A (for Alpha)
> Type **Notes payable (current)** (→)
> Type **3890** (RET)

· ·

ROW 60
Other current liabilities could include any other relatively current (short-term) obligations of the firm. Utility bills, repairs, and other such items may be expensed and yet still be unpaid and so would appear here on the balance sheet.

To enter
> *a label* to identify this as the row where other current liabilities will be entered
> *a value* of $5,900 in cell R60C2

Goto R60C1

Select A (for Alpha)
> Type **Other current liabilities** (→)
> Type **5900** (RET)

Entering the balance sheet Continued

ROW 62 — **Total current liabilities** are the sum of the above subaccounts.

To enter
>*a label* to identify this as the total current liabilities line of the balance sheet
>*a formula* in cell R62C2 that will add all of the individual current liabilities on the rows above

Goto R62C1

Select A (for Alpha)
>Type **Total current liabilities** →
>Type **= SUM(R55:61C2)** (RET)

Result You should get total current liabilities of $34,627.

....

ROW 64 — **Long-term debt** represents those obligations of the organization that are payable in more than one year; it is the net debt after the current portion of notes payable is subtracted.

To enter
>*a label* to identify this as the long-term debt line of the balance sheet
>*a value* of $44,110 in cell R64C2

Goto R64C1

Select A (for Alpha)
>Type **Long-term debt** →
>Type **44110** (RET)

....

ROW 66 — **Total liabilities** represent the total of the liability accounts and so summarizes the effect of the short-term (current) liabilities and the long-term liabilities.

To enter
>*a label* to identify this as the total liabilities line of the balance sheet
>*a formula* in cell R66C2 that will add total current liabilities and long-term debt

Goto R66C1

Select A (for Alpha)
>Type **Total liabilities** →
>Type **= R62C2 + R64C2** (RET)

Result Total liabilities should be $78,737.

ROW 68 — **Owner equity** appears on balance sheets in a number of forms, depending on the structure of the firm. Often referred to as net worth, it represents the owner's (or owners') investment in the operation. In this case, owner equity includes common stock and retained earnings.

To enter
>*a label* to identify this as the owner equity section of the balance sheet

Goto R68C1

Select A (for Alpha)
>Type <**Owner equity**> (RET)

....

ROW 69 — **Common stock** is the basic representative of the primary ownership investments in the firm. It may or may not actually represent the initial and subsequent investments in the firm. If not, it may be supplemented by accounts such as "paid-in surplus."

To enter
>*a label* to identify this as the row where common stock will be entered
>*a value* of $37,000 in cell R69C2

Goto R69C1

Select A (for Alpha)
>Type **Common stock** →
>Type **37000** (RET)

....

ROW 70 — **Retained earnings** are the residual profits (net income on row 26) that the owners have allowed to remain in the business. In this example, Mr. Adams leaves all of his net income in the business. Alternatively, he might have chosen to take some of it for his personal use. If the business has experienced operating losses, then retained earnings would be shown as a negative value.

To enter
>*a label* to identify this as the retained earnings line of the balance sheet
>*a formula* in cell R70C2 that will carry forward last year's retained earnings and add this year's net income to them
>*a value* of $10,855 in cell R70C4

Goto R70C1

Select A (for Alpha)
    Type **Retained earnings** (→)
    Type **= R70C4 + R26C2** (→) (→)
    Type **10855** (RET)

Recalculate the worksheet

Result Your retained earnings should be $13,767.

....

ROW 72	**Total owner equity** is the sum of owner equity and retained earnings.

To enter
    a label to identify this as the total owner equity
        line of the balance sheet
    a formula in cell R72C2 that will add common
        stock and retained earnings

Goto R72C1

Select A (for Alpha)
    Type **Total owner equity** (→)
    Type **= SUM(R67:71C2)** (RET)

Result Total owner equity at this point should be
$50,767.

....

ROW 74	**Total liabilities and equity** represents the total of the liability and equity accounts,

and equals total assets in the balance sheet equation.

To enter
    a label to identify this as the total liabilities and
        equity line of the balance sheet
    a formula in cell R74C2 that will add total liabilities
        and total owner equity

Goto R74C1

Select A (for Alpha)
    Type **TOTAL LIABILITIES & EQUITY** (→)
    Type **= R66C2 + R72C2** (RET)

Result Your result should be $129,504.

Step Six

Enter figures for "last year"

	1	2	3	4
54	LIABILITIES:			
55				
56	<Current liabilities>			
57	Accounts payable	18,480		17,000
58	Accrued wages & taxes	6,357		6,000
59	Notes payable (current)	3,890		3,890
60	Other current liabilities	5,900		5,900
61				
62	Total current liabilities	34,627		32,790
63				
64	Long-term debt	44,110		48,000
65				
66	Total liabilities	78,737		80,790
67				
68	<Owner equity>			
69	Common stock	37,000		37,000
70	Retained earnings	13,767		10,855
71				
72	Total owner equity	50,767		47,855
73				
74	TOTAL LIABILITIES & EQUITY	129,504		128,645
75				

COLUMN 4	**Enter comparison figures** for "last year." As before, the figures in this column will not

change once we've entered them.

To enter
    values on all the rows in the "last year" column

Goto R57C4
    Type **17000** (↓)
    Type **6000** (↓)
    Type **3890** (↓)
    Type **5900** (↓) (↓)
    Type **32790** (↓) (↓)
    Type **48000** (↓) (↓)
    Type **80790** (↓) (↓) (↓)
    Type **37000** (↓) (↓) (↓)
    Type **47855** (↓) (↓)
    Type **128645** (RET)

Entering the balance sheet Continued

Step Seven

Calculate cash. Now that both last year's and this year's balance sheets have been finished, we can go back to replace the cash value of $1,335 in cell R36C2 with a formula. This formula will automatically calculate this year's cash whenever changes are made anywhere on last year's or this year's balance sheets. Cash is a result of other changes on the balance sheet between the current and previous periods. It can be calculated by the following steps: (1) Begin with last year's cash; (2) subtract changes in assets (not including cash); (3) add changes in liabilities.

To enter

a formula that automatically calculates cash based on changes in other line items on the balance sheet

Goto R36C2

Select V (for Value)
Type **R36C4-SUM(R37:39C2)-R48C2-R50C2 + R74C2 + SUM(R37:39C4) + R48C4 + R50C4-R74C4** [RET]
(*Note:* The formula should be typed in one continuous string; we've broken it up here so you can see the logic of the formula more clearly.)

Recalculate the worksheet

Result The value in cell R36C2 shouldn't change since the calculated value of $1,335 was entered earlier. The formula will calculate a new value, however, whenever any other items on the balance sheet, either this year's or last year's, are changed.

Step Eight

Protect and save your work. Now that you have completed the balance sheet it's time again to save your work. Here you'll be saving the worksheet for the second time, so a file name doesn't have to be entered. You will be saving it on top of the old file on the disk. This erases the old file and replaces it with this latest version.

Select LC (for Lock Cells)
Type **R36:74C4** in the "cells" field [TAB]
Type **L** (for Locked) in the "status" field [RET]

Select LF (for Lock Formulas)
Type **Y** (to confirm) [RET]

Select TS (for Transfer Save)
Type **DECISION** in the "filename" field [RET]
(*Note:* Since you should already have saved an earlier disk copy of the worksheet, the name DECISION should automatically appear in the "filename" field as a proposed response from Multiplan. Unless you want to use a different file name, you can simply type [RET] to save the file.)

The message line reads
Overwrite existing file?
Type **Y** to confirm

Result The screen display and the worksheet in memory will remain unchanged, but the file is now saved to the disk. You can turn off the computer or you can continue. If anything goes wrong, your work won't be lost. Because saving your work is so easy to do, you should get into the habit of saving frequently.

MULTIPLAN TIPS Write-protecting your disks

Whenever you use the Transfer Save command, Multiplan checks the file directory on the designated disk drive to see if there is already a file stored under the same name. If there is, the message **OVERWRITE EXISTING FILE?** will appear on the message line. Multiplan will wait for you to answer yes or no before proceeding to save the file on disk. This error-trapping feature will save you from the all-too-common headache of overwriting a valuable file by using the same file name.

If you wish to further safeguard a worksheet from being overwritten or deleted, place a piece of opaque tape (usually included with the purchase of a box of disks) over the write-protect notch on the edge of the disk. The tape can be easily removed at a later time if you do wish to make changes.

MULTIPLAN TIPS Acceptable Multiplan file names

Multiplan has no say about the proper conventions for naming files or specifying the disk drives to save them to. This is determined by the operating system of your particular computer. There are many different operating systems available for microcomputers, and in this book we can't go into detail about every variation. Fortunately, the vast majority of microcomputers use either the CP/M or MS/DOS operating system. These two operating systems have identical conventions for naming files:

1 A file name can be up to eight characters long.

2 A file name can be any combination of letters and numbers, although the first character must be a letter. The name must be one continuous string of letters and numbers; no blank spaces are allowed.

3 A file can have an optional file extension, up to three letters and/or numbers in length. The file extension must be separated from the file name by a period, with no blank spaces before or after the period.

4 A disk drive can be specified by placing a single letter and a colon in front of the file name. If a disk drive is not specified, Multiplan will store your file on the default disk drive (the same disk drive that contains the Multiplan program disk).

MULTIPLAN TIPS How to overcome a Disk full message

A good housekeeping habit to get into when using floppy disks is the regular use of a file statistics command at the beginning and end of each work session. The exact name of the command will vary depending on the operating system. With MS/DOS, the command is **CHKDSK**, and in CP/M it's **STAT**. The File Statistics command will tell you how much room on the disk is taken up with data and how much free space remains.

Note: The **% Free** indicator on the status line (the bottom line on the Multiplan display) refers to core memory, not to disk space. There is no way of checking up on disk space availability from "inside" Multiplan; you must Quit to the operating system level first.

If, in spite of these precautions, you do get a DISK FULL message when you try to save a worksheet on disk, here are two possible courses of action:

1 Insert a fresh disk into the "data" disk drive, if your computer has more than one drive.

2 Use the Transfer Delete command to delete one or more unneeded or less valuable files. You should already have a backup copy of any important files.

3 If you have no extra disks, remove the Multiplan system disk from the drive, peel off the write-protect tape, return the disk to the drive, use the Transfer Options command to change the setup to the drive containing Multiplan, and attempt to save the file on this disk. Generally, it is wise to avoid writing data onto the system disk, but in a pinch it's okay. When you get back from the computer store with a new box of disks, copy the worksheet onto a fresh data disk, delete it from the system disk, and replace the tape over the write-protect notch.

Entering the balance sheet Continued

MULTIPLAN TIPS Protecting your worksheets

After a worksheet is finished and saved, it is normally reloaded and filled in with new data when needed. Problems can arise at this point. You, or others asked to use the worksheet, can inadvertently erase or change formulas, delete rows or columns, or cause an unending list of difficulties. This situation can be avoided by judicious use of the Lock command. There are two options to the Lock command.

1 Lock Cells protects a specified cell or range of cells. The contents of a locked cell cannot be changed, edited, or blanked; nor can its format or alignment characteristics be changed.

2 Lock Formulas protects every cell that contains either a label or a formula, at the time the command is invoked.

MULTIPLAN TIPS Eliminating error messages

Whenever you prepare a worksheet that uses division formulas, **DIV/0!** will appear in cells on the blank worksheet that contain those formulas. Any number divided by zero generates this error message automatically; when you enter data into the worksheet, the error messages will disappear. If you want to clean up your blank worksheet so that the **DIV/0!** messages won't appear, simply embed in an IF statement all formulas containing division by another cell. The IF function will carry out the division only if the divisor contains a non-zero value. For example, **IF(R2C10<>0,R2C3/R2C10,0)** will display a value of zero on the worksheet if R2C10 is blank or zero; otherwise it will perform the division and display the result.

MULTIPLAN TIPS Windows on the world

Multiplan's Window command is one of its most powerful and useful features. Up to eight windows at a time can be set up on the worksheet, allowing you to trace the effects of changed values in widely separated portions of the worksheet. In our example, two windows are enough to illustrate the business concepts we're trying to get across. However, you may wish to experiment by opening up three or four windows at once, and viewing changes in two or three ratios simultaneously.

A bit of practice (and trial and error) will help you take full advantage of the Window command. Don't worry — anything you do with this command can be easily undone using the Window Clear command. Keep in mind that the "window" itself takes up at least two lines of the twenty in the worksheet display area. Three lines are taken up if the windows are not linked, since the column numbers must also appear in the window.

Depending on the hardware characteristics of your computer system, the Window Border command may give you more visually interesting and more readable displays. For the ultimate in visual pyrotechnics, a color monitor on the IBM PC and similar machines will enable you to use the Window Paint command. This allows you to specify a palette of colors to distinguish the border, foreground, and background portions of your display.

4 Breakeven analysis

Introduction

Breakeven analysis is the first topic we discuss in depth because its understanding is central to effective business decision making. Very simply, breakeven is that point where the business neither makes a profit nor incurs a loss. It is the point where total costs exactly equal total revenues. Because the breakeven point is affected by changes in the total cost structure, it can illustrate the impact of various alternatives available to the business on the total sales required for the business to break even. It is for this reason that breakeven is so important as a critical decision-making tool.

Profits are the motivating force for any business in a free economic system. Breakeven analysis is a direct way to determine the relationships between cost, volume, and profit needed to ensure the best possible yield. Many business owner/managers tend to view increased sales as the cure-all for poor performance. Unfortunately, all too often they do not have the foggiest notion of what level of additional sales will be required to get them out of their inadequate or even loss condition and into a more profitable mode of operation. Again, the answer to this problem will often be revealed through breakeven analysis.

Of course, in any business, the objective is not just to break even but to make a profit. Nevertheless, understanding the balance point between expenses and revenues and the factors that affect or change that balance is essential as the first step in establishing targets and goals for the business's survival and in evaluating the total set of operating assumptions needed for a truly profitable operation.

Breakeven analysis provides the minimum sales objective that can be tolerated by the firm. This target can be expressed in dollars, units of production, sales, or whatever else is relevant. If the breakeven point is known, it can become a definite target to be reached and exceeded by carefully reasoned steps. Many businesses have destroyed themselves by ignoring the need for breakeven analysis. It is essential to remember that increased sales do not necessarily mean increased profits. For example, if the selling price is reduced in order to stimulate sales, the breakeven point may be forced upward to such an extent that, practically speaking, the business could never achieve sufficient sales to break even.

As an important general planning and decision-making tool, breakeven analysis is also a pricing tool and an expense control tool and can be invaluable when forecasting and predicting desired levels of activity for the organization. Breakeven analysis can be very helpful in determining whether to buy or lease, whether to expand into a new area, or whether to build a new plant and in a variety of other considerations. Breakeven analysis will not force a decision, of course, but it will provide additional insights into the effects of important business decisions on the bottom-line profits of the firm. Informed choices have a better chance of being correct than do random seat-of-the-pants decisions.

As a *planning tool*, breakeven analysis indicates the targets the business must reach and provides a quick and direct way of evaluating the impact of various alternative business strategies. It is possible that analysis of a certain strategy may indicate a breakeven point that is unrealistically high. It may also be clear that the business will never be able to achieve that level of sales because it would require an inordinately high percentage of the target market or the processing of more goods and services than the business has the capacity to handle. If this is the case, clearly such an alternative should not be pursued. On the other hand, if the breakeven is extremely low, it may suggest that a more profitable strategy could be pursued or at least seriously considered.

As a *decision-making tool*, breakeven helps in evaluating the various alternatives available to the business. Following these alternatives through a breakeven analysis is a far safer way of determining their impact on the business than actually experimenting with the real operation. A proactive anticipation of the negative impact of certain alternatives will automatically help to eliminate those alternatives and thereby avoid the negative impact. Problem solving by avoidance is far preferable to any other means that may be available to a business.

As an important *pricing tool*, breakeven analysis shows the relationship between price, gross profit, and volume. For example, breakeven provides a direct and straightforward approach to considering a series or range of prices and the potential effect of each on the business. It is generally assumed that as price goes down, volume is likely to increase. It is entirely possible, however, that this may not be desirable, especially for smaller firms. The volume required for breakeven may increase to such a point that it may never be achieved. The underlying focus must be on the relationship between gross profit and fixed costs. This is critical because as the gross profit decreases relative to the fixed costs, the breakeven point will increase. Again, under such conditions, the breakeven may increase to such a point that the sales required for breakeven are simply too high, thereby creating a totally unrealistic situation.

Finally, as an *expense control tool*, breakeven provides a way of evaluating the impact on the business of various expenses and also an interesting and sometimes very different way to consider the need or relevance of a given expense for the total operation. If removing that expense could significantly lower the breakeven and lowering the breakeven increases the feasibility of the operation, then it is advisable to assess the importance or relevance of that particular expense to the total operation. If it is not essential and the business is feasible without it, it can be eliminated and profits improved. If it is essential and the business is not feasible without it, and the resulting breakeven is too high with that expense, then the choice must be made not to pursue that particular alternative.

There is a simple and direct relationship between expenses, sales, and profit. Profit can typically be increased by increasing sales or decreasing expenses. Accordingly, it is useful for any business to view expenses as profits that would otherwise be available to the owners and, on that basis, to determine whether or not particular expenses are essential to the business operation. An ongoing breakeven analysis can be incorporated as part of the expense review and control process, which carefully observes the relationship between gross profits and expenses and helps to maintain a floating sales objective. The computer, of course, can calculate these target levels immediately and thereby show you the impact of present or proposed courses of action. Expenses have a tendency to increase in an almost invisible way in most operations. Accordingly, managers often feel that their operations are improving and yet find that their profits are in fact shrinking. An ongoing breakeven analysis will help to indicate the impact of any changes in spending and thus give you an opportunity to determine objectively whether these expenses are necessary and should be allowed to continue.

To sum all of this up, breakeven analysis is a powerful analytical tool that allows you to estimate with a fair degree of accuracy the level of sales you must reach for your business to at least survive; that is, to show neither profit nor loss. In addition, with a few modifications, it can produce (among other things) an indication of the sales volume necessary to cover only cash expenses or it can be expanded to cover all expenses plus full debt service — to cover both the interest and principal portions of a loan payment, for example.

For our purposes here, breakeven analysis is one of the primary tools we will use to show the impact on a business of various decision alternatives. We are greatly assisted by the fact that our computer can immediately calculate the breakeven level that will result from changes in any of the critical relationships within the business operation. Once this has been done, it then becomes a relatively straightforward task to choose among alternatives that may be available.

What is breakeven analysis?

Breakeven analysis is based on the proposition that the cost of doing business can be divided into two broad categories: fixed costs or expenses and variable costs or expenses. Once classified into these two broad categories, costs can be shown relative to sales. As we have seen earlier, categorizing expenses requires a separation of that portion of total costs which varies in direct proportion to the volume of sales (the variable costs) and that portion which exists regardless of the volume of sales (the fixed costs). Every time a sale is made, the business receives a certain amount of money. The variable costs are then subtracted from the sales revenues. Generally, these variable costs are those incurred in making the item available for sale; they reflect either the purchase price of the item or its direct manufacturing costs. When these costs are subtracted from the selling price, there is, you hope, something left over, which is the gross profit or gross margin. With breakeven analysis, our concern is to determine the level of sales that, after the variable costs are subtracted, will provide enough gross profit to exactly equal (cover) all of the fixed costs.

Determining breakeven

Calculating the breakeven point can be simple (for a one-product business) or complex (for a multiline business), but whatever the complexity, the technique is the same. Some of the figures you need to calculate the breakeven point may have to be estimates. If so, it is a good idea to make your estimates conservative by using somewhat pessimistic sales and margin figures and by slightly overstating your expected cost figures.

Technically, breakeven refers to the relationship between fixed costs, variable costs, gross margin, and sales. Change any one of these components and your breakeven will change. Understand the nature of the relationships between these components, understand which of them you can control, and you will be controlling your breakeven point. The basic breakeven equation is:

Breakeven in sales =

Fixed costs + Variable costs

Fixed costs are those costs that remain constant no matter what the sales volume may be. These are the costs that will be incurred even if you make no sales at all. Included here are overhead expenses such as rent, office and administrative costs, salaries, and so forth, and hidden costs such as interest and depreciation. Of course, these costs remain constant only within a relative range.

If, for example, you needed a new building because of a greatly increased sales volume, your fixed costs would rise.

The variable costs are those costs associated with sales, including cost of goods sold, variable labor costs, and sales commissions. Technically speaking, if you have no sales at all you will have no variable costs. This is true only up to a point for most small businesses since some and perhaps all of their variable costs (for instance, direct labor), which would normally vary directly with sales in a larger firm, may in fact be semivariable. This occurs because at low levels of sales you would simply not lay off your entire work force but would retain some or all of it in the expectation of sales increasing once again. Since these costs are now semivariable, they must be treated in a slightly different way. Semivariable costs can frequently be viewed as having both a fixed component and a variable component. These are discussed in greater detail later on. You will see in our example that we have divided the costs for Acme Hardware into three categories: fixed costs, variable costs, and semivariable costs. We have further allocated the semivariable costs back into the two main categories of fixed and variable. You should do the same as you analyze your own operation.

There is a five-step process that will help you in using breakeven analysis as a key management decision-making tool. The process is:

STEP ONE: Identify fixed and variable costs
STEP TWO: Analyze and allocate semivariable costs
STEP THREE: Calculate breakeven
STEP FOUR: Determine if breakeven is realistic
STEP FIVE: Monitor and control

STEP ONE: Identify fixed and variable costs

As a going concern, your business is generating expenses over the course of the year. Remember, those expenses that would continue whether or not you sold or made any item or product are the fixed expenses or costs; in the short run, these fixed costs are reasonably constant. Those costs that vary or change directly with output are variable costs or expenses. These are the costs that are associated with production and/or selling and are frequently the same as cost of goods sold. These variable costs do not accrue if you are not doing any business. By definition, variable costs are zero when no output is being produced or no sales are being realized. In this case, fixed costs are the only costs that will be incurred.

Fixed costs	Variable costs
rent	factory direct labor
depreciation of plant and equipment	materials inventory
executive and office staff salaries	freight-in (and -out)
general office expenses	variable office expenses
property taxes	utilities other than
insurance	fixed (e.g., electricity)
interest	sales commissions
	sales incentives

As you review your expense items for the past year or more, keep in mind that they may fluctuate seasonally. It is also critical to keep in mind that there should be a reason for each item. They must all, individually and/or jointly, serve a business purpose. If some do not, you must determine what justifies the expense. Ask yourself if the expense can reasonably be lowered or, in some cases, increased. Advertising, for example, is frequently underfunded to the detriment of a business.

By examining these costs one by one, you will reap several benefits: added understanding of where all these monies are dribbling away to, ideas for economies, and perhaps even warning of coming problems. The prodigious rise in oil cost should have been no surprise to any small business, but by not reviewing expenses on an annual basis and noting this trend, many companies were caught unprepared.

If you are involved in a start-up or an expansion, getting the necessary information may be something of a problem. Your accountant may be able to help with this process. You can also get some idea of the cost structure of your industry from some of the many business publications. If you are projecting costs that differ significantly from the trade averages, double-check your assumptions. If you continue to project expenses that are different from the norms, try to differ on the side of caution, either by overstating expenses or by putting any borderline items into fixed expense. Prudence and profit often seem to go together.

STEP TWO: Analyze and allocate semivariable costs

Semivariable costs represent a special problem for most small firms because, as their name suggests, they are neither really fixed nor truly variable. The problem comes about with costs that would normally be variable in larger-scale operations but that, in smaller operations, cannot be easily reduced or increased in a direct linear fashion. In a small firm, it is often difficult to increase or decrease partial "people units"; further, there may be economies of scale in your operation that mean you cannot go below a certain level without compromising or even destroying your ability to be effective.

A good example of semivariable costs can be seen in the case of a furniture manufacturer who had a balanced work force of five individuals. Each individual performed a different function and provided a separate set of skills, all of which were needed to keep the business operational. Being a knowledgeable person, the owner/manager, looking at his work force, recognized that it was direct labor and thus a variable cost. However, when he found that his sales had declined by 20 percent, he discovered that it was not really possible for him to lay off one worker (20 percent of the work force) without also eliminating some essential skills and therefore seriously compromising the firm's ability to stay in business. If he believed that the sales decline was to be of a long duration, then he would reduce his crew and realign responsibilities to maintain balanced production capacity. If he believed that the slump would be short-lived, however, he would grit his teeth and maintain the present crew, absorbing the attendant loss against a future profitable period.

Another useful example of costs that can behave in a semivariable manner is often found in sales departments in both small and large firms. It is not unusual to find compensation for salespersons with both fixed and variable components. For example, it is often common to see a base salary with a commission that kicks in above a given level of sales, or a guaranteed draw against commissions on sales that might not be fully achieved. In either case, at the lower level of sales, costs would be fixed, and at higher levels, costs become somewhat or fully variable. Rent is another example. It is not unusual to find rental rates including a fixed base and a percentage of sales above a prescribed level. This would have the same effect as the sales compensation problem noted above. You will find a more detailed discussion of these semivariable costs later on.

There is an important point here. Semivariable costs are difficult to analyze and budget for because of their erratic behavior. The tendency is to treat them arbitrarily as either fixed or variable. The problem is that if they are treated as fixed, you will overstate your expenses when sales are low and understate them when sales are high. Treating these expenses as variable creates exactly the reverse problem; they will be understated when sales are low and overstated when sales are high. The answer is to treat them as both fixed and variable in accordance with their actual composition and behavior. Normally this would be a complicated task due to the calculations involved. However, with a computer, this allocation function becomes quite easy. We merely instruct the computer to assign the fixed portion on a regular basis and calculate the variable portion based on whatever decision rule is appropriate. If a variable commission range kicks in above a given point in sales, then we can instruct our computer to calculate total sales compensation on that basis. Our later example shows how Mr. Adams treated these costs for his business.

STEP THREE: Calculate breakeven

If a firm's costs were all variable, the problem of breakeven would never arise because sales would automatically cover the cost of goods sold as long as each product or unit of service was priced at cost or above. By having some fixed as well as variable costs or expenses, the firm must suffer losses up to a given volume. Consequently, we look for that point where gross profit (gross margin), or the excess of selling price over costs, exactly equals the fixed expenses.

Breakeven is based on the relationship of fixed and variable expenses to sales. The breakeven level in sales is equal to fixed costs divided by 100 percent minus variable costs as a percentage of sales (variable costs divided by sales). As an example of breakeven analysis, let us assume that our furniture dealer has total sales of $500,000, variable costs of $300,000, and fixed costs of $170,000 per year.

$$\text{Breakeven} = 170{,}000 / (100\% - (300{,}000/500{,}000))$$
$$= 170{,}000 / (100\% - 60\%)$$
$$= 170{,}000 / 40\%$$
$$= \$425{,}000$$

In other words, this dealer needs sales of $425,000 a year to cover all of his fixed expenses. At this point, he will have neither a profit nor a loss. His business will break even.

The furniture industry has a high margin, whereas a grocery business has a low margin, say 17 percent as opposed to 40 percent. For the same fixed expenses, a grocer would need $170,000 divided by 17 percent, or $1,000,000 in sales. The lower the gross margin, the higher the sales must be to cover the same amount of fixed costs. Of course, you have to question whether you really need a fancy office (a fixed expense) or a Lear Jet. Maybe you do, but your decision should bear careful scrutiny, and breakeven analysis is a good place to start.

Another way to calculate your breakeven is by using a breakeven chart. Many people find the visual aspect of these charts more useful than the more accurate calculation process just described. However, the relationship between the elements will generally be relatively constant over a certain range, and any major decision would be made on more comprehensive grounds in any case. It is well to remember that the figures are not the only criteria; "Does it make sense?" must remain uppermost.

A breakeven chart may be constructed on a per unit

BREAKEVEN CHART

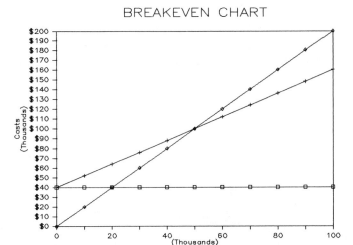

basis or a dollar basis. Often the vertical axis represents dollars and the horizontal axis represents volume, time, or dollars as well. The illustration above shows fixed costs of $40,000 represented by a horizontal line. Total costs (fixed plus variable) of $1.20 per unit rise from that fixed point. Sales are figured at $2.00 per unit, and we assume that each unit produced is sold. (While this last assumption is somewhat utopian, it may be justified as a working hypothesis or a goal; either way, we recognize that it is somewhat fictitious.) Since the ascent of the sales line is greater than that of the variable cost line, the two lines will eventually cross. Where they meet is the breakeven point. In the example, this occurs at 50,000 units, where total sales equals total costs (and where both are $100,000).

There are some critical assumptions involved in breakeven calculations. If we had zero sales, we would have fixed costs just as high as if we produced many units. The variable cost, on the other hand, is an ascending line that rises in direct relationship to the number of units produced. If there were zero units produced, there would be zero variable costs. As the number of units goes up, the variable costs directly associated with the production of goods or availability of a service will rise in a direct relationship to the units. If we were interested only in depicting variable costs, then the variable cost line would start at the zero point (point of origin) of our graph and rise in a direct linear fashion as quantity increases. However, since we are depicting a real-world situation, which has a base of fixed costs, the variable cost line will by necessity start at the base of the fixed costs, not at the origin of the graph. Consequently, at zero level of production, we will still have our base of fixed costs, which is shown by the fact that the variable cost line rises from the fixed cost base. Together, these two lines depict total costs.

The third element we need to add to our chart is sales. At zero sales there will of course be zero income, and so our sales line will start at the origin of the chart. Sales income is also a direct linear function of quantity made and sold, and so the sales line will rise in direct proportion to the increase in units. The sales line will rise at a faster rate than the variable cost line, assuming we have priced our product above our variable cost. The difference between the sales price and the variable cost per item will determine the difference in the slope of the two lines. The greater that difference, the shallower the slope of the variable cost line and the sooner (lower) the intersection. The junction point represents the breakeven point for the operation.

Keep in mind that this is a linear chart based on a constant selling price. By changing the assumptions, you can quickly adapt this chart to your advantage. For example, you can estimate the effect of price changes fairly precisely by varying the slope of the income line. (The effect of pricing on breakeven is critical and is discussed later on.) Similarly, by altering the slope of the variable cost line, you can approximate cost changes. Once they develop a working understanding of how a breakeven chart functions, managers generally find it to be a very thought-provoking tool.

Cash-flow considerations enter into this matter as well. For example, collection problems can frequently be identified by a breakeven analysis. Cash flow does not necessarily correspond with income flow, and of course a prudent person would not expect it to do so. If there are important differences between sales and cash flow, you may want to construct a breakeven chart for each.

STEP FOUR: Determine if breakeven is realistic

One of the important uses of breakeven is determining the potential viability of a given situation. Generally speaking, and as a useful rule of thumb, the lower the breakeven, the greater the potential viability. In our later discussions, we will be coming back to this concept quite often, especially in correlating breakeven to share of market. A related rule is that the smaller the share of the market required for breakeven, the greater the potential viability of the situation. We will also relate breakeven to overhead control, inventory management, and pricing. In each situation, similar rules of thumb will apply.

Determining the feasibility of your project is more subjective than objective. You can make some objective determinations with the help of your computer. However, the final conclusions must be based on your own good judgment. Your judgment will be helped by the objective analysis, but it cannot be replaced. The point here is that once you know the level of sales you must reach before making a profit, you must evaluate the reasonableness of this target. What are the odds of reaching this breakeven? One way to test this is to convert the gross dollar sales needed for breakeven into some other unit, which can then be compared against the capacity of the business and/or the size of the market. If the breakeven occurs at or near the capacity of the business or if your analysis shows that you must capture all (or more than all) of the available target market, the feasibility of your goal must be suspect. The odds of business success in such situations are against you. We repeat, this is clearly a subjective process. But then, so much of business management is exactly that. It is not possible or desirable to eliminate this subjective component of business decision making. The purpose of the analysis is to try to make your evaluation as reasonable as possible.

Suppose you own a soup restaurant. How many bowls of soup does breakeven represent? How many per working day, per hour? How does this match your capacity? Does it mean a larger number of tables? Fewer? More waiters? Are the numbers feasible? By putting your numbers into more concrete images, you may find the reasonableness criterion easier to use. Business is an interconnected system with each part related to all of the other parts. This is why piecemeal solutions often merely shift the problem to another area. If you are aware of how the parts interrelate, you have a great advantage over those in the competition who do not share this understanding. The unaware, of course, are the majority.

As noted earlier, another way of using your breakeven is to consider what share of the target market your breakeven represents. While defining your target market is extremely difficult (we will provide you with some suggestions later on), it is nevertheless very important. The effort you put into clearly defining that target and continually redefining it (nothing remains unchanged) will pay giant dividends.

This step is critical in determining the feasibility of your situation. If you can't say that your business deal makes sense at this point (for example, if it represents an expansion needing 110 percent of the market), then reexamine your plan. The process of reexamination may make you aware of new solutions. In any case, recognizing limitations through this type of analysis is much cheaper than charging blindly into a disaster. If it isn't going to work at all, acknowledging that fact at this point will save you the agony of future failure.

Of course, the final part of this step is to use the breakeven format to examine a wide range of possible alternatives, all with the objective of improving the profitability of the operation, possibly lowering the breakeven point, and improving the feasibility of the deal. Each of

our succeeding discussions will focus on the various components of the breakeven equation and give you some ideas on where you may be able to seek additional economies, provide new efficiencies, or increase sales. Your computer will be a valuable tool in examining each alternative. It can perform the calculations for you quickly and easily. What is required of you, though, is enough understanding of the process and what you are attempting to accomplish so that you will know which information you must enter into these decision models.

STEP FIVE: Monitor and control

Once you have established your breakeven and have examined some of the alternatives, you have automatically created a benchmark against which you can measure your progress. Once again, your computer can prove to be a very valuable tool. With the help of your machine, you can immediately examine the relationship between your actual performance and the set of assumptions that became the basis of your breakeven analysis. The point is simple: If you find your actual performance deviating significantly from your forecasted breakeven on the negative side, meaning margins are lower than you anticipated or fixed expenses are higher, then the feasibility of your plan may be suspect. If, on the other hand, you find your actual operation deviating positively, it may be that you left out something important or that you are actually doing a better job managing your operation than you had forecast. If this is the case, breakeven analysis can help you to understand better what it is you are doing right so that you can continue doing it.

Monitoring and controlling will be the integral part of each of the decision-making tools we suggest. Using these tools for planning purposes is great because then you will know what you ought to do in order to achieve your targeted goals. However, these plans by themselves will not prove very useful unless you develop action imperatives and actually use your tools for decision making and management control.

The following section will illustrate the applications of these tools to Mr. Adams's Acme Hardware. First we will show how to reload the DECISION worksheet into the computer, and then we will add an analysis section to the worksheet. Finally, we will suggest ways you can use these same tools in your own business.

Getting ready

You'll now enter an analysis section for the worksheet, which will be used for a number of purposes. It will be used to break down major line items on the income statement (cost of goods sold, general and administrative expenses, and selling expenses) into the items that contribute to these expenses. It will also be used to calculate breakeven, cash flow, and financial ratios. The rest of the DECISION worksheet will be gradually completed as you proceed through the following chapters.

STEP 1 **Reload the DECISION worksheet.** If you've continued directly from the end of Chapter 3 without leaving Multiplan, you can proceed directly to STEP 2. However, if you issued the QUIT command after saving a disk copy of the DECISION worksheet, you will now have to reload it into the computer memory to resume working.

Start up the Multiplan program in the primary disk drive, and insert your data disk (containing the copy of the DECISION worksheet) into the secondary drive.

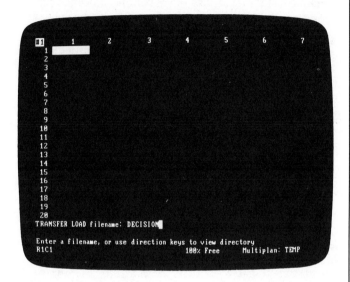

To enter

a command to reload the DECISION worksheet

Select TO (for Transfer Options) `TAB`
Type **B:** in the "setup" field `RET`

Select TL (for Transfer Load)
Type **DECISION** in the "filename" field `RET`

Result The DECISION worksheet should appear on the Multiplan screen exactly the way it appeared when you saved it. Column 1 should still be 30 characters in width, and numbers greater than 999 should have commas to separate thousands.

STEP 2 **Set recalculation to manual mode** to speed up data entry. This step must be repeated each time the Multiplan program is re-started; the program doesn't "remember" if recalculation was in manual mode the last time you QUIT, and always starts out with recalculation set to automatic operation.

To enter

a command that sets recalculation to manual

Select O (for Options)
Type **N** in the "recalc" field `RET`

Entering the analysis section

You will now set up the analysis section of the worksheet. This section will break down two major line items from the income statement (general and administrative expenses and selling expenses) into a detailed listing of the items that contribute to these expenses.

Up to this point we have generally determined the expenses that are sensitive to sales levels and those that remain constant regardless of the volume. Since the expense categories in Acme Hardware's income statement — general and administrative, selling expense, and cost of goods sold — are all totals of smaller expenses that conveniently fit into these categories, it is necessary that they now be further analyzed to assess their sensitivity to sales.

The general and administrative expenses can be explained as the office record keeping and administrative expenses of running Acme Hardware.

The selling expenses are exactly what the name implies, the costs associated with attracting the customer, selling the customer, and delivering the product to the customer.

MULTIPLAN TIPS Cell references

There are three different kinds of Multiplan cell references: absolute references, relative references, and named references. An *absolute reference* always refers to a particular cell, and uses the letters **R** and **C** and the actual row and column numbers (for instance, **R3C5**). A *relative reference* describes the location of another cell in relation to the current cell, and gives the direction of the cell (+ for right or down, − for left or up) and the number of columns or rows between the two cells. For example, **R[+2]C[−3]** means a cell two rows below and three columns to the left of the current cell. If you copied this cell reference to another cell, it would refer to the cell two rows below and three columns to the left of the new cell. A *named reference* is a word (or phrase) that identifies a cell or group of cells previously defined with the **Name** command. (Named references are a type of absolute reference, since they always refer to a specific cell or cells.)

Absolute and relative cell references can also be mixed. For instance, **R3C[+1]** always refers to row 3, but the column reference **C[+1]** means "one column to the right of the current cell."

Step One

Enter headings and ruled lines

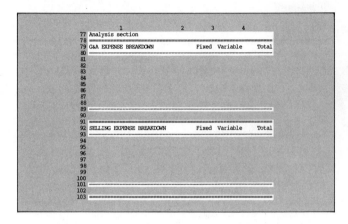

ROWS 77–103   **Headings and ruled lines** are entered for the analysis section of the worksheet. The single and double ruled lines will be "recycled" from the balance sheet section.

To enter
headings and ruled lines for the analysis section

Goto R77C1

Select A (for Alpha)
   Type **Analysis section** (RET)

Select CF (for Copy From)
   Type **shortline2** in the "cells" field (TAB)
   Type **R78C1,R91C1,R103C1** in the "to cells" field (RET)

Select CF (for Copy From)
   Type **shortline1** in the "cells" field (TAB)
   Type **R80C1,R89C1,R93C1,R101C1** in the "to cells" field (RET)

Select FC (for Format Cells)
   Type **R79C2:4** in the "cells" field (TAB)
   Type **R** (for Right) in the "alignment" field (RET)

Goto R79C1

Select A (for Alpha)
Type **G&A EXPENSE BREAKDOWN** (→)
Type **Fixed** (→)
Type **Variable** (→)
Type **Total** (RET)

Goto R92C1

Select A (for Alpha)
Type **SELLING EXPENSE BREAKDOWN** (RET)

Goto R92C2

Select CF (for Copy From)
Type **R79C2:4** in the "cells" field (RET)
(**R92C2** should already be in the "to cells" field)

Step Two

Enter labels for the G&A expense breakdown

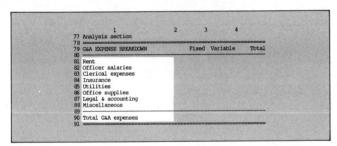

R O W S
81–88　 **Line item labels** for the general and administrative expense breakdown are entered. The breakdown of expenses is typical for a company such as Acme Hardware. The distribution of expenses between fixed and variable is based on the discussions of these expenses earlier in this chapter and the experienced judgment of Mr. Adams.

To enter
　 labels to identify the individual line items making up G&A expenses

---

Goto R81C1

Select A (for Alpha)
Type **Rent** (↓)
Type **Officer salaries** (↓)
Type **Clerical expenses** (↓)
Type **Insurance** (↓)
Type **Utilities** (↓)
Type **Office supplies** (↓)
Type **Legal & accounting** (↓)
Type **Miscellaneous** (RET)

....

R O W
90　 **Enter a label to identify the column totals row.**

To enter
　 a label to identify the G&A totals row

Goto R90C1

Select A (for Alpha)
Type **Total G&A expenses** (RET)

Step Three

Enter values in columns 2 and 3

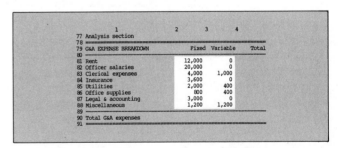

C O L U M N S **Enter values for fixed and variable expenses.**
2 and 3　 As noted earlier, the variable costs are those that are directly related to business activity; as activity increases, variable costs increase and as activity declines, so do variable costs. The relationship is directly proportional. Fixed costs, on the other hand, do not change relative to volume. In fact, they continue at the same level whether there is any business activity at all.

Entering the analysis section Continued

To enter

values for fixed and variable cost components of the
G&A breakdown

Goto R81C2

Type **12000** ⬇
Type **20000** ⬇
Type **4000** ⬇
Type **3600** ⬇
Type **2000** ⬇
Type **800** ⬇
Type **3000** ⬇
Type **1200** (RET)

Goto R81C3

Type **0** ⬇
Type **0** ⬇
Type **1000** ⬇
Type **0** ⬇
Type **400** ⬇
Type **400** ⬇
Type **0** ⬇
Type **1200** (RET)

Assign names to the "fixed" and "variable" expenses
columns so that they can be referenced in formulas.
Note that the cell ranges assigned to these two names
actually extend across both the the G&A breakdown
and the selling expense breakdown, and that the
boundaries of the named ranges are the ruled lines in
rows 80 and 101. This allows us to use one simple
formula in the "totals" column for both expense categories and also makes the itemization easily ex-
pandable by adding new rows between the ruled
lines.

To enter

a name for columns 2 and 3 so they can be called up
for formulas

Select N (for Name)
Type **fixed** in the "define name" field (TAB)
Type **R80:101C2** in the "to refer to" field (RET)

Select N (for Name)
Type **variable** in the "define name" field (TAB)
Type **R80:101C3** in the "to refer to" field (RET)

Enter formulas in column 4

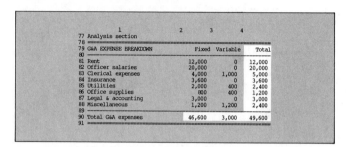

COLUMN 4   **Enter formulas in the "total" column.** The formula **fixed + variable** adds only the corresponding values in the current row; it is equivalent to the
formula **RC[-2]+RC[-1]**.

To enter

the formulas for column 4

Goto R81C4

Select V (for Value)
Type **fixed + variable** (RET)

Select CD (for Copy Down)
Type **7** in the "number of cells" field (RET)

Recalculate the worksheet

Result Your results should match those in the illustration.

. . . .

ROW 90   **Enter formulas for column totals.** Here we
build a formula using relative cell reference
notation in order to use the same formula repeatedly.

To enter

a formula to total G&A expenses

Goto R90C2

Select V (for Value)
Type **SUM(R[-10]C:R[-1]C)** (RET)

Select CR (for Copy Right)
Type **2** in the "number of cells" field (RET)

Recalculate the worksheet

Result The column totals should match the illustration.

Step Five

Enter a formula to link G&A on the worksheet to the income statement

```
        1        2      3      4      5      6       7
 1 DECISION worksheet
 2
 3 INCOME STATEMENT: January 1 through December 31, 19..
 4 ══════════════════════════════════════════════════════
 5                        This   % net  Last   % net  <——Deviation——>
 6                        year   sales  year   sales    $       %
 7 ══════════════════════════════════════════════════════
 8 Gross sales           336,000  100  312,000  100  24,000    8
 9 Sales discounts             0    0        0    0       0
10 Net sales             336,000  100  312,000  100  24,000    8
11
12 Cost of goods sold    221,760   66  201,240   65  20,520   10
13 Gross profit          114,240   34  110,760   36   3,480    3
14
15 General & administrative 49,600  15   52,000   17  -2,400   -5
16 Selling expenses       49,000   15   40,000   13   9,000   23
17 Depreciation
18
19 Operating income
20 Interest expense
21 Other income/expense
22
23 Income before taxes
24 Taxes
25
26 NET INCOME
27
```

```
                                    1        2       3       4
77 Analysis section
78
79 G&A EXPENSE BREAKDOWN           Fixed  Variable  Total
80
81 Rent                           12,000      0    12,000
82 Officer salaries               20,000      0    20,000
83 Clerical expenses               4,000   1,000    5,000
84 Insurance                       3,600      0     3,600
85 Utilities                       2,000     400    2,400
86 Office supplies                   800     400    1,200
87 Legal & accounting              3,000      0     3,000
88 Miscellaneous                   1,200   1,200    2,400
89
90 Total G&A expenses             46,600   3,000   49,600
91
```

CELL R15C2   **Link the G&A breakdown to the income statement.** When the income statement was entered in the last chapter, we entered a value for G&A expenses. Now that the breakdown is completed, the total G&A expenses on this worksheet should be carried to this year's G&A line on the income statement. Any changes in fixed or variable G&A expenses on the worksheet will then automatically be reflected in a changed G&A figure on the income statement. This allows you to explore "What Ifs" and immediately see the effect on the income statement (and on net income) of changes in such items as rent or salaries.

To enter
> *a formula* in cell R15C2 that will carry total G&A expenses in cell R90C4 to the income statement

Goto R15C2

Select V (for Value)
> Type **R90C4** (RET)

Result The value in cell R15C2 should be the same as the value in cell R90C4, $49,600.

Step Six

Enter labels for the selling expense breakdown

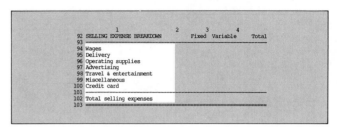

```
         1                      2      3         4
 92 SELLING EXPENSE BREAKDOWN      Fixed  Variable   Total
 93
 94 Wages
 95 Delivery
 96 Operating supplies
 97 Advertising
 98 Travel & entertainment
 99 Miscellaneous
100 Credit card
101
102 Total selling expenses
103
```

ROWS 94–102   **Labels** for the selling expense breakdown and totals are entered on the worksheet. As will be seen, included here are all of the costs directly related to the sales activities of the firm, from wages to travel and entertainment.

To enter
> *labels* to identify the individual line items making up selling expense

Goto R94C1

Select A (for Alpha)
> Type **Wages** (↓)
> Type **Delivery** (↓)
> Type **Operating supplies** (↓)
> Type **Advertising** (↓)
> Type **Travel & entertainment** (↓)
> Type **Miscellaneous** (↓)
> Type **Credit card** (RET)

Goto R102C1

Select A (for Alpha)
> Type **Total selling expenses** (RET)

| | Step Seven | | Step Eight |

Step Seven

Enter values in columns 2 and 3

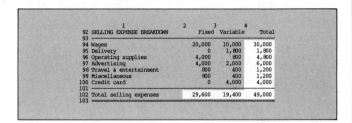

	1	2	3	4
92	SELLING EXPENSE BREAKDOWN		Fixed	Variable	Total
93					
94	Wages		20,000	10,000	
95	Delivery		0	1,800	
96	Operating supplies		4,000	800	
97	Advertising		4,000	2,000	
98	Travel & entertainment		800	400	
99	Miscellaneous		800	400	
100	Credit card		0	4,000	
101					
102	Total selling expenses				
103					

COLUMNS 2 and 3 **Fixed and variable selling expenses** are entered. Some selling expenses are directly related to sales, such as sales commissions, discounts, and co-op advertising allowances. Other selling expenses are essentially fixed, such as base salaries and advertising.

To enter

values for the fixed and variable cost components of each of the line items in the selling expense breakdown

Goto R94C2
Type **20000** ⬇
Type **0** ⬇
Type **4000** ⬇
Type **4000** ⬇
Type **800** ⬇
Type **800** ⬇
Type **0** (RET)

Goto R94C3
Type **10000** ⬇
Type **1800** ⬇
Type **800** ⬇
Type **2000** ⬇
Type **400** ⬇
Type **400** ⬇
Type **4000** (RET)

Step Eight

Enter formulas in column 4

	1	2	3	4
92	SELLING EXPENSE BREAKDOWN		Fixed	Variable	Total
93					
94	Wages		20,000	10,000	30,000
95	Delivery		0	1,800	1,800
96	Operating supplies		4,000	800	4,800
97	Advertising		4,000	2,000	6,000
98	Travel & entertainment		800	400	1,200
99	Miscellaneous		800	400	1,200
100	Credit card		0	4,000	4,000
101					
102	Total selling expenses		29,600	19,400	49,000
103					

COLUMN 4 **Enter formulas in the "total" column.** Having already named the "fixed" and "variable" columns, all we need to do is copy the "total" formula from the G&A expenses section.

To enter

a formula for the total column

Goto R94C4

Select CF (for Copy From)
Type **R88C4** in the "cells" field (RET)

Select CD (for Copy Down)
Type **6** in the "number of cells" field (RET)

Recalculate the worksheet

....

ROW 102 **Enter column totals formulas** for the total selling expenses.

To enter

a formula to add the total selling expenses

Goto R102C2

Select V (for Value)
Type **SUM(R[-9]C:R[-1]C)** (RET)

Select CR (for Copy Right)
Type **2** in the "number of cells" field (RET)

Recalculate the worksheet

Result Your worksheet should match the illustration.

Step Nine

Enter a formula that will link total selling expense to the income statement

```
         1          2     3      4      5       6     7
 1 DECISION worksheet
 2
 3 INCOME STATEMENT: January 1 through December 31, 19..
 4 ================================================================
 5                          This   % net   Last   % net   <----Deviation---->
 6                          year   sales   year   sales       $         %
 7 ================================================================
 8 Gross sales            336,000   100  312,000   100    24,000         8
 9 Sales discounts              0     0        0     0         0
10 Net sales              336,000   100  312,000   100    24,000         8
11
12 Cost of goods sold     221,760    66  201,240    65    20,520        10
13 Gross profit           114,240    34  110,760    36     3,480         3
14
15 General & administrative 49,600   15   52,000    17    -2,400        -5
16 Selling expenses        49,000    15   40,000    13     9,000        23
17 Depreciation             6,000     2    5,500     2       500         9
18
19 Operating income         9,640     3   13,260     4    -3,620       -27
20 Interest expense
21 Other income/expense
22
23 Income before taxes
24 Taxes
25
26 NET INCOME
27 ================================================================
```

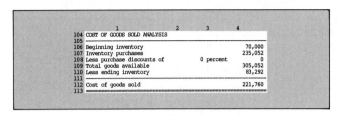

```
          1                2       3        4
 92 SELLING EXPENSE BREAKDOWN      Fixed  Variable   Total
 93 ================================================================
 94 Wages                         20,000   10,000    30,000
 95 Delivery                           0    1,800     1,800
 96 Operating supplies             4,000      800     4,800
 97 Advertising                    4,000    2,000     6,000
 98 Travel & entertainment           800      400     1,200
 99 Miscellaneous                    800      400     1,200
100 Credit card                        0    4,000     4,000
101 ----------------------------------------------------------------
102 Total selling expenses        29,600   19,400    49,000
103 ================================================================
```

CELL
R16C2

Link the selling expense breakdown to the income statement. When the income statement was entered in the last chapter, we entered a value for selling expense. Now that the breakdown is completed, the total selling expense on this worksheet should be carried to this year's selling expense line on the income statement. Any changes in fixed or variable selling expense on the worksheet will then automatically be reflected in a changed selling expense figure on the income statement. This allows you to explore "What Ifs" and immediately see the effect on the income statement (and on net income) of changes in such items as advertising.

To enter
> *a formula* in cell R16C2 that will carry total selling expense in cell R102C4 to the income statement

Goto R16C2

Select V (for Value)
> Type **R102C4** (RET)

Result The value displayed in cell R16C2 should be the same as the total selling expenses amount calculated in cell R102C4, $49,000.

Step Ten

Enter labels and formulas for the cost of goods analysis

```
          1                    2      3        4
104 COST OF GOODS SOLD ANALYSIS
105 ================================================================
106 Beginning inventory                         70,000
107 Inventory purchases                        235,052
108 Less purchase discounts of    0 percent          0
109 Total goods available                      305,052
110 Less ending inventory                       83,292
111 ----------------------------------------------------------------
112 Cost of goods sold                         221,760
113 ================================================================
```

ROWS
104–113

Enter ruled lines and a heading for the cost of goods sold analysis. Cost of goods is the true variable cost within the firm. A change in this section will raise or lower the breakeven in direct relation to the degree of change.

To enter
> *a label* to identify this section of the worksheet
> *ruled lines* to make the worksheet easier to read

Goto R104C1

Select A (for Alpha)
Type **COST OF GOODS SOLD ANALYSIS** (RET)

Select CF (for Copy From)
> Type **shortline2** in the "cells" field (TAB)
> Type **R113C1** in the "to cells" field (RET)

Select CF (for Copy From)
> Type **shortline1** in the "cells" field (TAB)
> Type **R105C1,R111C1** in the "to cells" field (RET)

. . . .

ROW
106

Beginning inventory for the present operating period is the same figure as the ending inventory from the preceding period. This helps to preserve the continuity from one period to the next.

To enter
> *a label* to identify this as the beginning inventory line of the worksheet
> *a formula* in cell R106C4 that will carry the beginning inventory from cell R38C4, last year's ending inventory

Entering the analysis section Continued

Goto **R106C1**

Select A (for Alpha)
Type **Beginning inventory** → → →
Type **= R38C4** (RET)

Result Beginning inventory should be $70,000.

··

ROW 107 **Inventory purchases** are entered next. Added to the beginning inventory are any new items purchased during the present period.

To enter
a label to identify this as the inventory purchases line of the worksheet
a value of $235,052 in cell R107C4

Goto **R107C1**

Select A (for Alpha)
Type **Inventory purchases** → → →
Type **235052** (RET)

··

ROW 108 **Purchase discounts** are subtracted from inventory purchases to show the net or actual cost of these purchases.

To enter
a label to identify this as the purchase discounts line of the worksheet
a data entry space in cell R108C2 that will be used to enter discounts (they will be entered as whole number percentages, not as decimals)
a formula in cell R108C4 that will multiply purchase discounts (as percentages) times inventory purchases to give the dollar discount value (The % sign at the end of the formula is equivalent to dividing by 100.)

Goto **R108C1**

Select A (for Alpha)
Type **Less purchase discounts of** →
Type **0** →
Type **percent** →
Type **-R107C4*R108C2%** (RET)

Result Since no discount percentage has yet been entered, the dollar column R108C4 should read zero.

ROW 109 **Total goods available** for sale are found by adding the net inventory to the beginning inventory.

To enter
a label to identify this as the total goods available line of the worksheet
a formula in cell R109C4 that will add beginning inventory to purchases and subtract discounts

Goto **R109C1**

Select A (for Alpha)
Type **Total goods available** → → →
Type **= SUM(R106:108C4)** (RET)

Result Total goods available should be $305,052.

··

ROW 110 **Ending inventory** is the next item to be entered. Subtracting the ending or remaining inventory will show what was sold by adjusting for what is left.

To enter
a label to identify this as the ending inventory line of the worksheet
a formula in cell R110C4 that will carry the inventory figure from this year's column on the balance sheet

Goto **R110C1**

Select A (for Alpha)
Type **Less ending inventory** → → →
Type **= R38C2** (RET)

Result Ending inventory should be $83,292.

··

ROW 112 **Cost of goods sold** are entered. Once we have subtracted the ending inventory from the total inventory, we will know how much has actually been sold. The net purchases are added to the beginning inventory to show total goods available for sale. Ending inventory is subtracted from this total with the correct understanding that the difference between total goods available and those remaining were sold.

To enter

a label to identify this as the cost of goods sold
line of the worksheet

a formula in cell R112C4 that will subtract ending
inventory from total goods available to give the
cost of goods sold

Goto R112C1

Select A (for Alpha)
Type **Cost of goods sold** → → →
Type **= R109C4 − R110C4** (RET)

Result The cost of goods sold should be $221,760.

Step Eleven

Enter a formula to link cost of goods sold to the income statement

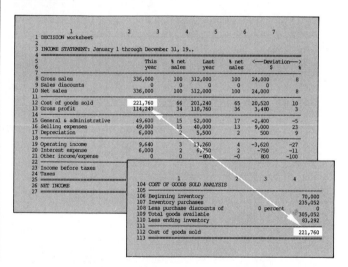

CELL
R12C2 **Linking the cost of goods sold analysis to the
income statement** is the last step in this section. When the income statement was entered in the last
chapter we entered a value for cost of goods sold. Now
that the analysis is completed, the total cost of goods sold
expenses on this worksheet should be carried to this
year's cost of goods line on the income statement. Any
changes in cost of goods sold expenses on the worksheet
will then automatically be reflected in a changed cost of
goods sold figure on the income statement. This allows

you to explore "What Ifs" and immediately see the effect
on the income statement (and on net income) of changes
in such items as inventory purchases and purchase discounts.

To enter

a formula in cell R12C2 that will carry total cost of
goods sold expenses in cell R112C4 to the income statement

Goto R12C2
Type **= R112C4** (RET)

Result The value in cell R12C2 should be the same as the
value in cell R112C4, $221,760.

Step Twelve

Enter labels and formulas for the breakeven calculations

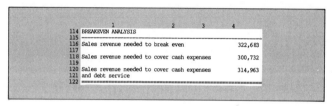

ROWS
114–122 **Breakeven calculations** are now entered
into the worksheet. The breakeven calculations we will explore will show the sales necessary to
reach breakeven, then show the sales necessary to cover
cash expenses, and finally the sales necessary to cover
cash expenses and debt service. In most businesses, there
are noncash expenses included along with cash expenses.
These are expenses we incur but don't actually pay for.
On the other hand, there are actual cash disbursements
that are made but that are not expenses, such as principal
portions of loan payments. Each of these breakeven targets is important because unless we reach the highest
level, we will be in trouble.

To enter

a label to identify this as the breakeven calculations
section of the worksheet

ruled lines to make the worksheet easier to read

Goto R114C1

Select A (for Alpha)
Type **BREAKEVEN ANALYSIS** (RET)

Entering the analysis section Continued

Select **CF** (for Copy From)
    Type **shortline2** in the "cells" field (TAB)
    Type **R122C1** in the "to cells" field (RET)

Select **CF** (for Copy From)
    Type **shortline1** in the "cells" field (TAB)
    Type **R115C1** in the "to cells" field (RET)

....

R O W 116   **Sales revenue needed to break even** is the first item. We will construct the breakeven sales level for this year based on the cost data in the income statement.

To enter

a label to identify this as the breakeven sales revenue line of the worksheet

a formula in cell R116C4 that will calculate the sales revenue needed to break even. The formula adds fixed G&A and selling expenses (from the worksheet) to depreciation and interest (from the income statement). The sum of these items is then divided by 1 minus the sum of variable G&A expense, selling expense, and cost of goods sold (from the income statement) divided by net sales. The formula in effect calculates the sales (100 percent), less the variable expense proportion (72.7 percent), necessary to generate the contribution (27.3 percent) remaining to cover fixed expenses. This contribution (27.3 percent) is then divided into the $88,200 in fixed expenses in order to produce the $322,683 in sales volume necessary to cover all expenses recorded on the income statement.

Select **FC** (for Format Cells)
    Type **R116C1:R120C3** in the "cells" field (TAB) (TAB)
    Type **C** (for Continuous) in the "format code" field (RET)

Goto R116C1

Select **A** (for Alpha)
    Type **Sales revenue needed to break even** (→) (→) (→)
    Type **(R90C2 + R102C2 + R17C2 + R20C2)/ (1-((R90C3 + R102C3 + R112C4)/R10C2))** (RET)

Result   Sales revenue needed to break even should be $322,683.

A N A L Y S I S   Mr. Adams's firm had sales at $336,000, but he breaks even with $13,317 (4.0 percent) less in sales ($322,683). This means that with his cost structure and pricing strategy he had a cushion of 4.0 percent to cover his costs. This is not much of a cushion in a business that is so competitive and so sensitive to business cycles.

....

R O W 118   **Sales revenue needed to cover cash expense** is now calculated. We will construct the sales level needed to cover the cash expense contained in this year's income statement.

To enter

a label to identify this as the sales revenue needed to cover cash expenses

a formula in cell R118C4 that will calculate the sales revenue needed to cover cash expense. The formula adds fixed G&A and selling expense (from the worksheet) to interest (from the income statement). The sum of those items is then divided by 1 minus the sum of variable G&A expense, selling expense, and cost of goods sold (from the income statement) divided by net sales. This formula differs from the initial breakeven sales computation in that it only accounts for expenses that require cash payments. This means expense items such as depreciation, which writes off assets previously paid, are deducted from the expenses. The net result is that there is a lower level of sales required to cover only the cash expense.

Goto R118C1

Select **A** (for Alpha)
    Type **Sales revenue needed to cover cash expenses** (→) (→) (→)
    Type **(R90C2 + R102C2 + R20C2)/(1-((R90C3 + R102C3 + R112C4)/R10C2))** (RET)

Result   Sales revenue needed to cover cash expenses should be $300,732.

A N A L Y S I S   Mr. Adams could have covered all his cash expenses with a sales level of only $300,732. Of course, this assumes all sales are for cash. This cushion of $35,268 (10.5 percent) is much greater than that required to cover all costs. The reason for the lower sales requirement is the elimination of a fixed expense, depreciation (or amortization). This item is usually the write-off over a period of years for an item paid for at an earlier date but that has value over the entire period. For example, a truck is paid for when you drive it from the dealer's lot. As an expense item, it is written off over its useful life, say five years. The annual writeoff is a noncash expense and thus excluded from cash breakeven. Another item that Mr. Adams might treat in a similar fashion is leasehold improvements. Although not a tangible fixed asset, it is an item that has value over the period of a lease, say five to ten years, and thus is so amortized.

It is important to note that the cash breakeven is the bottom line, so to speak. Sales below that level mean that the firm needs to obtain outside money to cover its day-to-day expenses, which inhibits acquisition of new assets.

....

ROWS 120–121. **Sales revenue needed to cover cash expenses and debt service** is the final item. Here we construct the sales level needed to cover this year's cash expenses plus the principal payments for notes or loans payable this year.

────────────────────

To enter

a label to identify this as the sales revenue needed to cover cash expenses and debt service line of the worksheet

a formula in cell R120C4 that will calculate the sales revenue needed to cover cash expenses and debt service. The formula adds fixed G&A and selling expenses (from the worksheet) to interest (from the income statement) and notes payable (current) from the balance sheet. The sum of these items is then divided by 1 minus the sum of variable G&A expense, selling expense, and cost of goods sold (from the income statement) divided by net sales. This formula differs from the previous two breakeven computations in that it adds, as if it were an expense, the principal payment for notes payable due in the next 12 months, to the cash expenses from the income statement. The breakeven sales necessary to cover these items are greater than the cash breakeven but less than the income breakeven.

Goto R120C1

Select A (for Alpha)
  Type **Sales revenue needed to cover cash expenses** ⬇
  Type **and debt service** ➡ ➡ ➡ ⬆
  Type **(R90C2 + R102C2 + R20C2 + R59C2)/ (1-((R90C3 + R102C3 + R112C4)/R10C2))** (RET)

────────────────────

Result Sales revenue needed to break even should be $314,963.

ANALYSIS The last breakeven exercise shows the sales _____ required to pay cash expenses plus fully pay the annual long-term debt payment required by the lenders. As in the above example, the noncash item depreciation is excluded, but the principal repayment due under the long-term debt agreement, $3,890, is included. Remember, part of the full payment to the bank is interest. This item, $6,000, is included in the income statement's cash costs. The sales necessary to cover the cash expenses and full debt service (as opposed to interest only) is $314,968, or $21,032 (6.3 percent) less than the sales level. Again, it is a margin that won't permit wide variations in sales without trouble.

Overall, the analysis tells us:

1 Mr. Adams, given his cost, price, and financial structure, has very little margin for error. The fallback is only 4 to 10 percent.

2 Mr. Adams has a short-term bottom line of approximately $300,000 in sales before he is beset with real problems.

3 Given the competitive nature of the business and its sensitivity to business cycles, Mr. Adams should be considering ways to improve his cushion. Especially when the economy is strong, it should be much larger.

────────────────────

Step Thirteen

Enter labels and formulas for the cash flow analysis

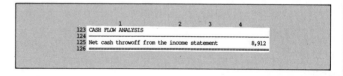

```
              1              2      3      4
123  CASH FLOW ANALYSIS
124
125  Net cash throwoff from the income statement    8,912
126  ════════════════════════════════════════════════════
```

ROWS 123–126 **Cash flow analysis** is next entered in the worksheet. The basic purpose of the concept of cash throwoff is simply to provide the manager of a small business, such as Mr. Adams, with some idea as to the cash that is being provided to the firm. Not all expenses are cash expenses; for example, depreciation is not. Thus the cash throwoff, assuming timely and consistent payment of accounts receivable and accounts payable, is usually greater than the net income. In effect, the cash throwoff subtracts from sales the expenses that require cash payments during the period.

Entering the analysis section Continued

To enter

a label to identify this as the cash flow analysis
section of the worksheet

a label to identify the net cash throwoff from the
income statement line of the worksheet

ruled lines to make the worksheet easier to read

a formula in cell R125C4 that will add operating income and depreciation and then subtract interest
and taxes

Select CF (for Copy From)
Type **shortline2** in the "cells" field (TAB)
Type **R126C1** in the "to cells" field (RET)

Select CF (for Copy From)
Type **shortline1** in the "cells" field (TAB)
Type **R124C1** in the "to cells" field (RET)

Select FC (for Format Cells)
Type **R125C1:3** in the "cells" field (TAB) (TAB)
Type **C** (for Continuous) in the "format code"
field (RET)

Goto R123C1

Select A (for Alpha)
Type **CASH FLOW ANALYSIS** (↓) (↓)
Type **Net cash throwoff from the income
statement** (→) (→) (→)
Type **=R19C2+R17C2-R20C2-R24C2** (RET)

Result Net cash throwoff should be $8,912.

Step Fourteen

Save your work Again, it's advisable to save your work
before you proceed. Here is a brief summary of how
to save (for detailed instructions see page 31).

To save
the analysis section of the worksheet

Select LF (for Lock Formulas)
Type **Y** (to confirm) (RET)

Select TS (for Transfer Save)
Type (RET)
The message line reads
Overwrite existing file?
Type **Y** to confirm

5 Overhead

Introduction

Why should we be concerned with overhead? Because overhead, the general expenses of any business, represents expenditures that if not made would, theoretically at least, be available as profits. Even worse than diverted profits, overhead may represent obligations that the firm cannot meet given its present level of sales and activity. Without overhead, breakeven would never be a problem as long as the product or service was priced at cost or above. Unfortunately, for most organizations no overhead is not even an option, no matter how carefully costs are planned. Even the sidewalk vendor generally must have a peddler's license, which for him may represent his total overhead. Nevertheless, even such a seemingly insignificant overhead cost must be taken into account in profit planning.

In virtually all organizations, there are those costs that will continue whether the operation is doing any business (incurring any sales) or not. Consequently, the purpose of this discussion is to carefully inspect these costs to determine whether they are truly essential and thus whether they can be reduced or eliminated.

Decision making is difficult at best in a small business. The better the information available, the better the decisions can be. Managers are often confronted with situations involving a variety of factors, many of which are overlapping, confusing, and/or conflicting. All of this seriously complicates effective decision making. As firms increase in size, these decision-making processes become more complex and so have a larger aggregate impact; but they nevertheless still remain essentially critical to the small firm, despite the smaller scale. Within the decision-making framework, the area of cost analysis and control is typically the most complex and the most critical. Understanding and being sensitive to cost implications can best be accomplished by aggregating costs into categories that simplify their analysis.

What is overhead?

In the broadest sense, overhead is a name for all of the expenses of a business. To be more technically correct, we would have to exclude the truly variable costs, those expenses directly associated with having goods or services available for sale and that, in the absence of such activity, would not exist. For small firms, however, we often consider many costs as overhead that, in larger firms, would be truly variable and therefore not technically part of overhead. The reason for this is that, in the smaller firm, these costs do not correlate directly to sales or other business activity. They are instead semivariable.

In all firms, costs can be divided into the categories of variable, fixed, and semivariable. Each of these classifications can, in turn, be separated into direct or indirect and, further, into long-term or short-term and incremental or nonincremental. It is by understanding how the costs function in each of these different categories that it is possible to bring them under control. Of course, your computer is a valuable tool to help you in this process, and we will show you how to apply its techniques.

Proper understanding of cost relationships within a firm helps in establishing a control system for expenses. The two parts of the profit equation are revenues and expenses. While these components have already been discussed as part of breakeven analysis, they will be investigated here in much greater detail to help you further your understanding of this critical area. Ways of stimulating revenues will be discussed later and certainly are an attractive option, but it is just as significant to note that controlling expenses is every bit as important as a means of improving profitability and one over which the firm frequently has the most control.

Cost expense categories

Analyzing costs is the first step toward their control. Accordingly, the first part of that analysis process is classifying costs into appropriate and related categories so that they can first be examined individually and in relation to each other, and then in relation to some outside standard, such as an industry average. Generally speaking, as we analyze these costs, it is useful to look at them both in terms of whole dollar amounts and in terms of their percentages relative to the total level of sales. There is nothing mysterious about the whole dollar amount; it is simply the amount of dollars represented by that cost category. The percentage of sales, however, sometimes seems to be confusing to individuals, particularly in terms of its calculation. This calculation is performed by simply dividing each of the cost categories by the net sales level for the operating period. The result will then express each one of the costs as percentage of sales. Using these percentage relationships greatly facilitates the comparison of costs for a given period with those of other operating periods, perhaps of different time durations or at different overall levels of activity, and with outside barometers such as industry averages, where expenses are always expressed as a percentage of sales.

As we get into our classification activities, we are interested in categorizing costs first in terms of whether they are variable, fixed, or semivariable, and then within these categories as direct or indirect and frequently also as short-term or long-term.

Variable expenses As we have discussed, variable expenses are those costs that vary directly and proportionately with the sales of the business. True variable expenses do not exist in the absence of sales. Examples of variable expenses include the following: commissions paid to the sales force, materials purchased for resale, direct materials used in manufacturing, the direct labor component of manufacturing (especially if payment is on a piece-rate basis), and so forth. As sales increase, these items should increase a fixed amount per unit of activity. Long term, the variability may change slightly based on such items as volume discounts, improved labor productivity, and other such "economies of scale," which we often at least hope to see above certain levels of activity.

It has often been said that all expenses are variable in the long run. In the strict sense this is true, but for small business managers this is not the case when their need is to run day-to-day operations. The statement really says that expenses only become fixed or are nonvariable when you make a commitment to incur the expense. For example, when you agree to rent a larger facility, you now have a regular "fixed" expense. The larger the firm grows, the greater will be the need to add to its present expense base. Many of these expenses will only increase at certain stages. The present facility may be capable of handling, for example, a volume of $350,000 per year. When you exceed that level, the facility (rent) expense must, by definition, be increased to handle the larger volume. If rent as a percent of sales is plotted over five to ten years, it may appear to be a consistent percentage of sales because capacity has been added as the volume increases. However, in the short term, say over a year or two, the proportion of sales relative to capacity is high and decreases as the business increases in capacity. In the interim, the expense itself was not variable since its level was fixed by contract regardless of the volume.

Fixed expenses Fixed expenses, as the name suggests, are "fixed" or constant relative to activity. Unlike variable expenses, fixed expenses are not influenced by the volume of sales. They will stay the same regardless of the level of activity. Because they do not vary relative to sales activity, as sales levels change, fixed expenses as a proportion of sales will change. In other words, the percentage of sales that a given expense represents will increase or decrease as a sales level changes and will be inversely related to the level of sales. This is a helpful bit of knowledge to keep in mind as you analyze sales and cost relationships in the organization. True variable costs will be the same percentage of sales at different volumes of activity, while the actual dollar amount of these costs will vary in a direct relationship to sales activity. Fixed costs, on the other hand, are fixed as far as the actual expenditures are concerned, but will change their percentage relationship to sales as sales levels increase or decrease.

Examples of fixed expenses include flat monthly rental rates, most insurance premiums, interest on loans, depreciation, and so forth. These expenses are the same each month, regardless of the sales volume. Again, it is important to note that, long term, these expenses may very well change (increase) in steps as volume increases. For example, expanded sales volume may well require additional space, and as additional space is typically only available in whole incremental units, the cost is very likely to increase in a stepped fashion rather than in a linear relationship.

Semivariable expenses For small firms particularly, most expenses do not vary directly or proportionately with sales. In reality, there are often widely differing degrees of variability. Thus, to be accurate, we should classify these costs as semivariable expenses. In other words, these are costs that change somewhat in response to different levels of sales activity but are not directly proportional to sales nor are they truly fixed. A discussion of some of the more common semivariable expenses will help to illustrate this point. Examples are:

- Cost of goods sold
- Rent expense with a percentage lease
- Utilities expense
- Advertising and sales promotion
- Sales salaries/wages and related expenses
- Managerial and administrative wages

Cost of goods sold is usually considered to be a true variable cost as it typically has a direct relationship to sales. This is especially true in retail businesses such as Acme Hardware. While inventory costs will vary somewhat depending upon the volume purchased, over time they will remain relatively constant as a percentage of sales. However, in manufacturing businesses the cost of goods sold contains not only direct materials and direct labor, but the factory overhead as well, which contains variable, fixed, and semivariable expense items. Consequently, in a manufacturing business we would not expect to see cost of goods sold vary quite as directly with sales as we would in a retail business where all of the goods are purchased.

Cost of goods sold is a derivative of several expense and inventory items and as such is an item of confusion in many smaller firms. The final figure is not necessarily the amount of money you spent on inventory and/or purchases during the preceding accounting period; it is, in simple terms, the cost that can be associated with goods or merchandise that have been sold. It is this distinction between purchases and cost of sales that is sometimes confusing. This confusion can be clarified somewhat by the following breakdown of cost of goods sold:

Beginning inventory + Purchases
= Cost of goods available for sale − Ending inventory
= Cost of goods sold

Thus, it can be seen from the model that it is the difference in inventory levels as well as purchases that we must concern ourselves with in order to directly associate the correct cost with our sales activity.

Regarding *rent expense*, during recent years, especially in shopping mall locations, landlords have indicated an awareness of the true value of a facility and a willingness to share in the risk associated with the productivity of a given location by setting up a two-tiered schedule, which has both a fixed and a variable component, resulting in a semivariable cost. Under typical arrangements, the landlord would charge a certain rate for a square foot of occupied space and then stipulate that, should sales exceed a certain specified level, the business will pay a percentage of its sales in addition to the base fixed monthly rental cost.

Utilities expense covers the cost of items such as water and gas. If the business is billed for these items on a flat rate, which is unusual, then of course the cost would be fixed; however, if the business is billed on a usage basis, which is far more typical, then this expense becomes a true variable cost. For a telephone bill, the cost is both fixed and variable; there is a base charge for the system with a variable portion, which is a function of the calls made. The variable portion may be directly correlated with sales activities, while the base portion is fixed. The heating or air-conditioning usage of electricity brings a monthly variability, but not necessarily in relation to sales. Where the monthly variations are small, it makes most sense to budget these items as fixed costs. The key to their proper treatment, however, comes through a true understanding of the nature and cause of their behavior.

Advertising and sales promotion can be fixed when a specific amount is budgeted or set aside to be spent on a regular basis. On the other hand, if the amount of this expenditure is related to current sales, the expense would be variable. In many situations, a regular amount is planned as a fixed expense, with an additional percentage of sales added as a variable cost. Sometimes an unfortunate side effect of this type of strategy can occur when the business is experiencing a sales downturn. Under such circumstances, the rule or formula would show that the business should spend less, when in reality the wise strategy might instead be to increase the expenditure and try to affect the factors that are contributing to the negative trend. It will not always be possible to change these negative factors, of course, but this certainly should at least be a consideration.

Sales salaries/wages and related expenses are often regarded as a variable cost of sales. Unfortunately, particularly in small firms, this is often not true. There are generally minimum levels of staffing that are required in any area of a business. Like rent, this human support must be provided at that minimum level, whether there is any sales activity or not. Whatever this level is for the sales force becomes a fixed expense. In the case of Mr. Adams, his cost in the hardware store is represented by the percentage of his time that he must spend on the sales floor, along with whatever sales clerks are required for his minimal staffing level. Mr. Adams may use additional staff people on peak days or weeks on a part-time basis, thus minimizing what would otherwise be an increase in fixed expenses if full-time sales clerks were added. Handled in this incremental fashion, the extra cost is a variable expense. Thus a small firm can make additions beyond the minimum that are correlated to the sales volume.

Managerial and administrative wages in most instances are relatively fixed in nature. However, in small struggling businesses, it often behooves the manager to minimize fixed expense and relate as many expenses as possible to the sales level. Even more desirable would be to develop a method of compensation that is based on profitability rather than sales volume. Compensation based on sales volume would tend to drive up the breakeven, as noted in the preceding discussion. Compensation related to profitability will not come into play until after breakeven has been reached. The problem in establishing a variable payment program for management is that the basic wage or the fixed component must be sufficient to cover an individual's basic living expenses. If not, the age-old problem of skimming can easily become a way of life in order to obtain an adequate level of income for the necessities of life. Beyond the basic wage, the compensation could well be geared to profit.

Direct expenses Once we have divided our costs into variable, fixed, and semivariable, it is useful to further subdivide each of these categories into direct or indirect expenses based on the degree of their relationship to actual operational activities. The more closely connected to the actual activities of running the operation, the more direct. But keep in mind that the reason for this classification is to be able to examine carefully each expense category to determine whether or not it is truly essential. Identifying and examining a direct expense enables us to try to determine whether we are getting the optimal impact for the funds invested. If we are not, then we should question the desirability of continuing with that particular expense at its present level.

An example here could be a small trucking firm, which has as direct expenses those costs that relate directly to the movement of goods, such as the drivers' wages, truck maintenance, and fuel. Truck ownership and depreciation costs would be classified as indirect. Classifying these costs on this basis permits analysis of the relative efficiency of various sizes of vehicles by a pertinent measure, such as vehicle miles. This knowledge then will assist management in selecting the optimal vehicle size, or combination of sizes, to perform a given task. Assume that the firm has a job of transporting 30,000 pounds to a destination and has trucks of three different capacities with these direct costs per mile:

	Pounds capacity	Direct cost per mile
Truck A	40,000	$2.00
Truck B	20,000	$1.40
Truck C	10,000	$0.90

The combination of Trucks B and C will enable the firm to use full vehicle capacity. However, from a cost standpoint, the cheapest way to transport the 30,000-pound load, assuming that there are no externalities or alternative uses of the vehicles, is to use Truck A. The combined direct cost of Trucks B and C is $2.30 per mile. The direct cost for use of Truck A is $0.30 per mile less, even though the load uses only 75 percent of its capacity.

Indirect expenses Indirect expenses are, by definition, all those expenses that are not direct. In the example of the small trucking firm, the expenses unaccounted for include marketing costs, terminal handling, and administrative expenses. These can also be further classified into variable, fixed, and semivariable. We will find, however, that indirect costs have a far greater tendency to be either fixed or semivariable than do direct costs. We would see that our direct costs are primarily variable. In the trucking firm, the direct expenses are the revenue producers. No revenues are earned unless trucks are moving. The indirect expenses are the support expenses. In a manufacturing organization, we would see indirect expenses included in our cost of goods sold, typically a variable expense, because we would include manufacturing overhead as part of the cost of production. If we were to examine the manufacturing overhead expenses, it would become clear that these costs are usually semivariable and more often fixed. However, our accounting objective is to try and assign costs to the various areas of activity in the most useful manner possible, and therefore our rule enables us to classify these "overhead" costs, normally seen as fixed, as variable.

Short-term expenses In addition to relating cost to sales activity, it is also very helpful to examine costs based on their duration. Dividing costs into short- and long-term categories enables us to predict the degree of control and impact represented by these costs. Generally speaking, the longer the time period we will be stuck with a given cost, the greater should be our concern for its long-term impact. Conversely, we may make a decision to withstand an unusually high short-term cost, knowing that it will soon disappear and so no longer affect our overall operation. Consequently, short-term costs are those that are, relative to the rest of the operation, of short duration. A more precise definition must be made by the user. To a real estate developer, short-term may be six months to a year; on the other hand, long-term for a Christmas tree business may be only two or three weeks. The reason for the use of these categories primarily relates to the type of finance obtained. For example, the mink farmer who pelts his mink only once a year has a very short selling period, one to two weeks, but he incurs expenses at an increasing rate over the entire year. He thus needs short-term financing during the year up to the time he sells his output. At this point he hopes to repay the loan. On the other hand, the real estate developer may require financing over a much longer period of time, often five or more years, before he too is able to repay what is, for practical purposes, his short-term loan.

Short-term expenses are those that require a short time, however defined, to turn on or off. Unskilled labor in the factory can often be hired or terminated with little notice. Similarly, other costs that have a short life span are classified as short-term. An example may be the rental of a tent for a tent sale in the parking lot of a retail store. Short-term costs may also be subject to further subclassification into fixed, variable, and semivariable.

Long-term expenses Spending activities that are represented by obligations into the future and/or that take a long time to terminate are referred to as long-term costs. As noted in the preceding discussion, we are particularly concerned with these costs because we are stuck with their consequences for a long period of time. Facility rental is a typical long-term expense because a lease is generally required, typically for a period of years. If you have a five-year lease, and you find the facility too large or too small or the location inappropriate for your purposes after the first year, you have a cost that may be very difficult to change. Consequently, it is very important to be especially sensitive to these longer-term obligations and particularly to try to determine at the time of their inception whether circumstances will change substantially in the future. If their usefulness or appropriateness changes, you may find an asset becoming an important liability.

Incremental versus nonincremental expenses In many individual and/or short-term managerial decisions, it is often the incremental costs associated with a particular plan or alternative course of action that can be the critical deciding factor. These incremental costs, often referred to as marginal costs, are the extra or variable costs of an activity and are to be contrasted with the so-called average or total cost of a particular action. We need to be cautious in using incremental or marginal costing because we are typically considering only a small component of the total cost of that particular choice to the firm. This is a valid approach, however, when our choice involves using resources that we have on hand anyway (the fixed portion of a semivariable cost), which with a small additional (incremental) cost we can use to gain some benefit for the firm. This is especially relevant when we are not using these available resources at all and consequently are not utilizing our base investment. Under such circumstances, of course, it would be wise to pursue the additional activity. In the longer run, however, such incremental-cost decision making will automatically also represent an obligation for the base or fixed component and thereby stand to increase the total operating costs of the firm. Through this process of reasoning, it may be seen that a project that may be viable on an incremental or marginal basis could prove to be inappropriate when judged on a full-cost basis. Again, the key to analysis is: If there are no alternative uses for a base fixed cost and this resource would not be fully utilized without this particular project, then incremental or marginal cost analysis is justified. If, on the other hand, there are alternative purposes for those base resources, then a full-cost analysis must be used to make a choice between the alternatives.

Looking back at the earlier example of the trucking firm, we found it most economical to use the 40,000-pound capacity truck (Truck A) to carry the 30,000-pound load. This, of course, gives us 10,000 pounds of excess capacity, and therefore, the use of the 10,000 pounds of unused capacity will not entail the same variable costs as the initial 30,000 pounds. The truck driver and most of the maintenance and fuel will be covered by the initial 30,000 pounds. The only incremental costs will be loading, unloading, and perhaps a small additional maintenance and fuel cost due to the heavier load. Thus, the rate we charge per pound of the "filler" 10,000 pounds could be very small, but it would still make a meaningful contribution to our overall operating costs.

Another familiar example of the incremental or marginal cost approach to business management decision making is in the so-called "make or buy" decision. If your firm is currently purchasing an item, perhaps from a subcontractor, and it has the excess capacity to produce the item required, it may be well advised to reconsider manufacturing the item itself. On a full-cost basis, the company may not be able to manufacture the product as efficiently as the subcontractor, who may, for example,

enjoy economies of scale not available to the contracting firm. However, as long as the firm's incremental cost is less than the outside purchase price (which it would be if excess internal capacity is available), then the firm's profit will be improved.

Of course, the incremental or marginal costing technique cannot be used all of the time. At some point, the entire fixed costs of the firm must be covered. In utilizing only incremental costing, the risk is that neither all variable nor all fixed costs will ever be covered. In other words, by using these techniques it is easy to fool yourself into believing that false economies may be available, when in fact the reverse is true. Consequently, the techniques must be used knowingly and judiciously.

Can overhead be controlled?

The answer to this question is obvious. Of course overhead can be controlled. In order to do so, however, the managers of any firm must have a proper control system and the willingness and inclination to use such tools. The grouping of costs into appropriate categories is the first step in developing a useful control system. Once done, this permits the setting of standards for performance. The rest of the control process comes about by comparing actual performance with the plan, then evaluating any discrepancies or deviations that may exist between the two. As these discrepancies are identified, it is essential to determine their causes. When the underlying causes have been identified, the way has been made clear for developing a plan of action to remedy the situation. Each of these activities is a subject for further discussion. However, for now there are certain characteristics to keep in mind that should be a part of any business control system. The control system should provide information that is:

- Timely
- Inexpensive
- Accurate
- Quantifiable
- Measurable
- Able to identify causes
- Assignable

For the most part, the analysis can be made for specific time periods. Once this has been done, information can be verified and costs compared quickly, accurately, and simply by use of the microcomputer. In fact, the microcomputer has made available, especially to the smaller business owner/manager, analytic capacity that was never possible in the past. Consequently, control by an owner/manager is now possible both in the early and expanded growth stages of a firm by using these microcomputer processes. In addition, the decision-making process is improved with the ability to measure the impact of many "What If" scenarios, such as varying inventory levels. Reducing our investment in inventory is clearly going to have a beneficial effect as far as our cash position and our balance sheet accounts are concerned. However, there are some important down-side risks that are associated with reducing our inventory investment. One may be stockouts. Another may be a higher cost of goods because our order unit is becoming smaller than our supplier's economic shipment unit and/or we are ordering more frequently and through more expensive channels, and so we would have additional charges of order preparation and transportation, which we might not otherwise incur.

The following two examples will illustrate impacts on the overhead structure of Acme Hardware. The first "What If" we will consider is this: What if we change cost of goods sold from $235,052 to $221,612? Our computer analysis will quickly show the effect of this change on the income statement, balance sheet, and breakeven. It will also help us to analyze the impact on the cash flow of the operation. The second "What If" involves changing the method of depreciation; specifically, lengthening the writeoff time for assets. The same series of effects will be quickly calculated by our computer.

The analytical routine follows. As with the other exercises, it will be most useful to you if you follow the steps of the example by entering it into your own computer. When you truly understand this tool, you can play this "What If" game with your own business.

If you have continued from the previous chapter without turning off the computer, you can proceed with the "What Ifs" that follow. If, however, you turned off the computer after saving the example, you will have to reload it to continue working. (See page 49.)

Exploring "What Ifs"

Cost of goods sold is reduced. Once Mr. Adams had gained an understanding of overhead in general and had begun to apply this understanding to his own business, he began to wonder what would happen if he made some changes in his expenses. After he had studied his income statement, he noticed that his cost of goods sold expense was the largest single expense item on the statement. It comprised 66 percent of his total costs. If savings were to be made, this would be the best place to start. Perhaps savings could be made by finding new suppliers, negotiating better discounts on selected merchandise, or taking more advantage of special offers from suppliers.

He wondered what would happen if he could reduce these expenses even by a small amount — about 6.06 percent, or $13,440. How much impact would this savings have on the financial condition of his company?

Using the worksheet on the computer and the principles we have been discussing, we can quickly examine "What Ifs" of this kind. Let's explore with Mr. Adams the impact of decreasing the cost of goods sold. He could accomplish this by decreasing inventory purchases or by obtaining purchase discounts, for example. We will use the worksheet and the computer to help us determine the impact of reduced cost of goods sold expense from a number of angles. How will these savings affect the income statement? How will they affect the company cash position? Will they affect the sales revenue needed to break even?

(*Note*: Since you don't want to save the "What If" examples, check that you have put a piece of tape that came with your disk over the square write-protect notch on the disk.)

To enter

a change in inventory purchases in cell R107C4 decreasing them from $235,052 to $221,612. This reduction of $13,440 in inventory purchases will cause a reduction in the cost of goods sold by the same amount.

Goto R107C4 and type **221612** (RET)

Recalculate the worksheet

Result The cost of goods sold in cell R112C4 on the worksheet drops to $208,320. This lower cost of goods sold figure is automatically carried to the cost of goods sold line on the income statement (cell R12C2). With the drop in cost of goods sold, gross profit increases to $127,680, and the gross margin increases to 38 percent in cell R13C3.

The cost of goods sold is reduced $13,440, from $221,760 to $208,320. This improves the gross profit (net sales minus cost of goods sold) by the same amount and the gross margin (gross profit expressed as a percentage of sales) increases from 34 percent in the original example to 38 percent of sales.

Income before taxes (cell R23C2) increases the same amount as gross profit — $13,440, from $3,640 to $17,080. The increase in gross profit and income before taxes is identical because no expenses such as G&A or selling have been increased; thus, the entire savings in cost of goods sold have dropped from the gross profit to the income before taxes line.

Net income increases from $2,912 to $13,664 in cell R26C2. This is an increase of only $10,752 because taxes (cell R24C2) increased $2,688 from $728 to $3,416. This increase in taxes, resulting from the higher income before taxes, partially offsets the savings in cost of goods sold so all of the savings do not drop to the bottom line.

Savings in cost of goods sold	$13,440
Increase in taxes	2,688
Improvement in net income	$10,752

Even though all of the savings didn't drop to the bottom line, net income as a percentage of sales (cell R26C3) has risen from 1 percent to 4 percent. This is a more respectable income level for Acme Hardware.

The net cash throwoff (net income plus depreciation and amortization) in cell R125C4 is improved by the increase in net income ($10,752) from $8,912 in the original example to $19,664. This extra $10,752 in cash appears on the balance sheet in cell R36C2, increasing it from the original $1,335 to $12,087. This extra cash could be used in a variety of ways, such as reducing debt by paying off loans, and thereby increasing the equity base, or maintaining a more comfortable cash balance (the former $1,335 is not a comfortable level).

The sales revenue needed to break even in cell R116C4 has been reduced to $281,489 from the $322,683 in the original example, a reduction of $41,194. More importantly, it has improved Mr. Adams's margin of error in case sales don't meet expectations. The margin for error is simply the difference between what you expect to sell and what you need to sell to break even, expressed as a percentage. The margin for error in the original example and this "What If" can be calculated as follows:

"What If" 1

	1	2	3	4	5	6	7
1	DECISION worksheet						
2							
3	INCOME STATEMENT: January 1 through December 31, 19..						
4							
5		This	% net	Last	% net	<—Deviation—>	
6		year	sales	year	sales	$	%
7							
8	Gross sales	336,000	100	312,000	100	24,000	8
9	Sales discounts	0	0	0	0	0	
10	Net sales	336,000	100	312,000	100	24,000	8
11							
12	Cost of goods sold	208,320	62	201,240	65	7,080	4
13	Gross profit	127,680	38	110,760	36	16,920	15
14							
15	General & administrative	49,600	15	52,000	17	-2,400	-5
16	Selling expenses	49,000	15	40,000	13	9,000	23
17	Depreciation	6,000	2	5,500	2	500	9
18							
19	Operating income	23,080	7	13,260	4	9,820	74
20	Interest expense	6,000	2	6,750	2	-750	-11
21	Other income/expense	0	0	-800	-0	800	-100
22							
23	Income before taxes	17,080	5	7,310	2	9,770	134
24	Taxes	3,416	1	1,462	0	1,954	134
25							
26	NET INCOME	13,664	4	5,848	2	7,816	134
27							
28	BALANCE SHEET: December 31, 19..						
29							
30		This		Last			
31		year		year			
32							
33	ASSETS:						
34							
35	<Current assets>						
36	Cash	12,087		4,750			
37	Accounts receivable	17,777		16,000			
38	Inventory	83,292		70,000			
39	Prepaid expenses	3,400		3,400			
40							
41	Total current assets	116,556		94,150			
42							
43	<Fixed assets>						
44	Buildings & equipment	33,000		38,950			
45	Less accumulated depreciation	-13,000		-7,000			
46	Land	0		0			
47							
48	Total fixed assets	20,000		31,950			
49							
50	Other assets	3,700		2,545			
51							
52	TOTAL ASSETS	140,256		128,645			
53							
54	LIABILITIES:						
55							
56	<Current liabilities>						
57	Accounts payable	18,480		17,000			
58	Accrued wages & taxes	6,357		6,000			
59	Notes payable (current)	3,890		3,890			
60	Other current liabilities	5,900		5,900			
61							
62	Total current liabilities	34,627		32,790			
63							
64	Long-term debt	44,110		48,000			
65							
66	Total liabilities	78,737		80,790			
67							
68	<Owner equity>						
69	Common stock	37,000		37,000			
70	Retained earnings	24,519		10,855			
71							
72	Total owner equity	61,519		47,855			
73							
74	TOTAL LIABILITIES & EQUITY	140,256		128,645			
75							

	1	2	3	4
77	Analysis section			
78				
79	G&A EXPENSE BREAKDOWN	Fixed	Variable	Total
80				
81	Rent	12,000	0	12,000
82	Officer salaries	20,000	0	20,000
83	Clerical expenses	4,000	1,000	5,000
84	Insurance	3,600	0	3,600
85	Utilities	2,000	400	2,400
86	Office supplies	800	400	1,200
87	Legal & accounting	3,000	0	3,000
88	Miscellaneous	1,200	1,200	2,400
89				
90	Total G&A expenses	46,600	3,000	49,600
91				
92	SELLING EXPENSE BREAKDOWN	Fixed	Variable	Total
93				
94	Wages	20,000	10,000	30,000
95	Delivery	0	1,800	1,800
96	Operating supplies	4,000	800	4,800
97	Advertising	4,000	2,000	6,000
98	Travel & entertainment	800	400	1,200
99	Miscellaneous	800	400	1,200
100	Credit card	0	4,000	4,000
101				
102	Total selling expenses	29,600	19,400	49,000
103				
104	COST OF GOODS SOLD ANALYSIS			
105				
106	Beginning inventory			70,000
107	Inventory purchases			221,612
108	Less purchase discounts of		0 percent	0
109	Total goods available			291,612
110	Less ending inventory			83,292
111				
112	Cost of goods sold			208,320
113				
114	BREAKEVEN ANALYSIS			
115				
116	Sales revenue needed to break even			281,489
117				
118	Sales revenue needed to cover cash expenses			262,340
119				
120	Sales revenue needed to cover cash expenses			274,755
121	and debt service			
122				
123	CASH FLOW ANALYSIS			
124				
125	Net cash throwoff from the income statement			19,664
126				

	Original Example	This "What If"
Sales expected (cell R10C2)	$336,000	$336,000
Sales needed to break even	322,683	281,489
Difference in dollars	13,317	54,511
Margin for error (difference in %)	3.96%	16.22%

This increased margin for error means breakeven will be reached even if sales are $54,000, or 16 percent below expectations. Before cost of goods was reduced and gross margin improved, the room for error was only $13,317, or about 4 percent. Having this much room for error, without having to achieve it by raising expected sales, is very reassuring.

....

WHAT IF 2 **Depreciation expense is reduced.** The second change to experiment with is reducing the depreciation expense from $6,000 to $2,500. This could be accomplished by selling equipment or by changing terms to a longer writeoff period, for example from five years to ten years. We can use the original worksheet to help determine the impact on the income statement cash position and the sales revenue needed to break even. (See page 136 for a printout of the entire, original worksheet.)

To restore
the worksheet to its original values

Goto R107C4 and type **235052** (RET)

To enter
a change in depreciation in cell R17C2 decreasing it from $6,000 to $2,500

Goto R17C2 and type **2500** (RET)

Recalculate the worksheet

Result When depreciation is reduced to $2,500, the operating income in cell R19C2 increases from $9,640 to $13,140.

ANALYSIS When a fixed expense, depreciation, is reduced by $3,500, operating income (cell R19C2) and income before taxes (cell R23C2) are improved by the reduced amount (each increases $3,500 from the original example). This causes the payment of more taxes (cell R24C2), an increase of $700 from $728

to $1,428. The end result is an improvement in net income (cell R26C2) of only $2,800 from $2,912 to $5,712.

The net cash throwoff (cell R125C4) is reduced by $700 from the previous level of $8,912 to $8,212 because depreciation indirectly contributes to the cash flow that is generated. (Remember net cash throwoff equals net income plus depreciation and amortization.)

The sales revenue needed to break even (cell R116C4) with the lower fixed expenses is now $309,878; this is a reduction of $12,805 and thus an increase of 3.8 percent in the margin of error to achieve breakeven sales. (Margin of error equals sales expected minus sales needed to break even divided by sales expected: ($336,000 − $309,878)/$336,000, or 7.8 percent. "What If" 1 showed us that the margin for error in the original example was 4 percent.) For now, we are only considering the impact on the profitability breakeven. However, the cash flow breakeven will not change significantly (aside from the tax impact) because we are changing a noncash expense. We talked about the cash breakeven (sales revenue needed to cover cash expenses) when we entered the breakeven analysis section in Chapter 4.

"What If" 2

	1	2	3	4	5	6	7	
1	DECISION worksheet							
2								
3	INCOME STATEMENT: January 1 through December 31, 19..							
4								
5		This	% net	Last	% net	<----Deviation---->		
6		year	sales	year	sales	$	%	
7								
8	Gross sales	336,000	100	312,000	100	24,000	8	
9	Sales discounts	0	0	0	0	0		
10	Net sales	336,000	100	312,000	100	24,000	8	
11								
12	Cost of goods sold	221,760	66	201,240	65	20,520	10	
13	Gross profit	114,240	34	110,760	36	3,480	3	
14								
15	General & administrative	49,600	15	52,000	17	-2,400	-5	
16	Selling expenses	49,000	15	40,000	13	9,000	23	
17	Depreciation	2,500	1	5,500	2	-3,000	-55	
18								
19	Operating income	13,140	4	13,260	4	-120	-1	
20	Interest expense	6,000	2	6,750	2	-750	-11	
21	Other income/expense	0	0	-800	-0	800	-100	
22								
23	Income before taxes	7,140	2	7,310	2	-170	-2	
24	Taxes	1,428	0	1,462	0	-34	-2	
25								
26	NET INCOME	5,712	2	5,848	2	-136	-2	
27								
28	BALANCE SHEET: December 31, 19..							
29								
30		This		Last				
31		year		year				
32								
33	ASSETS:							
34								
35	<Current assets>							
36	Cash	635		4,750				
37	Accounts receivable	17,777		16,000				
38	Inventory	83,292		70,000				
39	Prepaid expenses	3,400		3,400				
40								
41	Total current assets	105,104		94,150				
42								
43	<Fixed assets>							
44	Buildings & equipment	33,000		38,950				
45	Less accumulated depreciation	-9,500		-7,000				
46	Land	0		0				
47								
48	Total fixed assets	23,500		31,950				
49								
50	Other assets	3,700		2,545				
51								
52	TOTAL ASSETS	132,304		128,645				
53								
54	LIABILITIES:							
55								
56	<Current liabilities>							
57	Accounts payable	18,480		17,000				
58	Accrued wages & taxes	6,357		6,000				
59	Notes payable (current)	3,890		3,890				
60	Other current liabilities	5,900		5,900				
61								
62	Total current liabilities	34,627		32,790				
63								
64	Long-term debt	44,110		48,000				
65								
66	Total liabilities	78,737		80,790				
67								
68	<Owner equity>							
69	Common stock	37,000		37,000				
70	Retained earnings	16,567		10,855				
71								
72	Total owner equity	53,567		47,855				
73								
74	TOTAL LIABILITIES & EQUITY	132,304		128,645				
75								

	1	2	3	4
77	Analysis section			
78				
79	G&A EXPENSE BREAKDOWN	Fixed	Variable	Total
80				
81	Rent	12,000	0	12,000
82	Officer salaries	20,000	0	20,000
83	Clerical expenses	4,000	1,000	5,000
84	Insurance	3,600	0	3,600
85	Utilities	2,000	400	2,400
86	Office supplies	800	400	1,200
87	Legal & accounting	3,000	0	3,000
88	Miscellaneous	1,200	1,200	2,400
89				
90	Total G&A expenses	46,600	3,000	49,600
91				
92	SELLING EXPENSE BREAKDOWN	Fixed	Variable	Total
93				
94	Wages	20,000	10,000	30,000
95	Delivery	0	1,800	1,800
96	Operating supplies	4,000	800	4,800
97	Advertising	4,000	2,000	6,000
98	Travel & entertainment	800	400	1,200
99	Miscellaneous	800	400	1,200
100	Credit card	0	4,000	4,000
101				
102	Total selling expenses	29,600	19,400	49,000
103				
104	COST OF GOODS SOLD ANALYSIS			
105				
106	Beginning inventory			70,000
107	Inventory purchases			235,052
108	Less purchase discounts of	0 percent		0
109	Total goods available			305,052
110	Less ending inventory			83,292
111				
112	Cost of goods sold			221,760
113				
114	BREAKEVEN ANALYSIS			
115				
116	Sales revenue needed to break even			309,878
117				
118	Sales revenue needed to cover cash expenses			300,732
119				
120	Sales revenue needed to cover cash expenses			314,963
121	and debt service			
122				
123	CASH FLOW ANALYSIS			
124				
125	Net cash throwoff from the income statement			8,212
126				

6 Market analysis

Introduction

Marketing in the classical sense is getting goods from where they are made to where they are needed. As with many other broad-based statements, this generalization by itself is not particularly useful. What is needed to make it useful is a very precise definition of "where they are needed." Once made, this specification will provide the key for developing effective and profitable strategies.

The first step toward answering the "where are they needed" question is to use the marketing concept as a guide to developing marketing strategy. The marketing concept calls for quite a different look at the entire business operation than is traditionally the case. What is needed here is a view of a business as a system satisfying customers' needs and wants rather than an operation providing whatever its owners want to produce.

A *push marketing strategy* is production based. You decide what you want to make or sell and then try to get somebody to buy it. On the other hand, with a *pull strategy*, you determine what the market wants and then produce it. Consequently, the marketing concept is pull-focused rather than push-focused, and so, using the marketing concept, all of the activities of a business become focused on satisfying customer wants and needs.

There are three key components of the marketing concept that help us to frame our overall operating philosophy:

1 A focus on customer needs and wants as a means of establishing the direction of the firm's activities.

2 Maintenance of a marketing orientation throughout all activities of the firm.

3 A concern for profits rather than volume.

The first of these considerations again deals with the difference between push and pull marketing strategies. The second is geared toward helping the firm maintain an external focus rather than becoming overly preoccupied with its internal operations. The third notion is often a startling concept for many individuals. For many people, unfortunately, there is a correlation between volume and profit. This is unfortunate because the correlation does not necessarily hold true, and for many small firms it tends to be untrue more often than not. The reason for this has to do with the economic level of operation within the organization. Organizations have capacities. As you reach and begin to exceed the reasonable capacity of your firm, your costs will start to increase; machinery and personnel are working overtime, the product is starting to clog up the aisles, waste and mistakes tend to increase, and a variety of other problems come into play, all of which have a tendency to drive up costs faster than revenues.

Marketing costs may also go up with increasing volume. Prices are often reduced in order to attract more buyers, but there is not always a valid correlation here either. (This is discussed further in the section on pricing.) In addition, advertising expenditures may be increased disproportionately to yield. This concept takes us back to our main point: Some market segments are more expensive to reach than others, and so our marketing strategy should be concerned with producing the maximum profit on sales for the lowest marketing costs. Keeping the three components of the marketing strategy firmly in mind as we develop our overall operational plan will help us to make sure that our decisions are as productive as possible.

Market segmentation/Target marketing

The marketing concept is an especially important guiding philosophy for a small firm. It is often said that advertising can be used to create demand. This is simply not true for most small firms; that level of demand-creating advertising is too costly. What advertising can do for the small firm is stimulate the demand that already exists, especially by informing the target customers that the business has what they want at an appropriate price. The question then arises, "Who are you selling what to?" One way to answer it is through market segmentation and target marketing.

Market segmentation involves dividing the total market into groups of potential customers based on common characteristics and/or shared needs. Target marketing involves identifying the group or groups of potential customers that appear to include your most desirable customer type. There are a variety of reasons why you might select one group over another. One business may want to sell the greatest volume possible, while another may want the greatest profit possible (again, volume and profit are not necessarily synonymous and often do not coincide at all). Still another firm may want to provide customer service, work with a particular socioethnic group, or whatever.

The first part of this market segmentation process is to divide the total universe of possible customers into groups. This is often a highly subjective activity. Be specific with yourself as you perform this analysis and take the time and trouble to write down your thoughts. Many times ideas on paper take on quite a different character than they possessed when floating through your head. Putting your ideas on paper forces you to select words, and this helps you to be more specific than you usually are. In addition, having your ideas on paper may permit a more objective review the next day, after the first blush of your enthusiasm subsides.

The way to determine the various groups or segments in your market is by identifying common characteristics and/or shared interests. In our hardware business, for example, Mr. Adams identified major customer groups as homeowners, local merchants, and small building contractors. Each of these categories could be further divided using more specific and detailed information. Knowing the size of each group will become quite important to us later in this analysis. The more specific and objective your analysis, the easier it will be to determine the size of each market segment. Consequently, an emphasis on characteristics is more helpful than one on interests. Characteristics are objective; interests are subjective. We can go to census data and industry profiles to determine how many individuals or firms share certain characteristics. With census data, for example, we can look for socioeconomic characteristics such as age, sex, income, education, and so on. With industry data we can look for similar types of operations, as categorized by the Standard Industrial Classification Code (SIC). On the other hand, you must rely on tools such as opinion market surveys, your own or someone else's, to determine what percentage of the population shares given interests and then hope that this data holds true for your particular universe.

Once we have divided our total market into distinguishable market segments such as various educational and/or income levels of private families, we can proceed to select our targets. Target marketing is a process of selecting specific market segments as the target for all of our marketing efforts. In this selection process, we want to choose the segment or segments where we can best meet our overall business objectives at the lowest possible cost and thus produce the greatest possible profits.

In order for us to select the most appropriate target segment(s), we must first determine how many customers are needed to produce a profit. This is why we said earlier that specificity was so important in market segmentation. Once we have determined how many customers we need, we can begin to compare the number needed with the number available, adjusting, of course, for our competition's share of the market. The problem of how many customers we need is a considerably more complicated question than it may appear at first glance. This question is related to the whole issue of breakeven, and its answer may influence the breakeven level as well, as our marketing strategy may affect the key characteristics that determine what the breakeven level is.

Determining how many customers we need is a matter of dividing our breakeven by the average price per sale. Adjusted for sales returns, this will give us the total number of sales units we require to reach breakeven. We can then divide that number by the repeat purchase cycle of our average customers, and we will have the number of customers that we require to support our venture at the breakeven level of operation. The average sale and repeat purchase cycle information must be derived through an analysis of our own business. If we are a new firm, we must make some assumptions.

This suggested analysis is not easy, because it requires a very detailed understanding of how your customers are going to behave. It can become even more complicated when you begin to consider that different groups of customers may behave in different ways; the weekend handyman might purchase items from Acme Hardware in small volumes on an as-needed basis with no set frequency of repurchase, while a professional carpenter might come back once or twice a week.

Mr. Adams's second group was local businesses who were purchasing various supply items as needed to maintain their own operations. These purchases tended to be more regular and so easier to plan on. The third group, small building contractors, were even more dependable. These individuals would pick up the supply items needed for their small jobs on a very regular basis. The benefit for Mr. Adams in having made this analysis was that he could now begin to make some thoughtful decisions about his target market segments and then attempt to determine how many customers he needed in each of his major categories.

Target marketing and breakeven

Once we have performed the first stage of our target segment evaluation, the identification of likely markets, we can begin to evaluate the effect of changing some of the variables and assumptions in our marketing "equation." One of the decisions we have to make that hasn't necessarily already been made concerns the overall style or image of our business operation. Is this business going to be a low-margin, high-volume operation? Or is it going to be an expensive, high-margin operation? If it is going to be a low-margin (low-price) operation, then we will need more space to handle a higher volume of goods than we would require if we were to aim for a lower level of activity. This may well drive up our fixed costs and, consequently, drive up our breakeven. Interestingly enough, not all expenses will increase directly with an increase in volume. For example, the number of sales clerks is not necessarily a function of volume but more often a function of style. In fact, if we maintain a low-margin, high-volume operation, we may well be expecting our customers to serve themselves and so will not require a large number of sales clerks. Alternatively, with an expensive, low-volume operation, we may put a premium on customer service and so actually have a higher number of sales clerks than we might have in our higher-volume, lower-margin operation. This cost will, of course, drive up the breakeven as well.

The breakeven equation is simple: higher operating expenses per unit equals higher breakeven. Lower margin also equals higher breakeven. We've already seen these effects in our previous discussions. Now we can begin to use our understanding of these effects to evaluate our decision alternatives. If we have a low-margin, high-volume operation, we assume that we need more customers than if we had a high-margin, low-volume operation. We also expect that these margin considerations, and thus the style of our overall operation, will affect the type of customer we expect to attract and thereby affect our choice of target customers.

There are some additional cost considerations affected by volume along with space costs and margin expectations. We also need to consider the overall cost of reaching the market and the variable costs of production at different volumes. Reaching the market has both before- and after-the-fact components. Before-the-fact costs include advertising and marketing expenses as well as any product development activities. After-the-fact costs include packaging, shipping, or other expenses and any later-stage support that may be needed. The variable costs of production, as we saw in the discussion on breakeven, may well include some semivariable components. The extent to which production costs are semivariable will help to determine the incremental costs of moving from one level of activity to another. That is, there may be economies of scale that come into play at higher volumes that are simply not available at lower levels.

Another consideration in evaluating various target segments is that some segments are easier to reach than others. When this is the case, it normally makes sense to pursue the easiest-to-reach segment first and then move on to the next, recognizing that the degree of marketing effort and cost will increase proportionately with the increasing difficulty of reaching later segments. Consequently, the net return from these additional sales will be lower than from the initial segments. It may be found that it does not make sense to seek any additional segments along this scale of diminishing returns.

There may be not only additional direct marketing costs associated with further market development but indirect costs as well. A cash-and-carry operation may need to offer credit to attract a new segment. If this is the case, even though additional sales may result, additional cash will be absorbed in the working capital equation through increased (or new) accounts receivable.

In considering his own operation, Mr. Adams had to ask still another question: "What business am I in?" "Clearly," we might say, "Acme Hardware is a hardware store." Not so simply, we might conclude that a hardware store is a collection of service/product subcenters, including paint and wallpaper in some stores, sporting goods in others, and garden/farm supplies in still others. Acme Hardware may in fact be subtly diversifying even if Mr. Adams is not consciously aware of the change. He must determine if, through this subtle changing process, he is in fact becoming a different business and, if so, whether he is now appealing to different target segments.

One problem that sometimes occurs as firms start to change their marketing image, either directly or indirectly, is the creation of a mixed image that confuses potential target segments. Some segments may be mutually exclusive. The quality-product buyer may not be particularly interested in shopping in a discount store environment. In fact, this type of customer may actually feel that his or her quality needs cannot be met in a discount environment and so, regardless of the actual quality of products offered, might never want to shop there at all. This situation is *image incongruence*. Especially in a small operation, it is important to determine the target segments that are compatible and to then gear the style of the operation to meet their needs as closely as possible.

Mr. Adams has thought through the analysis format suggested here and has begun to develop an improved understanding of his operation. To illustrate using the computer as an aid in marketing problem solving, we assume basic facts about the Acme operation in the next two "What Ifs" and then use the computer to measure the consequences of changing these assumptions. We will examine the impact on the income statement, cash flow, and sales revenue needed to break even.

Mr. Adams wants to do some speculating as to revenue and profit results if he goes after different market segments. For example, he could provide a higher level of service and increase prices. One of the reasons that Mr. Adams may have in the back of his mind for this change is a new discount hardware store moving into the area. There are two ways that Mr. Adams might deal with this challenge. One would be to reduce his prices and his service to directly compete on a price basis but thereby drive up his own breakeven. On the other hand, he could significantly improve his service, the depth of his inventory, his credit capacity, and his sales support in order to provide a more helpful environment for his customers. Further analysis of the market will be required before he can determine which of these two alternatives might be the best way to go, but for now, we can examine the impact of changing some of these assumptions.

Exploring "What Ifs"

WHAT IF 3 **Prices are increased and services improved.** Mr. Adams has decided to explore a change toward an expensive, high-margin operation. He will start with assuming an increase in gross margin to 40 percent, which automatically assumes an increase in prices (or more effective purchasing to result in a lower cost of goods at the same price). Gross margin is the gross profit expressed as a percentage of sales.

$$\text{Gross profit} = \text{Net sales} - \text{Cost of goods sold}$$

In this case, net sales are the same as gross sales, and with the gross margin increasing to 40 percent:

$$\text{Gross sales} = \text{Gross profit} + \text{Cost of goods sold}$$

$$100\% = 40\% \text{ of sales} + 60\% \text{ of sales}$$

Acme Hardware's cost of goods sold (cell R112C4) is $221,760. If cost of goods sold is now 60 percent of sales, Mr. Adams can calculate the new level of gross sales:

$$\text{Gross sales} \times .60 = \$221,760$$

$$\text{Gross sales} = \frac{\$221,760}{.60} = \$369,600$$

He further assumes the following:

1 A 10-percent increase in average inventory, thus providing a wider selection for customers. Average inventory is determined by adding a period's beginning and ending inventories and dividing the total by two. In the original worksheet, the average inventory is $76,646 (add $70,000 from cell R106C4 and $83,292 from cell R110C4 and divide the sum by two). To increase the average inventory by 10 percent, twice the increase of $7,665 (10 percent of $76,646) could be added to either the beginning or ending inventory or to the inventory purchases figures. In this "What If," the 10-percent increase in average inventory will be achieved by adding $15,330 to the inventory purchases (cell R107C4), reflected here in ending inventory:

	Original Example	"What If" 3
Beginning inventory	$70,000	$70,000
Ending inventory	83,292	98,622
Sum of both	153,292	168,622
Average inventory	76,646	84,311
Increase in dollars	—	7,665
Increase in percent	—	10%

2 No change in level of credit card sales. They will remain at their former level of 1.2 percent of total sales. However, because gross sales have increased (cell R8C2), the dollar figure for credit card sales also increases in cell R100C3 ($369,600 × .012 = $4,435).

3 Increase of $100 per month in rent due to the expansion of lease space required for the increased inventory (cell R81C2).

4 A leasehold improvement (paid-in-cash) of $5,000 to provide storage space to accommodate the increased inventory. Buildings and equipment (cell R44C2) increases from $33,000 to $38,000. These improvements are written off over five years and appear as a $1,000 increase in depreciation (cell R17C2).

5 The addition of one selling clerk at half-time ($400 per month) fixed wages (cell R94C2) plus the 3-percent commission. This is the same commission rate that is given to all selling clerks in order to provide better in-store service to customers. Therefore, variable wages in cell R94C3 increase to 3 percent of the new gross sales ($369,600 × .03 = $11,088).

6 Delivery expense is anticipated to increase to 0.6 percent of sales in order to provide improved service. Thus the increase of $418 from $1,800 to $2,218 appears in cell R95C3.

7 All of the other fixed costs will remain constant.

8 All of the other variable costs will remain constant.

As seen from the foregoing, this problem makes a variety of adjustments to inventory, gross profit, prices, leasehold improvements, rent, wages of selling clerks, and delivery expense. These are all important parts of the Acme marketing mix that may be influential in helping Acme to reach its desired markets.

To enter

changes increasing gross sales, depreciation, buildings and equipment, rent, wages, delivery expense, credit card expenses, and inventory purchases

"What If" 3

```
            1              2      3        4      5       6           7
 1 DECISION worksheet
 2 ═══════════════════════════════════════════════════════════════════════
 3 INCOME STATEMENT: January 1 through December 31, 19..
 4 ═══════════════════════════════════════════════════════════════════════
 5                         This    % net   Last   % net   <----Deviation---->
 6                         year    sales   year   sales        $        %
 7 ───────────────────────────────────────────────────────────────────────
 8 Gross sales            369,600   100   312,000  100    57,600       18
 9 Sales discounts              0     0         0    0         0
10 Net sales              369,600   100   312,000  100    57,600       18
11 ───────────────────────────────────────────────────────────────────────
12 Cost of goods sold     221,760    60   201,240   65    20,520       10
13 Gross profit           147,840    40   110,760   36    37,080       33
14 ───────────────────────────────────────────────────────────────────────
15 General & administrative 50,800   14    52,000   17    -1,200       -2
16 Selling expenses        55,741    15    40,000   13    15,741       39
17 Depreciation             7,000     2     5,500    2     1,500       27
18 ───────────────────────────────────────────────────────────────────────
19 Operating income        34,299     9    13,260    4    21,039      159
20 Interest expense         6,000     2     6,750    2      -750      -11
21 Other income/expense         0     0      -800   -0       800     -100
22 ───────────────────────────────────────────────────────────────────────
23 Income before taxes     28,299     8     7,310    2    20,989      287
24 Taxes                    5,660     2     1,462    0     4,198      287
25 ───────────────────────────────────────────────────────────────────────
26 NET INCOME              22,639     6     5,848    2    16,791      287
27 ═══════════════════════════════════════════════════════════════════════
28 BALANCE SHEET: December 31, 19..
29 ═══════════════════════════════════════════════════════════════════════
30                         This            Last
31                         year            year
32 ───────────────────────────────────────────────────────────────────────
33 ASSETS:
34 ───────────────────────────────────────────────────────────────────────
35 <Current assets>
36 Cash                     1,732           4,750
37 Accounts receivable     17,777          16,000
38 Inventory               98,622          70,000
39 Prepaid expenses         3,400           3,400
40 ───────────────────────────────────────────────────────────────────────
41 Total current assets   121,531          94,150
42 ───────────────────────────────────────────────────────────────────────
43 <Fixed assets>
44 Buildings & equipment   38,000          38,950
45 Less accumulated depreciation -14,000   -7,000
46 Land                         0               0
47 ───────────────────────────────────────────────────────────────────────
48 Total fixed assets      24,000          31,950
49 ───────────────────────────────────────────────────────────────────────
50 Other assets             3,700           2,545
51 ───────────────────────────────────────────────────────────────────────
52 TOTAL ASSETS           149,231         128,645
53 ═══════════════════════════════════════════════════════════════════════
54 LIABILITIES:
55 ───────────────────────────────────────────────────────────────────────
56 <Current liabilities>
57 Accounts payable        18,480          17,000
58 Accrued wages & taxes    6,357           6,000
59 Notes payable (current)  3,890           3,890
60 Other current liabilities 5,900          5,900
61 ───────────────────────────────────────────────────────────────────────
62 Total current liabilities 34,627        32,790
63 ───────────────────────────────────────────────────────────────────────
64 Long-term debt          44,110          48,000
65 ───────────────────────────────────────────────────────────────────────
66 Total liabilities       78,737          80,790
67 ═══════════════════════════════════════════════════════════════════════
68 <Owner equity>
69 Common stock            37,000          37,000
70 Retained earnings       33,494          10,855
71 ───────────────────────────────────────────────────────────────────────
72 Total owner equity      70,494          47,855
73 ═══════════════════════════════════════════════════════════════════════
74 TOTAL LIABILITIES & EQUITY 149,231     128,645
75 ═══════════════════════════════════════════════════════════════════════
```

```
            1                  2         3        4
 77 Analysis section
 78 ═══════════════════════════════════════════════════════
 79 G&A EXPENSE BREAKDOWN          Fixed   Variable    Total
 80 ────────────────────────────────────────────────────────
 81 Rent                         13,200         0    13,200
 82 Officer salaries             20,000         0    20,000
 83 Clerical expenses             4,000     1,000     5,000
 84 Insurance                     3,600         0     3,600
 85 Utilities                     2,000       400     2,400
 86 Office supplies                 800       400     1,200
 87 Legal & accounting            3,000         0     3,000
 88 Miscellaneous                 1,200     1,200     2,400
 89 ────────────────────────────────────────────────────────
 90 Total G&A expenses           47,800     3,000    50,800
 91 ════════════════════════════════════════════════════════
 92 SELLING EXPENSE BREAKDOWN      Fixed   Variable    Total
 93 ────────────────────────────────────────────────────────
 94 Wages                        24,800    11,088    35,888
 95 Delivery                          0     2,218     2,218
 96 Operating supplies            4,000       800     4,800
 97 Advertising                   4,000     2,000     6,000
 98 Travel & entertainment          800       400     1,200
 99 Miscellaneous                   800       400     1,200
100 Credit card                       0     4,435     4,435
101 ────────────────────────────────────────────────────────
102 Total selling expenses       34,400    21,341    55,741
103 ════════════════════════════════════════════════════════
104 COST OF GOODS SOLD ANALYSIS
105 ────────────────────────────────────────────────────────
106 Beginning inventory                             70,000
107 Inventory purchases                            250,382
108 Less purchase discounts of      0 percent           0
109 Total goods available                          320,382
110 Less ending inventory                           98,622
111 ────────────────────────────────────────────────────────
112 Cost of goods sold                             221,760
113 ════════════════════════════════════════════════════════
114 BREAKEVEN ANALYSIS
115 ────────────────────────────────────────────────────────
116 Sales revenue needed to break even            284,909
117 ────────────────────────────────────────────────────────
118 Sales revenue needed to cover cash expenses   263,959
119 ────────────────────────────────────────────────────────
120 Sales revenue needed to cover cash expenses   275,601
121 and debt service
122 ════════════════════════════════════════════════════════
123 CASH FLOW ANALYSIS
124 ────────────────────────────────────────────────────────
125 Net cash throwoff from the income statement    29,639
126 ════════════════════════════════════════════════════════
```

Goto **R8C2** and type **369600** (RET)
R17C2 and type **7000** (RET)
R38C2 and type **98622** (RET)
R44C2 and type **38000** (RET)
R81C2 and type **13200** (RET)
R94C2 and type **24800** (RET)
R94C3 and type **11088** (RET)
R95C3 and type **2218** (RET)
R100C3 and type **4435** (RET)
R107C4 and type **250382** (RET)

Recalculate the worksheet

Result The combination of the detailed changes results in a net income improvement to $22,639, which is an increase of $19,727 from the old level in cell R26C2. The cash position is increased to $1,732 from the original example of $1,335, for a net increase of $397.

Exploring "What Ifs" Continued

ANALYSIS This "What If" makes a variety of adjustments to inventory, gross profit, prices, leasehold improvements, rent, wages of selling clerks, and delivery expense. These are all important parts of the marketing strategy Mr. Adams is developing to reach different market segments. The combination of the detailed changes results in an improvement in net income in cell R26C2 to $22,639. The cash position is increased to $1,732 for a net increase of $397. The reason for this increase is that the increase in net income is larger (by $397) than the increase in inventory and fixed assets. The increase in net income of $19,727 was partially spent on inventory ($15,330) and fixed assets ($4,000), leaving only $397 as cash. This table shows the changes and where they occurred when the results of "What If" 3 are compared to the original worksheet.

	Original	"What If" 3	Difference
Net income (cell R26C2)	$2,912	$22,639	+$19,727
Inventory (cell R38C2)	$83,292	$98,622	+$15,330
Total fixed assets (cell R48C2)	$20,000	$24,000	+$ 4,000

Cash equals change in net income minus the change in inventory minus the change in total fixed assets or

$$\$397 = \$19,727 - \$15,330 - \$4000$$

The sales revenue needed to break even (cell R116C4) falls to $284,909. This reduction of $37,774 (from $322,683 in the original example) means an increased margin for error of 22.9 percent ([$369,600 − $284,909]/$369,600). In other words, the wider spread between the sales that are needed and the sales that are expected provides more margin for error in the sales estimates. This is quite an improvement, since the original example provided only a 4-percent error range.

WHAT IF 4 **Prices are decreased and inventory turnover is improved.** The other set of marketing alternatives that Mr. Adams wants to consider is what happens if he attempts to become more price competitive, reducing his prices and increasing his inventory turnover. The process will reduce his gross profit and, as he will see, increase the breakeven. Inventory turnover is the ratio between the cost of goods sold and the base inventory. This shows how many times the base inventory has been sold and replaced during the year. We will discuss this further in Chapter 8. For now, Mr. Adams assumes a 30-percent gross margin (a 4-percent decrease in cell R13C3) for Acme Hardware with the original level of cost of goods sold ($221,760). As in "What If" 3, cost of goods divided by 70 percent will give him the new gross sales ($316,800 in cell R8C2). He will use the computer to measure the new impact on the income statement cash flow and breakeven.

Mr. Adams assumes:

1 Inventory turnover is increased to 3.0 times, thus reducing inventory in cell R37C2 from $83,292 to $77,840, a net decrease of $5,452. Lower prices, which produce more sales, are the way faster turnover is achieved.

2 Accounts receivable are decreased 20 percent (fewer customers will be extended credit at the reduced prices), and the total decrease is $3,555. Cell R36C2 shows the decrease from $17,777 to $14,222.

3 One selling clerk who is half-time is eliminated due to the need for lower overhead and less service with reduced prices. The basic wage eliminated is $400 per month, or a reduction of $4,800, from $20,000 to $15,200 in cell R94C2.

4 Delivery service and expense will be eliminated (cell R95C3).

5 Commissions of 2.5 percent on all sales will be paid to all selling clerks in addition to their base wages. This represents a .5-percent decrease in commissions. Variable wages are reduced to $7,920 in cell R94C3 (2.5 percent of gross sales = $316,800 × .025).

6 Credit card sales will remain at 1.2 percent of sales. Because gross sales in cell R8C2 are reduced with lower prices and a 4-percent decrease in gross profit, the credit card figure in cell R100C3 will also decrease ($316,800 × .012 = $3,802).

7 All of the other fixed costs will remain constant.

8 All of the other variable costs will remain constant.

```
           1              2        3        4        5      6        7
 1 DECISION worksheet
 2 ═══════════════════════════════════════════════════════════════════
 3 INCOME STATEMENT: January 1 through December 31, 19..
 4 ───────────────────────────────────────────────────────────────────
 5                       This    % net    Last    % net  <────Deviation────>
 6                       year    sales    year    sales      $         %
 7 ───────────────────────────────────────────────────────────────────
 8 Gross sales          316,800   100    312,000   100    4,800       2
 9 Sales discounts            0     0          0     0        0
10 Net sales            316,800   100    312,000   100    4,800       2
11 ───────────────────────────────────────────────────────────────────
12 Cost of goods sold   221,760    70    201,240    65   20,520      10
13 Gross profit          95,040    30    110,760    36  -15,720     -14
14 ───────────────────────────────────────────────────────────────────
15 General & administrative 49,600 16     52,000    17   -2,400      -5
16 Selling expenses      40,122    13     40,000    13      122       0
17 Depreciation           6,000     2      5,500     2      500       9
18 ───────────────────────────────────────────────────────────────────
19 Operating income        -682    -0     13,260     4  -13,942    -105
20 Interest expense       6,000     2      6,750     2     -750     -11
21 Other income/expense       0     0       -800    -0      800    -100
22 ───────────────────────────────────────────────────────────────────
23 Income before taxes   -6,682    -2      7,310     2  -13,992    -191
24 Taxes                      0     0      1,462     0   -1,462    -100
25 ───────────────────────────────────────────────────────────────────
26 NET INCOME            -6,682    -2      5,848     2  -12,530    -214
27 ═══════════════════════════════════════════════════════════════════
28 BALANCE SHEET: December 31, 19..
29 ═══════════════════════════════════════════════════════════════════
30                       This            Last
31                       year            year
32 ───────────────────────────────────────────────────────────────────
33 ASSETS:
34 ───────────────────────────────────────────────────────────────────
35 <Current assets>
36 Cash                    748            4,750
37 Accounts receivable  14,222           16,000
38 Inventory            77,840           70,000
39 Prepaid expenses      3,400            3,400
40 ───────────────────────────────────────────────────────────────────
41 Total current assets 96,210           94,150
42 ───────────────────────────────────────────────────────────────────
43 <Fixed assets>
44 Buildings & equipment 33,000          38,950
45 Less accumulated depreciation -13,000 -7,000
46 Land                      0               0
47 ───────────────────────────────────────────────────────────────────
48 Total fixed assets   20,000           31,950
49 ───────────────────────────────────────────────────────────────────
50 Other assets          3,700            2,545
51 ───────────────────────────────────────────────────────────────────
52 TOTAL ASSETS        119,910          128,645
53 ═══════════════════════════════════════════════════════════════════
54 LIABILITIES:
55 ───────────────────────────────────────────────────────────────────
56 <Current liabilities>
57 Accounts payable     18,480           17,000
58 Accrued wages & taxes 6,357            6,000
59 Notes payable (current) 3,890          3,890
60 Other current liabilities 5,900        5,900
61 ───────────────────────────────────────────────────────────────────
62 Total current liabilities 34,627      32,790
63 ───────────────────────────────────────────────────────────────────
64 Long-term debt       44,110           48,000
65 ───────────────────────────────────────────────────────────────────
66 Total liabilities    78,737           80,790
67 ───────────────────────────────────────────────────────────────────
68 <Owner equity>
69 Common stock         37,000           37,000
70 Retained earnings     4,173           10,855
71 ───────────────────────────────────────────────────────────────────
72 Total owner equity   41,173           47,855
73 ───────────────────────────────────────────────────────────────────
74 TOTAL LIABILITIES & EQUITY 119,910   128,645
75 ═══════════════════════════════════════════════════════════════════
```

```
            1                   2         3         4
 77 Analysis section
 78 ═══════════════════════════════════════════════════════
 79 G&A EXPENSE BREAKDOWN       Fixed   Variable    Total
 80 ───────────────────────────────────────────────────────
 81 Rent                       12,000       0      12,000
 82 Officer salaries           20,000       0      20,000
 83 Clerical expenses           4,000    1,000      5,000
 84 Insurance                   3,600       0       3,600
 85 Utilities                   2,000     400       2,400
 86 Office supplies               800     400       1,200
 87 Legal & accounting          3,000       0       3,000
 88 Miscellaneous               1,200    1,200      2,400
 89 ───────────────────────────────────────────────────────
 90 Total G&A expenses         46,600    3,000     49,600
 91 ───────────────────────────────────────────────────────
 92 SELLING EXPENSE BREAKDOWN   Fixed   Variable    Total
 93 ───────────────────────────────────────────────────────
 94 Wages                      15,200    7,920     23,120
 95 Delivery                        0       0           0
 96 Operating supplies          4,000     800       4,800
 97 Advertising                 4,000    2,000      6,000
 98 Travel & entertainment        800     400       1,200
 99 Miscellaneous                 800     400       1,200
100 Credit card                     0    3,802      3,802
101 ───────────────────────────────────────────────────────
102 Total selling expenses     24,800   15,322     40,122
103 ───────────────────────────────────────────────────────
104 COST OF GOODS SOLD ANALYSIS
105 ───────────────────────────────────────────────────────
106 Beginning inventory                            70,000
107 Inventory purchases                           229,600
108 Less purchase discounts of      0 percent          0
109 Total goods available                         299,600
110 Less ending inventory                          77,840
111 ───────────────────────────────────────────────────────
112 Cost of goods sold                            221,760
113 ───────────────────────────────────────────────────────
114 BREAKEVEN ANALYSIS
115 ───────────────────────────────────────────────────────
116 Sales revenue needed to break even           344,393
117 ───────────────────────────────────────────────────────
118 Sales revenue needed to cover cash expenses  319,616
119 ───────────────────────────────────────────────────────
120 Sales revenue needed to cover cash expenses  335,680
121 and debt service
122 ───────────────────────────────────────────────────────
123 CASH FLOW ANALYSIS
124 ───────────────────────────────────────────────────────
125 Net cash throwoff from the income statement     -682
126 ═══════════════════════════════════════════════════════
```

Mr. Adams reviewed the effects of price increases in the previous "What If." After considering the various implications of his pricing structure, it was pretty clear to Mr. Adams that he should also examine the impact of a price decrease; using the computer model, he is able to do this relatively easily.

To restore
the worksheet to its original values

Goto **R17C2** and type **6000** (RET)
     R44C2 and type **33000** (RET)
     R81C2 and type **12000** (RET)

Exploring "What Ifs" Continued

To enter

changes in gross sales, accounts receivable, inventory, wages, delivery expense, credit card expenses, and inventory purchases

Goto **R8C2** and type **316800** (RET)
R37C2 and type **14222** (RET)
R38C2 and type **77840** (RET)
R94C2 and type **15200** (RET)
R94C3 and type **7920** (RET)
R95C3 and type **0** (RET)
R100C3 and type **3802** (RET)
R107C4 and type **229600** (RET)

Recalculate the worksheet

Result Gross profit in cell R13C2 drops by $19,200 from $114,240 to $95,040, and the gross margin decreases to 30 percent. Operating income in cell R19C2 decreases by $10,322 to show a loss of −$682. Net income also becomes a loss of −$6,682 ($2,912 − $9,594 in cell R26C2).

ANALYSIS The marketing alternative of reduced prices and increased inventory turnover reduces the gross profit and makes appropriate adjustments to inventory, accounts receivable, and expense items to match the new market segments. The net result is a disaster for Acme Hardware. Sales decrease and profits are turned into losses.

The net cash throwoff (cell R125C4) from the income statement is reduced by $9,594, from $8,912 to −$682. The original cash balance (cell R36C2) of only $1,335 now changes to a balance of only $748. It is almost impossible to run a business with no cash.

The breakeven computation is the final blow to the revised program. The sales revenue needed to break even shown in cell R116C4 is now up to $344,393. This means that sales would have to increase 8.7 percent (using the margin for error formula ($316,800 − $344,393)/$316,800) in order to merely break even.

Without additional information, it appears that the course outlined in the second problem should not be pursued.

7 | Pricing

Introduction

Effective pricing requires careful thought and attention. How much should you charge for your products or services? As much as you can get, of course, but charge too much and you lose sales; charge too little and you lose profits. Pricing is a skill and an art that must be developed over time. There are some mechanical techniques that can be used and we will show you these, but to be successful, their use must be governed by good judgment and experience.

Setting goals, developing strategies for achieving those goals, and monitoring the effectiveness of those strategies are important components of an effective pricing policy. However, to have these strategies be successful, you must take into account all the factors that influence your business objectives and all the factors and forces that are relevant in the market in which you are trying to deal.

It is always important to note that the best price is not necessarily the price that will sell the most units nor the price that will bring in the most sales dollars. The best price is the one that will maximize the profits of the company. To achieve this, the best price must be both cost based and market or demand oriented.

Pricing decisions are a critical part of your business strategy. The story is often told about the retailer whose pricing structure was somewhat out of balance. He summed up his problem by saying, "Sure we lose $2 per unit, but we make it up in the volume." There is something wrong here, and that something is an important symptom of a pricing problem.

In our earlier discussion on marketing, we described the need for a marketing strategy. You must come up with a pricing strategy as well. A pricing strategy is actually the core of your marketing strategy, particularly since prices help to determine the amount of revenue that your firm will receive. The other elements of an effective marketing strategy are supportive; they make it possible for a particular good or service to be sold at a price that will yield profits to the firm.

There is no one correct formula to use in determining the best price. All pricing methodologies are subject to question and none have proven acceptable to all businesses. Our purpose here is to describe some of the different approaches to pricing. You can then select the approach or the combination of techniques that will be most appropriate for you, your products, your target market, and your business.

Methods of pricing

There are four major approaches to pricing:

- full cost
- flexible
- gross margin
- suggested and going rate

Of these pricing techniques, full-cost pricing, also known as cost-plus or percent over cost, is the most widely used. For many businesses, though, the most successful strategy is a combination of all four approaches. Often firms will use the cost-plus or full-cost pricing method to identify a low-end price within a relevant range of contribution or gross profit, check with the competition to see how that price fits in with their pricing structure, and finally engage in some price-sensitivity testing to see what the market will bear. With all that information in hand, the firm will then select a price that it thinks will be most effective. The use of each approach as a working tool will be explained in the following sections.

Here is the main problem in pricing: There are various mechanical techniques for establishing prices, but ultimately, the question of pricing must be one of judgment. That judgment can be developed only through experience, research, and careful thought.

Full-cost approach to pricing The full-cost or cost-plus approach to pricing seeks to take into consideration every single operating cost, such as rent, utilities, salaries, delivery costs, returns, and many others. These basic costs are added to the cost of the merchandise itself and to that is added a percentage high enough to provide a "reasonable" profit. Of course, many of the figures that will be used come out of your breakeven analysis, which is itself substantially influenced by your overhead.

Full-cost pricing simplifies making pricing decisions since you develop a formula and then automatically plug all your products into that formula to come up with a consistent set of prices. To use this approach, add up the direct (variable) costs; add on the percentages, which will include an allocation for overhead (indirect or fixed costs) and profit margin; and there's the price. Part of the charm of this method is its safety. If all costs are taken into consideration and a profit margin is put on top of that, then the seller must make money whenever any merchandise is sold.

But it is not quite that simple. Two problems are hidden in this approach. First, for the business to make a profit, the merchandise must be sold using a rigid, inflexible method of pricing, which may result in prices higher than the competition is charging for similar merchandise. If this occurs, sales that are expected may not occur. Similarly, some prices may be too low, meaning that they could be higher without compromising the salability of the goods. A second hidden danger is that even though each sale is itself a "profitable" sale, until the aggregate or gross sales exceed the breakeven point, the business will still not make a profit.

Many seasonal businesses get caught in this trap. They price their products so that each sale is indeed profitable, they add up their sales for their active periods of the year, and they recognize that they're making a lot of money. However, when they get to the end of the year, they discover that they have been operating at a loss.

Why does this occur? It happens because their active period of sales is extended over only a portion of the year. Even though there are no sales over the rest of the year, they are forced to carry their fixed costs for the balance of the fiscal period. Remember, fixed costs are those costs that a business incurs no matter what the level of sales. They're the regular expenses of a business, such as rent, telephone, office staff, and so forth. These fixed costs may in fact exceed the gross profit that was accumulated during the active period, so these so-called "profitable" businesses wind up with a loss. Small contractors, in particular, have been caught in this bind.

It is important to note that rigid adherence to full-cost pricing is the exception rather than the rule. Even though many small firms claim to prefer a full-cost pricing policy, when it comes down to actually establishing their prices, the decisions are influenced by other factors as well, especially consumer demand and competition.

The flexible approach to pricing Flexibility in pricing helps to avoid the problems of applying an overly rigid pricing formula. Sensitivity testing is one way to approach flexible pricing. This can be a very simple process. Observe your customers' behavior when confronted with different prices. If they buy more of a product when it is priced at $1.25 than at $2.00, you can conclude that the demand for your product is price sensitive. Under these conditions, if you lower the price you will sell more. The objective of pricing, though, is to maximize profits. You maximize profits by maximizing the price/volume relationship. Consequently, it is important to be certain that lowering the price will truly increase sales and profits; don't lower the price simply because you *hope* it will increase sales. Consider the other side of this pricing approach and experiment with raising the price of your product as well, noting just as carefully the impact of higher prices on your sales. If higher prices do not lower sales, then of course you make more money in the long run with higher prices.

It is also important to consider the impact of different prices for a given product on the total product mix. Experimenting with loss leaders may be useful. Perhaps by pricing one or two items well below the normal mar-ket price, maybe even below your costs, you will stimulate sales for other products in your mix. The overall result would be increased profitability. Using such loss leaders is actually a marketing investment; you are using these products to "purchase" additional sales of other more profitable items. Acme Hardware finds that a seasonal loss leader is an inevitable sales promoter. In the spring it is a garden hose, and in winter snow shovels. These items are sold at cost and advertised widely. Customers come in for the low price of the loss leaders and buy other items at the same time.

It is possible to take advantage of techniques such as full-cost pricing to establish a floor for a flexible pricing strategy. You know what your relevant costs are and so can establish a reference point below which you will not permit prices to fall. Generally, it is not desirable to sell below cost. However, given inventory carrying costs, there are times when it makes sense to liquidate merchandise at practically any cost. The floor below which you do not want to go can be established by analysis and strategy and, once established, becomes your guide. The seller who uses the flexible method of pricing can adjust to changes in consumer demand or competition while still protecting the business from errors in pricing the merchandise too low. If $100 per unit is the floor, then don't sell for $99 without a good reason.

Gross margin pricing Prices are often determined on the basis of product costs rather than full costs. This strategy involves the concepts of gross margin and the contribution to profits that each sale of a particular product provides. Gross margin can be calculated in two ways. To calculate it as *markup*, you would take a percentage of your wholesale cost and add it back to wholesale cost to give you a selling price. *Mark-on*, on the other hand, refers to the percentage of the retail price that the gross margin (gross profit) represents. (A *markdown* is a reduction in price you may make in order to move a slow-selling item.)

The actual amount of contribution that each product in the product mix makes to total profit is the determining consideration in setting prices. Gross margin pricing takes into account internal costs, demand, purchasing habits, the competition, and a variety of other factors, all of which affect the sales volume.

Firms using the gross margin method of pricing often do not apply the same margin to all items and may not even apply the same margin to a family of products or to the same product at all times. It may be more profitable to take into account the effect of sales volume on different prices for different products at different times. Careful analysis will reveal which items will bear higher markups and which require lower markups to achieve a desired sales level.

Markup strategy doesn't solve your pricing problem, but it gives you a guide to use in establishing an initial price. Pricing is an art, so you must develop the skill to weigh volume possibilities, consumer resistance, variable expenses, and reductions.

For example, if Mr. Adams has handsaws that cost him $4.85 and he applies a 60 percent ($2.91) markup ($4.85 × .60), the normal price of the item would be $7.76. This price also represents a gross margin contribution or a mark-on of 37.5 percent ($2.91/$7.76 = .375). Either way, once you've identified your selling price of $7.76, you can examine the specific product more closely. Is it a highly speculative item? Does it carry the risk of a large seasonal markdown? Will it move slowly? These questions, which are not expressed in numbers, relate to customer reaction and possible sales levels, which are important in determining the final price. Your analysis may suggest that the final price you actually put on the product or service should be higher or lower than the calculated price. Mr. Adams felt that these handsaws were an especially good value for the price he paid, so he actually priced them at $8.95, a price comparable to that of similar products.

If you have experience with a particular type of merchandise, base your expectation of a reasonable price on past performance. Also, especially if this is your initial experiment with the product, question your supplier, check with the merchants' association, and do some comparison shopping of your competitors to help determine the final price.

Careful analysis of sales performance throughout a complete sales cycle will help you in pricing for the following year. A *sales cycle* is the period during a year that a product is in demand. Snow shovels have a sales cycle of the winter, garden tools of the summer. Other items, hand tools for example, have a more stable demand throughout the year. If an item is a fast mover, if the risk is low, and perhaps even because expenses per unit are lower due to the fast turnover, you may wish to price the item lower to stimulate still more action. However, remember that just because volume goes up, profits do not necessarily follow.

As noted earlier, many sellers will establish the markup or mark-on range or a gross profit range within which they choose to operate. Within this range, they determine whether a given product should be priced toward the high end, the low end, or in the middle, based on their assessment of other variables that are relevant to their businesses at that point. The pricing guides give only ranges. Experience and intelligence turn these ranges (shared by most competitors) into your profits.

Suggested pricing and going-rate pricing Suggested pricing and going-rate pricing are the simplest of all.

They may also be the least satisfactory. Suggested pricing means going with the recommendation of the manufacturer or some other external adviser. Sometimes, of course, this "list price" is simply a base from which to discount. However, many manufacturers work hard to maintain their list price structure. It is important to remember also that along with this strategy goes the need to make sure that expenses within your organization are consistent with industry averages, and that sales levels approximate the normal sales level volumes of the industry as well.

Going-rate pricing places emphasis on the competition and the prices that people seem willing to pay. There are some industries where costs become almost irrelevant and market prices are determined almost exclusively by external demand conditions. Think of various kinds of food products, particularly where spoilage is a factor. If many producers have bumper crops, the price will be low no matter what the product costs an individual producer. An individual producer's choice in this case is either to sell at that price or to lug the stuff home and throw it away. The choice is between setting prices that are consistent with the market and not selling. The more standard the product is, the less flexibility the producer and/or the seller is likely to have.

There is an important exception to these generalizations. Price differences between different sellers for so-called "standard" products may be valid due to different concepts of the total product package. The total product package certainly includes the basic standard product, but it also includes any special advantages or benefits that an individual seller may be able to provide in addition to the basic product. Add-ons may include specialized services, special assistance in product selection, explanations for product use, return privileges, guarantees, product assembly, credit, delivery service, and a variety of other services. The point is that each of these different add-ons represents an additional cost to the seller and therefore justifies a higher retail price. A specialty shop may be able to charge and get considerably more for a given product than a high-volume discount dealer can. Consequently, it is important in your own business to make sure that you recognize the differences between your operation and that of your competitors, and that these differences are reflected in your pricing strategy.

Product categories

Different types of products may carry the need for different pricing strategies, even within the same business. Some products may be high volume, and some may have a very slow turnover. In addition, some products may have a highly seasonal demand, which introduces further complications. In the hardware business, for example, Mr. Adams has his high-turnover items (nails, screws, small tools, window shades, and various other such accessories), which are generally available in other stores throughout the town. Therefore, he must price these products with two considerations in mind. First, he can consider the relatively high-volume nature of the products and perhaps therefore assign a lower contribution margin than he would be comfortable with for slower turnover items, simply because he will be cycling his money back more quickly and consequently reducing his carrying costs. Secondly, he must also take into account the demand-based pricing of what similar items are selling for in other stores within the town.

Mr. Adams may even go a step further than pricing relative to the trade. He may consider using some of these more commonly traded items as loss leaders to attract more buyers into his store, hoping they will also buy items that they could pick up in any other store. The logic here is that as these buyers purchase other more normally priced items while they are in the store purchasing the loss leaders, they help to improve overall sales performance. The slower turnover items carry a higher margin for these same two reasons. Because these items have a slower turnover, there are higher costs involved in keeping them in the store; and so Mr. Adams must price with this consideration in mind. Also, since these items are hardware specialty items, they are generally not available in other stores within the town and so there is not a popular consumer price with which he must contend. These are the items that people would feel they have to go to a hardware store to purchase.

Seasonality includes the same two considerations just discussed, as well as a third; some items are only in demand a certain portion of the year. For Acme, seasonal items would include lawnmowers and snowblowers. These items must be priced with a view to what the competition is offering, cost recovery (both direct and indirect), contribution versus volume, and specifically, the possible need for post-seasonal markdowns to liquidate end-of-season inventories. The alternative, of course, is to keep leftover merchandise until the next selling season. The down-side risk of this strategy is that the stored products may go out of style and/or may be damaged while they are in storage, and capital will be tied up while the goods are sitting up in the attic. The discussion on inventory control will take these matters into consideration.

Exploring "What Ifs"

We have developed four "What If" situations to illustrate the impact of pricing decision alternatives on the Acme Hardware store. An outline of these decisions follows:

"What If" 5 Increase prices 5 percent and show the impact on the income statement, cash flow, and breakeven. In the case of this price change, the experience of Mr. Adams suggests that a 5-percent increase in prices usually results in a 2-percent decrease in net sales. Thus, the revised sales are:

Old sales	$336,000
Plus 5-percent price increase	16,800
Minus 2-percent lost sales	(6,720)
Revised sales	$346,080

"What If" 6 Decrease prices 5 percent and show the impact on the income statement, cash flow, and breakeven. In this case, the experience of Mr. Adams suggests that a 5-percent decrease in prices usually generates a net sales increase of 7 percent. Thus, the revised sales are:

Old sales	$336,000
Minus 5-percent price decrease	(16,800)
Plus 7-percent increased sales	23,520
Revised sales	$342,720

"What If" 7 Maintain the 5-percent price increase and 2-percent loss in net sales of "What If" 5, but also make the following expense changes:

■ Adjust variable wages to the new sales level (3-percent commission to all sales clerks).

■ Adjust credit card charges to the new level (1.2 percent of sales). Measure impact of these changes on the income statement, cash flow, and breakeven sales.

"What If" 8 Maintain the 5-percent price decrease and the 7-percent net sales increase of "What If" 6, but also make the following expense changes:

■ Adjust variable wages to the new sales level (3-percent commission to all sales clerks).

■ Adjust credit card charges to the new level (1.2 percent of sales).

The basic decision for Mr. Adams regarding price increases or price decreases must relate to many factors, including his view of the image he wishes for Acme Hardware. In the extreme, he must decide whether Acme should be a high-price, quality store or a low-price, high-volume store.

Exploring "What Ifs"

WHAT IF 5 **Prices are increased by 5 percent.** Mr. Adams knows from past experience that as he increases prices, he is very likely to experience a loss in sales. However, he now also understands that the overall result could be increased profitability, so he assumes here that a 5-percent increase in prices will result in a 2-percent decrease in sales. Consequently, his revised sales will be:

Old sales	$336,000
5% price increase	+16,800
2% lost sales	−6,720
Revised sales	$346,080

This is a net increase of 3 percent, or $10,080, in gross sales. The computer can show us what other outcomes result from a 5-percent price increase.

To restore
the worksheet to its original values

> **Goto** **R37C2** and type **17777** (RET)
> **R38C2** and type **83292** (RET)
> **R94C2** and type **20000** (RET)
> **R94C3** and type **10000** (RET)
> **R95C3** and type **1800** (RET)
> **R100C3** and type **4000** (RET)
> **R107C4** and type **235052** (RET)

To enter
a change in gross sales in cell R8C2

> **Goto** **R8C2** and type **346080** (RET)

> **Recalculate** the worksheet

Result Net income in cell R26C2 increased $8,064 to $10,976. This is $2,016 less than the $10,080 increase in gross sales and operating income because that amount was paid out in increased taxes.

ANALYSIS The price increase has improved profit and cash to a much more acceptable level for Mr. Adams. Net income and cash have both increased $8,064, net income from $2,912 to $10,976, and cash from $1,335 to $9,399 (cell R36C2). The sales revenue needed to break even has been reduced by $23,191 (cell R116C2). Thus, the difference between actual sales ($346,080) and breakeven ($299,492) is $46,588, or 13.5 percent of sales. This is a comfortable cushion for the margin of error in expected sales.

WHAT IF 6 **Prices are decreased by 5 percent.** The other side of looking at a price increase is looking at a price decrease. Mr. Adams has observed in the past that a 5-percent decrease in prices will usually generate a net sales increase of 7 percent. He feels this relationship should hold constant for the present as well. Consequently, the revised sales are:

Old sales	$336,000
5% price decrease	−16,800
7% increased sales	+23,520
Revised sales	$342,720

Gross sales are increased by 2 percent, or $6,720.

To enter
a change in gross sales in cell R8C2

> **Goto** **R8C2** and type **342720** (RET)

> **Recalculate** the worksheet

Result Net income in cell R26C2 is increased by $5,376 from $2,912 to $8,288. Cash is increased by the same amount from $1,335 to $6,711 (cell R36C2). Sales revenue needed to break even decreased by $15,988 in cell R116C4 from $322,683 to $306,695.

ANALYSIS Overall, the financial improvements resulting from a 5-percent price decrease are encouraging. However, improvement is not as good as that produced by the price increase problem.

Net income and cash have both increased by a healthy $5,376. The difference between actual sales and breakeven is $36,025 ($342,720 − $306,695). This leaves the margin for error at a still comfortable 10.5 percent ($36,025 divided by $342,720).

"What If" 5

```
            1              2      3      4      5      6        7
 1 DECISION worksheet
 2 ════════════════════════════════════════════════════════════════
 3 INCOME STATEMENT: January 1 through December 31, 19..
 4 ════════════════════════════════════════════════════════════════
 5                        This   % net   Last   % net  <────Deviation───>
 6                        year   sales   year   sales     $         %
 7 ────────────────────────────────────────────────────────────────
 8 Gross sales           346,080  100   312,000  100   34,080      11
 9 Sales discounts             0    0         0    0        0
10 Net sales             346,080  100   312,000  100   34,080      11
11 ────────────────────────────────────────────────────────────────
12 Cost of goods sold    221,760   64   201,240   65   20,520      10
13 Gross profit          124,320   36   110,760   36   13,560      12
14 ────────────────────────────────────────────────────────────────
15 General & administrative 49,600  14   52,000  17   -2,400      -5
16 Selling expenses       49,000   14    40,000   13    9,000      23
17 Depreciation            6,000    2     5,500    2      500       9
18 ────────────────────────────────────────────────────────────────
19 Operating income       19,720    6    13,260    4    6,460      49
20 Interest expense        6,000    2     6,750    2     -750     -11
21 Other income/expense        0    0      -800   -0      800    -100
22 ────────────────────────────────────────────────────────────────
23 Income before taxes    13,720    4     7,310    2    6,410      88
24 Taxes                   2,744    1     1,462    0    1,282      88
25 ════════════════════════════════════════════════════════════════
26 NET INCOME             10,976    3     5,848    2    5,128      88
27 ════════════════════════════════════════════════════════════════
28 BALANCE SHEET: December 31, 19..
29 ════════════════════════════════════════════════════════════════
30                        This              Last
31                        year              year
32 ────────────────────────────────────────────────────────────────
33 ASSETS:
34 ────────────────────────────────────────────────────────────────
35 <Current assets>
36 Cash                    9,399             4,750
37 Accounts receivable    17,777            16,000
38 Inventory              83,292            70,000
39 Prepaid expenses        3,400             3,400
40 ────────────────────────────────────────────────────────────────
41 Total current assets  113,868            94,150
42 ────────────────────────────────────────────────────────────────
43 <Fixed assets>
44 Buildings & equipment  33,000            38,950
45 Less accumulated depreciation -13,000    -7,000
46 Land                        0                 0
47 ────────────────────────────────────────────────────────────────
48 Total fixed assets     20,000            31,950
49 ────────────────────────────────────────────────────────────────
50 Other assets            3,700             2,545
51 ────────────────────────────────────────────────────────────────
52 TOTAL ASSETS          137,568           128,645
53 ════════════════════════════════════════════════════════════════
54 LIABILITIES:
55 ────────────────────────────────────────────────────────────────
56 <Current liabilities>
57 Accounts payable       18,480            17,000
58 Accrued wages & taxes   6,357             6,000
59 Notes payable (current) 3,890             3,890
60 Other current liabilities 5,900           5,900
61 ────────────────────────────────────────────────────────────────
62 Total current liabilities 34,627         32,790
63 ────────────────────────────────────────────────────────────────
64 Long-term debt         44,110            48,000
65 ────────────────────────────────────────────────────────────────
66 Total liabilities      78,737            80,790
67 ────────────────────────────────────────────────────────────────
68 <Owner equity>
69 Common stock           37,000            37,000
70 Retained earnings      21,831            10,855
71 ────────────────────────────────────────────────────────────────
72 Total owner equity     58,831            47,855
73 ════════════════════════════════════════════════════════════════
74 TOTAL LIABILITIES & EQUITY 137,568      128,645
75 ════════════════════════════════════════════════════════════════
```

```
             1                 2        3         4
 77 Analysis section
 78 ══════════════════════════════════════════════════════
 79 G&A EXPENSE BREAKDOWN      Fixed   Variable    Total
 80 ──────────────────────────────────────────────────────
 81 Rent                     12,000        0      12,000
 82 Officer salaries         20,000        0      20,000
 83 Clerical expenses         4,000    1,000       5,000
 84 Insurance                 3,600        0       3,600
 85 Utilities                 2,000      400       2,400
 86 Office supplies             800      400       1,200
 87 Legal & accounting        3,000        0       3,000
 88 Miscellaneous             1,200    1,200       2,400
 89 ──────────────────────────────────────────────────────
 90 Total G&A expenses       46,600    3,000      49,600
 91 ══════════════════════════════════════════════════════
 92 SELLING EXPENSE BREAKDOWN  Fixed   Variable    Total
 93 ──────────────────────────────────────────────────────
 94 Wages                    20,000   10,000      30,000
 95 Delivery                      0    1,800       1,800
 96 Operating supplies        4,000      800       4,800
 97 Advertising               4,000    2,000       6,000
 98 Travel & entertainment      800      400       1,200
 99 Miscellaneous               800      400       1,200
100 Credit card                   0    4,000       4,000
101 ──────────────────────────────────────────────────────
102 Total selling expenses   29,600   19,400      49,000
103 ══════════════════════════════════════════════════════
104 COST OF GOODS SOLD ANALYSIS
105 ──────────────────────────────────────────────────────
106 Beginning inventory                            70,000
107 Inventory purchases                           235,052
108 Less purchase discounts of      0 percent           0
109 Total goods available                         305,052
110 Less ending inventory                          83,292
111 ──────────────────────────────────────────────────────
112 Cost of goods sold                            221,760
113 ══════════════════════════════════════════════════════
114 BREAKEVEN ANALYSIS
115 ──────────────────────────────────────────────────────
116 Sales revenue needed to break even            299,492
117 ──────────────────────────────────────────────────────
118 Sales revenue needed to cover cash expenses   279,119
119 ──────────────────────────────────────────────────────
120 Sales revenue needed to cover cash expenses   292,328
121 and debt service
122 ══════════════════════════════════════════════════════
123 CASH FLOW ANALYSIS
124 ──────────────────────────────────────────────────────
125 Net cash throwoff from the income statement    16,976
126 ══════════════════════════════════════════════════════
```

```
          1                    2      3      4      5      6      7
 1 DECISION worksheet
 2
 3 INCOME STATEMENT: January 1 through December 31, 19..
 4 =========================================================================
 5                         This    % net   Last    % net   <---Deviation--->
 6                         year    sales   year    sales       $         %
 7 -----------------------------------------------------------------------
 8 Gross sales            342,720   100   312,000   100    30,720      10
 9 Sales discounts              0     0         0     0         0
10 Net sales              342,720   100   312,000   100    30,720      10
11 -----------------------------------------------------------------------
12 Cost of goods sold     221,760    65   201,240    65    20,520      10
13 Gross profit           120,960    35   110,760    36    10,200       9
14 -----------------------------------------------------------------------
15 General & administrative 49,600   14    52,000    17    -2,400      -5
16 Selling expenses        49,000    14    40,000    13     9,000      23
17 Depreciation             6,000     2     5,500     2       500       9
18 -----------------------------------------------------------------------
19 Operating income        16,360     5    13,260     4     3,100      23
20 Interest expense         6,000     2     6,750     2      -750     -11
21 Other income/expense         0     0      -800    -0       800    -100
22 -----------------------------------------------------------------------
23 Income before taxes     10,360     3     7,310     2     3,050      42
24 Taxes                    2,072     1     1,462     0       610      42
25 =======================================================================
26 NET INCOME               8,288     2     5,848     2     2,440      42
27 =======================================================================
28 BALANCE SHEET: December 31, 19..
29 =======================================================================
30                          This            Last
31                          year            year
32 -----------------------------------------------------------------------
33 ASSETS:
34 -----------------------------------------------------------------------
35 <Current assets>
36 Cash                     6,711           4,750
37 Accounts receivable     17,777          16,000
38 Inventory               83,292          70,000
39 Prepaid expenses         3,400           3,400
40 -----------------------------------------------------------------------
41 Total current assets   111,180          94,150
42 -----------------------------------------------------------------------
43 <Fixed assets>
44 Buildings & equipment   33,000          38,950
45 Less accumulated depreciation -13,000   -7,000
46 Land                         0               0
47 -----------------------------------------------------------------------
48 Total fixed assets      20,000          31,950
49 -----------------------------------------------------------------------
50 Other assets             3,700           2,545
51 =======================================================================
52 TOTAL ASSETS           134,880         128,645
53 =======================================================================
54 LIABILITIES:
55 -----------------------------------------------------------------------
56 <Current liabilities>
57 Accounts payable        18,480          17,000
58 Accrued wages & taxes    6,357           6,000
59 Notes payable (current)  3,890           3,890
60 Other current liabilities 5,900          5,900
61 -----------------------------------------------------------------------
62 Total current liabilities 34,627        32,790
63 -----------------------------------------------------------------------
64 Long-term debt          44,110          48,000
65 -----------------------------------------------------------------------
66 Total liabilities       78,737          80,790
67 -----------------------------------------------------------------------
68 <Owner equity>
69 Common stock            37,000          37,000
70 Retained earnings       19,143          10,855
71 -----------------------------------------------------------------------
72 Total owner equity      56,143          47,855
73 =======================================================================
74 TOTAL LIABILITIES & EQUITY 134,880     128,645
75 =======================================================================
```

```
           1                        2        3        4
77 Analysis section
78 ===================================================================
79 G&A EXPENSE BREAKDOWN          Fixed   Variable      Total
80 -------------------------------------------------------------------
81 Rent                          12,000        0      12,000
82 Officer salaries              20,000        0      20,000
83 Clerical expenses              4,000    1,000       5,000
84 Insurance                      3,600        0       3,600
85 Utilities                      2,000      400       2,400
86 Office supplies                  800      400       1,200
87 Legal & accounting             3,000        0       3,000
88 Miscellaneous                  1,200    1,200       2,400
89 -------------------------------------------------------------------
90 Total G&A expenses            46,600    3,000      49,600
91 ===================================================================
92 SELLING EXPENSE BREAKDOWN      Fixed   Variable      Total
93 -------------------------------------------------------------------
94 Wages                         20,000   10,000      30,000
95 Delivery                           0    1,800       1,800
96 Operating supplies             4,000      800       4,800
97 Advertising                    4,000    2,000       6,000
98 Travel & entertainment           800      400       1,200
99 Miscellaneous                    800      400       1,200
100 Credit card                       0    4,000       4,000
101 ------------------------------------------------------------------
102 Total selling expenses        29,600   19,400      49,000
103 ==================================================================
104 COST OF GOODS SOLD ANALYSIS
105 ------------------------------------------------------------------
106 Beginning inventory                             70,000
107 Inventory purchases                            235,052
108 Less purchase discounts of      0 percent            0
109 Total goods available                          305,052
110 Less ending inventory                           83,292
111 ------------------------------------------------------------------
112 Cost of goods sold                             221,760
113 ==================================================================
114 BREAKEVEN ANALYSIS
115 ------------------------------------------------------------------
116 Sales revenue needed to break even             306,695
117 ------------------------------------------------------------------
118 Sales revenue needed to cover cash expenses    285,832
119 ------------------------------------------------------------------
120 Sales revenue needed to cover cash expenses    299,358
121 and debt service
122 ==================================================================
123 CASH FLOW ANALYSIS
124 ------------------------------------------------------------------
125 Net cash throwoff from the income statement     14,288
126 ==================================================================
```

Exploring "What Ifs" Continued

WHAT IF 7 **Selling expense changes accompany the 5-percent price increase.** As Mr. Adams thinks through the effects of price increase and decrease changes on the business, he further realizes that he will require changes in other expense categories to support the upward or downward movement. In the first case, the 5-percent price increase requires changes in some of the other expense categories. Therefore, Mr. Adams will:

1 Experience sales commissions of 3 percent of the new sales level.

2 Experience credit card charges at 1.2 percent of the new sales level.

To enter
> *a change* in gross sales in cell R8C2
> *changes* in wages (cell R94C3) and credit card expenses (cell R100C3)

> **Goto R8C2** and type **346080** (RET)
> **R94C3** and type **10382** (RET)
> **R100C3** and type **4153** (RET)

> **Recalculate** the worksheet

Result When minor adjustments to expenses are made in this third pricing problem, the adjustments are carried almost directly to the net income line with a corresponding impact on cash. Net income increases by $7,636 from $2,912 to $10,548 (cell R26C2). Cash increases by the same amount from $1,335 to $8,971 (cell R36C2).

ANALYSIS This problem is meant to be a comparison to "What If" 5, which was a simple approach to examining the consequences of a 5-percent price increase. When the factors of increased selling expenses are included, a more complete analysis can be made.

	"What If" 5	"What If" 7	Difference
Variable wages	$10,000	$10,382	+$382
Credit card expense	4,000	4,153	+ 153
Selling expense increase			+ 535

The expense increases (wages in cell R94C3, and credit card expenses in cell R100C3) of $535 showed up on the income statement as a $428 decrease in net income and on the balance sheet as a $428 decrease in cash.

	"What If" 5	"What If" 7	Difference
Net income	$ 10,976	$ 10,548	−$428
Cash	9,399	8,971	−428
Sales revenue needed to break even	299,492	301,073	+1,581

The point to note here is that although the expenses were only increased $535, the breakeven sales increased $1,581 from "What If" 5 or almost triple the expense increase.

Left panel — columns 1-7

```
   1                           2       3        4       5        6         7
 1 DECISION worksheet
 2
 3 INCOME STATEMENT: January 1 through December 31, 19..
 4 =================================================================
 5                          This    % net    Last    % net   <----Deviation---->
 6                          year    sales    year    sales       $          %
 7 ---------------------------------------------------------------------------
 8 Gross sales            346,080    100    312,000    100    34,080        11
 9 Sales discounts              0      0          0      0         0
10 Net sales              346,080    100    312,000    100    34,080        11
11 ---------------------------------------------------------------------------
12 Cost of goods sold     221,760     64    201,240     65    20,520        10
13 Gross profit           124,320     36    110,760     36    13,560        12
14 ---------------------------------------------------------------------------
15 General & administrative 49,600    14     52,000     17    -2,400        -5
16 Selling expenses        49,535     14     40,000     13     9,535        24
17 Depreciation             6,000      2      5,500      2       500         9
18 ---------------------------------------------------------------------------
19 Operating income        19,185      6     13,260      4     5,925        45
20 Interest expense         6,000      2      6,750      2      -750       -11
21 Other income/expense         0      0       -800     -0       800      -100
22 ---------------------------------------------------------------------------
23 Income before taxes     13,185      4      7,310      2     5,875        80
24 Taxes                    2,637      1      1,462      0     1,175        80
25 =================================================================
26 NET INCOME              10,548      3      5,848      2     4,700        80
27 =================================================================
28 BALANCE SHEET: December 31, 19..
29 ---------------------------------------------------------------------------
30                          This               Last
31                          year               year
32 ---------------------------------------------------------------------------
33 ASSETS:
34 ---------------------------------------------------------------------------
35 <Current assets>
36 Cash                     8,971              4,750
37 Accounts receivable     17,777             16,000
38 Inventory               83,292             70,000
39 Prepaid expenses         3,400              3,400
40 ---------------------------------------------------------------------------
41 Total current assets   113,440             94,150
42 ---------------------------------------------------------------------------
43 <Fixed assets>
44 Buildings & equipment   33,000             38,950
45 Less accumulated depreciation -13,000      -7,000
46 Land                         0                  0
47 ---------------------------------------------------------------------------
48 Total fixed assets      20,000             31,950
49 ---------------------------------------------------------------------------
50 Other assets             3,700              2,545
51 ---------------------------------------------------------------------------
52 TOTAL ASSETS           137,140            128,645
53 =================================================================
54 LIABILITIES:
55 ---------------------------------------------------------------------------
56 <Current liabilities>
57 Accounts payable        18,480             17,000
58 Accrued wages & taxes    6,357              6,000
59 Notes payable (current)  3,890              3,890
60 Other current liabilities 5,900             5,900
61 ---------------------------------------------------------------------------
62 Total current liabilities 34,627           32,790
63 ---------------------------------------------------------------------------
64 Long-term debt          44,110             48,000
65 ---------------------------------------------------------------------------
66 Total liabilities       78,737             80,790
67 ---------------------------------------------------------------------------
68 <Owner equity>
69 Common stock            37,000             37,000
70 Retained earnings       21,403             10,855
71 ---------------------------------------------------------------------------
72 Total owner equity      58,403             47,855
73 =================================================================
74 TOTAL LIABILITIES & EQUITY 137,140        128,645
75 =================================================================
```

Right panel — columns 1-4

```
    1                           2        3         4
77 Analysis section
78 =================================================================
79 G&A EXPENSE BREAKDOWN        Fixed  Variable    Total
80 ---------------------------------------------------------------------------
81 Rent                        12,000       0     12,000
82 Officer salaries            20,000       0     20,000
83 Clerical expenses            4,000   1,000      5,000
84 Insurance                    3,600       0      3,600
85 Utilities                    2,000     400      2,400
86 Office supplies                800     400      1,200
87 Legal & accounting           3,000       0      3,000
88 Miscellaneous                1,200   1,200      2,400
89 ---------------------------------------------------------------------------
90 Total G&A expenses          46,600   3,000     49,600
91 =================================================================
92 SELLING EXPENSE BREAKDOWN    Fixed  Variable    Total
93 ---------------------------------------------------------------------------
94 Wages                       20,000  10,382     30,382
95 Delivery                         0   1,800      1,800
96 Operating supplies           4,000     800      4,800
97 Advertising                  4,000   2,000      6,000
98 Travel & entertainment         800     400      1,200
99 Miscellaneous                  800     400      1,200
100 Credit card                     0   4,153      4,153
101 ---------------------------------------------------------------------------
102 Total selling expenses      29,600  19,935     49,535
103 =================================================================
104 COST OF GOODS SOLD ANALYSIS
105 ---------------------------------------------------------------------------
106 Beginning inventory                            70,000
107 Inventory purchases                           235,052
108 Less purchase discounts of   0 percent              0
109 Total goods available                         305,052
110 Less ending inventory                          83,292
111 ---------------------------------------------------------------------------
112 Cost of goods sold                            221,760
113 =================================================================
114 BREAKEVEN ANALYSIS
115 ---------------------------------------------------------------------------
116 Sales revenue needed to break even            301,073
117
118 Sales revenue needed to cover cash expenses   280,592
119
120 Sales revenue needed to cover cash expenses   293,870
121 and debt service
122 =================================================================
123 CASH FLOW ANALYSIS
124 ---------------------------------------------------------------------------
125 Net cash throwoff from the income statement    16,548
126 =================================================================
```

Exploring "What Ifs" Continued

Selling expense changes accompany the 5-percent price decrease. The 5-percent price decrease will also carry changes in certain expense categories. Just as with the price increase, Mr. Adams will:

1 Bear 3-percent commission to all sales clerks in addition to the base wages.

2 Experience credit card charges to reflect 1.2 percent of the new sales level.

Mr. Adams very wisely wants to include exactly the same changes for the price decrease that he had factored in for the price increase. He has learned to examine the aggregate net effect of the price change on the business as a whole. It is important to do this with any change. If Mr. Adams had grouped many factors together for each assumption he made, it would have been impossible to compare the impact of the two basic assumptions. By using the methods of these four pricing problems, the effect of the assumptions can be isolated, and therefore similar factors can be compared in terms of their net effect on the overall operation. This permits an intelligent choice to be made between the two alternatives.

To enter
 a change in gross sales in cell R8C2
 changes in wages (cell R94C3) and credit card expenses (cell R100C3)

 Goto R8C2 and type **342720** (RET)
 R94C3 and type **10282** (RET)
 R100C3 and type **4113** (RET)

 Recalculate the worksheet

Result Net income increases by $5,060 from $2,912 to $7,972 (cell R26C2). Cash increases by the same amount from $1,335 to $6,395 (cell R36C2).

ANALYSIS The $395 in increased expenses (wages increase by $282 in cell R94C3; credit card expenses by $113 in cell R100C3) goes almost entirely to a reduction in cash and net income as compared to "What If" 6.

	"What If" 6	"What If" 8	Difference
Net income	$8,288	$7,972	−$316
Cash	6,711	6,395	−316
Sales revenue needed to break even	306,695	307,930	+1,235

As in the last problem, the effect on breakeven is almost three times the increase in expenses. Overall, the critical item in all of the above problems is the sensitivity of sales to price increases. The judgments of Mr. Adams in this area, if incorrect, can make significant changes in the results. If, for example, a 5-percent price decrease results in only a 4-percent increase in sales, profits would be almost wiped out, as would cash. The lesson is that the decision to change prices should not be taken lightly, and supporting data must be taken into consideration.

1	2	3	4	5	6	7

1 DECISION worksheet
2
3 INCOME STATEMENT: January 1 through December 31, 19..
4 ==

	This year	% net sales	Last year	% net sales	<——Deviation——> $	%
8 Gross sales	342,720	100	312,000	100	30,720	10
9 Sales discounts	0	0	0	0	0	
10 Net sales	342,720	100	312,000	100	30,720	10
11						
12 Cost of goods sold	221,760	65	201,240	65	20,520	10
13 Gross profit	120,960	35	110,760	36	10,200	9
14						
15 General & administrative	49,600	14	52,000	17	-2,400	-5
16 Selling expenses	49,395	14	40,000	13	9,395	23
17 Depreciation	6,000	2	5,500	2	500	9
18						
19 Operating income	15,965	5	13,260	4	2,705	20
20 Interest expense	6,000	2	6,750	2	-750	-11
21 Other income/expense	0	0	-800	-0	800	-100
22						
23 Income before taxes	9,965	3	7,310	2	2,655	36
24 Taxes	1,993	1	1,462	0	531	36
25						
26 NET INCOME	7,972	2	5,848	2	2,124	36

27 ==
28 BALANCE SHEET: December 31, 19..
29 ==

	This year	Last year
30		
31		
32		
33 ASSETS:		
34		
35 <Current assets>		
36 Cash	6,395	4,750
37 Accounts receivable	17,777	16,000
38 Inventory	83,292	70,000
39 Prepaid expenses	3,400	3,400
40		
41 Total current assets	110,864	94,150
42		
43 <Fixed assets>		
44 Buildings & equipment	33,000	38,950
45 Less accumulated depreciation	-13,000	-7,000
46 Land	0	0
47		
48 Total fixed assets	20,000	31,950
49		
50 Other assets	3,700	2,545
51		
52 TOTAL ASSETS	134,564	128,645
53		
54 LIABILITIES:		
55		
56 <Current liabilities>		
57 Accounts payable	18,480	17,000
58 Accrued wages & taxes	6,357	6,000
59 Notes payable (current)	3,890	3,890
60 Other current liabilities	5,900	5,900
61		
62 Total current liabilities	34,627	32,790
63		
64 Long-term debt	44,110	48,000
65		
66 Total liabilities	78,737	80,790
67		
68 <Owner equity>		
69 Common stock	37,000	37,000
70 Retained earnings	18,827	10,855
71		
72 Total owner equity	55,827	47,855
73		
74 TOTAL LIABILITIES & EQUITY	134,564	128,645

75 ==

1	2	3	4

77 Analysis section
78 ==

79 G&A EXPENSE BREAKDOWN	Fixed	Variable	Total
80			
81 Rent	12,000	0	12,000
82 Officer salaries	20,000	0	20,000
83 Clerical expenses	4,000	1,000	5,000
84 Insurance	3,600	0	3,600
85 Utilities	2,000	400	2,400
86 Office supplies	800	400	1,200
87 Legal & accounting	3,000	0	3,000
88 Miscellaneous	1,200	1,200	2,400
89			
90 Total G&A expenses	46,600	3,000	49,600

91 ==

92 SELLING EXPENSE BREAKDOWN	Fixed	Variable	Total
93			
94 Wages	20,000	10,282	30,282
95 Delivery	0	1,800	1,800
96 Operating supplies	4,000	800	4,800
97 Advertising	4,000	2,000	6,000
98 Travel & entertainment	800	400	1,200
99 Miscellaneous	800	400	1,200
100 Credit card	0	4,113	4,113
101			
102 Total selling expenses	29,600	19,795	49,395

103 ==

104 COST OF GOODS SOLD ANALYSIS
105 --

106 Beginning inventory			70,000
107 Inventory purchases			235,052
108 Less purchase discounts of	0 percent		0
109 Total goods available			305,052
110 Less ending inventory			83,292
111			
112 Cost of goods sold			221,760

113 ==

114 BREAKEVEN ANALYSIS
115 --

116 Sales revenue needed to break even			307,930
117			
118 Sales revenue needed to cover cash expenses			286,982
119			
120 Sales revenue needed to cover cash expenses 121 and debt service			300,563

122 ==

123 CASH FLOW ANALYSIS
124 --

125 Net cash throwoff from the income statement			13,972

126 ==

8 Inventory control

Introduction

Control your inventory and you control a major cost of your business. Inventory typically represents 45 to 90 percent of all expenses for businesses engaged in the sale of products, whether they manufacture these products or buy them from others. The Acme Hardware Company, as is typical in its industry, has 66 percent of its assets tied up in inventory. Unless the inventory is controlled, it can easily get out of balance. Additionally, maintaining too much or too little inventory means that there may be excessive carrying costs or a loss of sales. Control is needed to assure that you have the right goods on hand to avoid stockouts, to prevent shrinkage (spoilage and/or theft), and to provide proper accounting. The objective of sound inventory management is to maintain the balance that helps you to achieve the highest profit possible.

Many businesses have too much of their most limited resource, capital, tied up in their major asset, inventory. Worse, they have their capital tied up in the wrong kind of inventory. Inventory may be old, worn out, shopworn, obsolete, the wrong sizes or colors, or there may be an imbalance between different product lines, which lowers the overall appeal of the total operation. For example, in our discussion on marketing, we emphasized the need to have the right goods for your target market segments.

Inventory control systems range from eyeball systems to "brown bag" or reserve stock systems to perpetual systems. One of the earliest purposes for which large businesses used computers was controlling inventory, often on a worldwide basis. This is an ideal job for a computer because it merely involves the adding and subtracting of units to and from totals held in storage or memory. We will briefly describe the operation of each of these informal inventory control systems and then focus our discussion on the use of your microcomputer in performing this important control task. You will then be able to select a system that best serves your own needs for your products and your business.

What is inventory?

Inventory consists of goods for sale. These may be items in, or to be used in, various stages of manufacturing a product or that are to be expended in the completion of a service. Alternatively, inventory may consist of goods that have been purchased for resale, as in the case of most retail businesses. Inventory is normally listed at original cost, market value, or current replacement cost, whichever is the lowest. Such evaluation is in accordance with generally accepted accounting practices because it minimizes the possibility of overstating earnings and assets. Inventory evaluation and accounting practices are

worth a separate discussion. However, since our focus here is on the management aspects of inventory control, we will not discuss these accounting implications further. In any event, inventory management and accounting are essentially two different approaches to the same concern: the control of this important asset.

The ideal amount of merchandise inventory will vary from one business and one market to another. Average inventory balances or ending figures serve as guides for comparison. Too large an inventory at a particular location may not be justified because the turnover does not support the investment. On the other hand, too small an inventory minimizes sales and profits because it can cause a loss of profitable sales. This dynamic situation warrants close attention in all small firms. The minimum inventory required is based on the reorder time needed. Understanding this relationship can become especially important in your buying activities. Inventory investment, purchasing costs, support materials, and storage costs are expensive. However, stockouts are also expensive. All of these costs can be minimized by efficient inventory practices. Proper control of inventory can help save money and increase the return on investment.

Inventory control involves the procurement, care, and disposition of materials. There are three types of inventory that are of concern to managers in manufacturing firms: raw materials, in-process or semifinished goods (work in process), and finished goods. If the manager effectively controls these three types of inventory, he can release capital that may be tied up in unnecessary inventory; improve production control; protect against obsolescence, deterioration, and/or theft; and gather useful information for planning ahead.

Inventory control can come about through a variety of methods, some more efficient than others. These can be generally grouped into three categories:

The eyeball system The eyeball system is very simple in application. The manager stands in the middle of the store or manufacturing inventory area and looks around. If he or she happens to notice that some of the items are missing, then he or she will order more. The difficulty with the eyeball system is that you may not notice that some particularly good (or even essential) item is out of stock. It may stay out of stock for a long time before it happens to be brought to your attention. Throughout the time that it is out of stock, you are losing sales. Such unsystematic but simple inventory control systems are practiced by many small retailers to their disadvantage.

The brown bag or reserve stock system In the "brown bag system," a reserve stock of an item is maintained, often literally in a brown bag placed at the back of a bin or storage area. When the last unit of open inventory or open stock is used, the bag is opened and the new supplies that it contains are placed in the bin. An order for new stock is then immediately placed. The quantity of the reserve stock is established by calculating the time from order to delivery of the product and the rate of sales of the product. Thus, if the order/delivery time cycle is two weeks and the rate of sale is 100 units per week, the reserve stock should consist of 200 units. This is fine if you can plan on a two-week delivery cycle. However, it may be necessary for you to maintain a little slush in the reserve stock so that you do not experience stockouts. You may decide that a one-week additional supply of safety stock is wise. When the new inventory supplies are received, a new bag is filled with the reserve quantity of stock and placed in the back of the stock bin; the rest of the stock is placed in the open part of the bin. It's a very simple system and one that's highly effective for a great many different types of operations.

Perpetual inventory systems Perpetual inventory systems include card-operated, computer-operated, and other systems, all of which tally either the unit use or the dollar use of different product lines. The benefits are avoidance of stockouts and maintenance of a constant record of the sales of different products. This record helps you to see where you should be placing your emphasis in terms of selling and buying activities.

The observation method, or eyeball system, fails to keep a satisfactory check on merchandise depletion unless you have an unusually alert sense of quantities. It means that you record shortages of goods or reorder as the need occurs to you. Without a better checking system, orders are usually placed only at the time of the saleman's regular visit. This plan may be the simplest, but it often results in lost sales. The perpetual inventory system avoids these problems.

Detachable stubs on tickets placed on merchandise afford a good means of control. The stubs, containing information identifying the articles, are removed at the time the items are sold. The accumulated stubs can then be posted regularly to a perpetual inventory.

A checklist, sometimes provided by wholesalers, is another simple counting device. The list provides space to record the items carried and the selling price, cost, and minimum order quantities for each. It also typically contains a column in which to note whether stock on hand is sufficient and when to reorder. You might also keep a chart of slow-moving merchandise, listing each brand and noting items that begin to lag in sales. The checklist system is very similar to the brown bag system, but it's on paper and is preferred where actually keeping the items in bags would not be feasible.

Because the key to inventory control is counting, keeping track of merchandise that enters the system as new stock and leaves the system as sales, your computer

is an ideal tool for this function. The computer can maintain the perpetual tally that is so essential to good decision making and can even be set up to show the critical reorder points based on whatever logic seems to be most appropriate to your particular situation.

Inventory turnover

Before we proceed with developing an inventory control system, we must know how much of each item we actually need. One of the key questions that must be asked in evaluating inventory is, *How much should I have tied up in inventory?*

The answer to this question relates to *inventory turnover* and establishing the best balance between the actual experience of a firm and the industry average. Once understood, turnover can be used as a measure that helps control purchases. Turnover is an important concept because it helps you determine what your inventory level should be in order to achieve or support the sales levels you predict or desire. Turnover, also known as stock turns, is the number of times the average inventory of a given product is sold in a year. This is normally calculated by dividing the average inventory by the gross sales or the cost of goods sold, as will be seen later. For Acme Hardware, the inventory turnover is 2.89 times per year. Once calculated or projected from historical experience, the inventory turnover rate in a given business can be compared against the industry averages as a means of evaluating the efficiency of the total sales operation.

Inventory turns 4 times on the average for many businesses; but a jewelry store, for instance, may turn only 2 times per year, while a grocery store may turn as many as 25 times per year. You can consult industry averages to determine the appropriate turnover for your business. Of course, it is important to recognize that in the accumulation of comparative statistical data, a wide variation will be found for any particular type of firm. Averages are just that, and most firms in a group are at variance with the final result. Nevertheless, these averages serve as a very useful guide for measuring the adequacy of industry turnover. The important consideration for each individual business manager is to see how his firm compares with the averages and to determine whether his deviation from that average is to his benefit or disadvantage. In the hardware industry, inventory turns 2.4 times, and so with a turnover of 2.89 times, Mr. Adams may be somewhat more efficient in his inventory management than others in the industry.

Inventory turnover is computed by dividing the volume of goods sold by the average inventory held throughout a given period. If the inventory is recorded at cost, as is most often the case, then:

$$\text{Turnover} = \frac{\text{Cost of goods sold}}{\text{Average inventory}}$$

$$\text{Average inventory}$$

$$= \frac{\text{Beginning inventory} + \text{ending inventory}}{2}$$

If the inventory is recorded at retail, then

$$\text{Turnover} = \frac{\text{Sales}}{\text{Average inventory}}$$

As noted, in the case of Acme Hardware, the inventory turnover is 2.89 times for the year using the cost basis. This was calculated as follows:

$$\text{Turnover} = \frac{\text{Cost of goods sold}}{\text{Average inventory}}$$

$$\text{Turnover} = \frac{\$221,760}{\text{Average inventory}}$$

$$\text{Average inventory} = \frac{\$70,000 + \$83,292}{2}$$

$$\text{Turnover} = \frac{\$221,760}{\$76,646} = 2.89 \text{ times}$$

The cost of goods sold ($221,760) comes from the income statement. The average inventory is somewhat more difficult to determine. In theory, the average inventory would be the average of the inventory levels for each period of change throughout the year — a month, a quarter, or a season. Using this series of figures would allow us to adjust for seasonal cycles that the business may experience. This is difficult in reality, however, as many firms, particularly small ones, are hard pressed to determine their inventory level even semiannually and rarely measure it for shorter time periods. In the case of Acme Hardware, inventory is actually only taken once a year, at the year's end. Thus, the average inventory figure we have to work with would be the average of the inventory at the beginning of the year (the previous period's ending inventory) and the inventory at the end of this year. (We should be somewhat concerned about the resulting figure, though, because it fails to take into account the possible inventory fluctuations throughout the year.) Thus, dividing the cost of goods sold ($221,760) by the average inventory (beginning inventory of $70,000 plus ending inventory of $83,292 divided by 2) will equal the inventory turnover calculated of 2.89 times.

If we had additional inventory totals available to us for intermediate periods throughout the year, we would total all of the available inventory balances and divide by the number of inventories. This process would give us our average inventory for that operating period.

We just looked at turnover on a cost basis. However, in many retail businesses, inventory is often taken (recorded) at retail price. When this is done, average inventory would be divided into net sales. In the case of Acme Hardware, the resulting inventory turnover would be 4.4 times. The computation would be:

$$\text{Turnover} = \frac{\text{Sales}}{\text{Average inventory}}$$

$$= \frac{\$336,000}{\$76,646} = 4.38 \text{ or } 4.4$$

There is clearly a wide difference between Acme Hardware's inventory turnover at cost, 2.89 times, and at retail, 4.4 times. In order to know which turnover figure we should use for comparative purposes, we have to know whether our inventory has been taken at cost or retail. Assuming the more conservative approach (which is generally recommended), our inventory figure would most probably be at cost, and so the turnover figure of 2.89 times is the figure we would find more useful for comparing with the industry average. Of course, Mr. Adams should know how his inventory was recorded. The point here, though, is that to use comparative inventory turnover ratios, we must know how the industry averages have been calculated or we may be comparing apples and oranges. It is a simple enough matter to determine whether the industry average has been calculated at cost or retail. In fact, this information is always provided as part of the statistical data. Still, we have to be aware of this difference in order to know that we should be on the lookout for its clarification.

Inventory planning

Once we have determined what our average inventory is and what we think it should be (based on industry averages and other such considerations), we can then start planning to achieve our goal. However, in order to do this, we must have a good understanding of what our sales level is likely to be for the next operating period. Consequently, proper planning for inventory requires forecasting of sales as well. The problems of forecasting for small businesses are many. We are not going to discuss the methodology of forecasting beyond a restatement of the fact that it is essential for inventory management and as a target for planning purposes.

If we take the case of Acme Hardware and assume that sales are forecast to increase 10 percent over the next year, we would anticipate a sales level of $369,600

($336,000 times 110 percent equals $369,600). Further, assuming that Acme feels that the 34-percent gross profit experienced in the past operating period is a realistic expectation for the next, then the cost of goods will equal 66 percent of sales, or $243,936. If we expect that inventory management practices will remain unchanged, we will require an average inventory of $84,116 calculated as follows:

$$\frac{\text{Cost of goods sold}}{\text{Inventory turnover}} = \text{Average inventory}$$

$$= \frac{\$243,936}{2.9} = \$84,116$$

Mr. Adams may now decide that he wants to try for an improved inventory turnover of 3 times. He may conclude that, after all, interest rates are high and the money for any added inventory would have to be raised through borrowing. (In order to meet increased sales demands of 10 percent, either increased inventory turnover or increased inventory will have to be achieved.) With these figures at hand, he can calculate his new average inventory requirements for the next operating period as follows:

$$\frac{\text{Cost of goods sold}}{\text{Inventory turnover}} = \frac{\$243,936}{3} = \$81,312$$

Since the beginning inventory of the next period will be the same as the ending inventory of this period ($83,292), the ending inventory for the next period would have to be less than the average of $81,312. The target ending inventory is calculated as follows:

Total beginning and ending inventory

$$= \$81,312 \times 2 = \$162,624$$

Total inventory − beginning inventory

= ending inventory

$$\$162,624 - \$83,292 = \$79,332$$

If this goal can be achieved by year end, the inventory level will be reduced by $3,960. This inventory reduction will also reduce cash needs by the same amount plus any savings in interest costs or other carrying charges. However, as we reduce our inventory level by increasing our stock turns, we must keep aware of the potential problem of stockouts or not having goods available as they are needed. We earlier noted the extra costs that too much or not enough inventory can represent.

Inventory control

Inventory control means having the right amounts of the right items on hand when they are needed. Consequently, the basic inventory control questions that must be answered are:

- What should be ordered?
- In what quantity?
- When should it be ordered?

In answering the questions, it is necessary to determine the minimum level of inventory that is the indication of time to reorder. This reorder point must take into consideration the time needed to place and process an order, the delivery time cycle, and a time contingency factor. Estimates of the sales that would occur during this time period will help to derive the minimum order quantity. Manufacturers have the same problems as retailers except that a second dimension is included. In addition to finished goods, manufacturers must have adequate supplies of raw materials to support planned production and must consider labor and other costs represented by work-in-process as well.

In the case of Acme Hardware, if putty is sold at the rate of a case of 24 cans per month, and it takes 15 days to get a new order placed and delivered, an order should be placed when putty is down to 12 cans. If this pattern is followed, the new order will arrive just as the last can is being sold. However, this does not leave any contingency factor (safety stock). If we want 5 cans as a buffer, then the reorder point will be reached when in-store supplies reach 17 cans.

Of course, in the case of hardware stores, where there are thousands of different items, regular review of each is a difficult task. This monitoring is typically done through inspection by an experienced person. But today the computer can do this for the manager. The idea is to establish a numbering system that identifies each item that is for sale. Once the basic format is set up, it is easy to record purchases and sales for each item at either the time of the transaction or later, by use of sales slips. This input in the form of sales of each individual item is the starting point. Daily posting of sales and purchases by item number will do the trick. Once this information has been entered, it then is a simple matter to ask the computer to provide a list of items in inventory at a given time. Such a listing would probably look like this:

Stock no.	Item	Qty on hand	Reorder no.	Sales last 30 days	Latest unit cost	Value of inventory on hand
0620	Hammers —small	12	5	20	$ 2.25	$ 27.00
0621	Hammers —large	10	3	5	$ 3.75	$ 37.50
1859	Rake —grass	24	12	2	$ 4.19	$ 100.56
1860	Rake —garden	8	6	4	$ 6.23	$ 49.84
5216	Snowblower —Type A	3	3	6	$415.00	$1,245.00

A quick glance tells us that rakes are not moving too well. At the rate of sales during the last 30 days, it would take 12 months to get rid of the inventory of grass rakes. The question now is why these sales are moving so slowly. Perhaps it is December and there is no need to cut and rake grass. If this is so, then we are stuck with $100.56 in inventory until spring unless we have a special sale. On the other hand, we notice that the large dollar item in this abbreviated listing is the Snowblower—Type A, with an on-hand value of $1,245.00. The other four items listed are somewhat less critical, adding up to only $214.90 of inventory value. Thus, the item to watch carefully is the Snowblower—Type A. Close scrutiny suggests that sales of this item have been reasonably good during the last 30 days and that the inventory level is at the reorder point. If indeed it is December, then it behooves Acme to place an order or it will run the risk of a stockout at a time when sales should be strong. If it is February, a close-out sale may well be in order to avoid carrying this inventory over into the next period.

Another use of the microcomputer is to ask for an inventory listing that displays only items that are at or near the reorder point. Such a listing might look like this for Acme:

Stock no.	Item	Qty on hand	Reorder no.	Sales last 30 days	Latest unit cost	Value of inventory on hand
5216	Snowblower —Type A	3	3	6	$415.00	$1,245.00
6743	Lawnmower —Type D	3	3	1	$267.00	$ 801.00
7169	Handsaw —Type B	5	5	10	$ 4.37	$ 21.85

This listing says that at the current rate of sales, unless Acme immediately reorders its Snowblower—Type A and Handsaw—Type B, there will be stockouts within 15 days. On the other hand, although the Lawnmower—Type D is at the reorder point, sales have been slow, so it might be possible to delay ordering this item if cash is tight or if the model is old. In the latter case, Acme may wish to take some other action, such as a special sale, to reduce the inventory level and free cash to purchase faster-moving items.

The point of this analysis is that the reorder process should not be automatic. Problems can come into play when the total system is automated and the computer directly reorders when minimum levels are reached. The computer's ability is limited. It can only compare sets of data. It does not have any judgment and cannot make decisions for you. No matter how helpful we make our computer tool, it can never become a substitute for good judgment. Unfortunately, this is an important fact that people all too frequently lose sight of.

Economic order quantity

As we have discussed, they key to inventory control is having exactly the right amount of goods on hand — neither too many nor too few. One way to help ensure that this optimal objective is met is to use the *economic order quantity* (EOQ) approach to inventory management. The EOQ is the order size that costs the least and still ensures adequate inventory levels to minimize stockouts. Certain data is required in order to apply the EOQ approach. This includes:

- Forecast of annual sales or usage of a specific item.

- Cost per unit to purchase that particular item.

- Internal cost of ordering, regardless of order size (often this is merely the administrative cost of issuing a purchase order).

- Annual inventory carrying cost (often the prevailing interest rate), along with storage cost, inventory insurance, and a provision for inventory obsolescence (usually an arbitrary percentage of the inventory cost value). In today's environment, with moderately high interest rates, the annual inventory carrying cost would be around 30 percent.

When the above information is gathered and entered into your microcomputer, the machine will perform the necessary calculations and show you the most economic levels that should be ordered. Of course, this can also be calculated by hand through the application of a fairly complex formula. With a microcomputer, however, it is not necessary to memorize this formula because the computer will do so for you.

All of this can be best illustrated by way of example. Mr. Adams has examined his records and determined the following data for his most popular hammers:

	Item	Value
Q	Number of hammers sold per year	1,200
C	Cost of each hammer	$6.00
B	Cost of issuing purchase order	$20.00
P	Cost of possession as percentage of inventory costs (inventory carrying, storage, obsolescence, and insurance)	30%

The formula is calculated as follows:

$$\text{EOQ} = \sqrt{\frac{2\,QB}{CP}} = \sqrt{\frac{2 \times 1{,}200 \times \$20}{\$6 \times 30\%}} =$$

$$\sqrt{\frac{\$48{,}000}{\$1.80}} = \sqrt{26{,}667} = 163.3 \text{ units}$$

The EOQ formula automatically compares the purchasing and possession costs for various purchase quantity levels in order to find the minimum cost level. We can prove that the derived answer is correct by using a trial-and-error method. We will illustrate this approach by constructing an analysis of six different order sizes as follows:

Order size	Number of orders per year	Ordering cost per year	Possession cost per year	Total cost per year
100	12.00	$240.00	$ 90.00	$330.00
120	10.00	200.00	108.00	308.00
140	8.57	171.43	126.00	297.43
160	7.50	150.00	144.00	294.00
180	6.67	133.33	162.00	295.33
200	6.00	120.00	180.00	300.00

This analysis shows that if Mr. Adams orders hammers in quantities of 100, his total annual cost for ordering and holding inventory would be $330. If he ordered in quantities of 200, the total cost would be only $300. However, somewhere between 100 and 200 the total cost would be lower, since the cost to order 180 was only $295.33. After many such trial calculations, we could finally determine that the lowest cost would occur at 163

units. At that point, the cost is only $293.24. Using the formula, we can derive this answer quite quickly. Using the computer, we can have an answer almost instantaneously and so avoid the large number of hand computations otherwise needed to find the minimum total annual cost point.

The geometry of the situation helps to explain why and how the situation works. Quite simply, as quantities increase, possession cost per unit tends to increase and ordering costs per unit decrease. This can best be shown by way of a graph (see below). The EOQ occurs at the point where the ordering cost line intersects with the possession cost line.

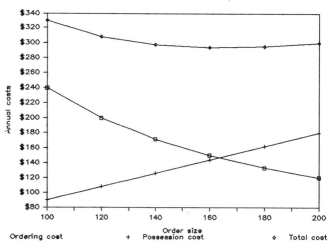

ECONOMIC ORDER QUANTITY

There are a variety of adjustments that can be made to the basic EOQ formula that can produce a great deal of sophistication and refinement in inventory planning. For example, adjustments can be made for:

- Transportation costs
- Cost of inventory in transit
- Volume transportation rates
- Private carrier transportation
- Purchasing for uncertain sales levels

Each of these situations can be evaluated using the same basic approaches shown above. Again, the computer can perform the calculations for a wide range of situations and thus allow us to quickly and easily inspect the impact of each of these variables.

The EOQ worksheet

Getting ready

The EOQ worksheet that we will develop is simply the data that is needed to determine the optimal economic order quantity for an item considering the basic elements of ordering and possession costs. In addition, it requires the forecasting of sales for the particular item.

STEP 1   **Load Multiplan** into the computer. The program disk should be inserted into or removed from the disk drive only when the drive isn't working (when it isn't humming and the helpful red light is off).

STEP 2   **Clear the screen.** Data, labels, formulas, or formats could be on the Multiplan worksheet and not appear on the screen display. To be sure the computer's memory and the spreadsheet are clear of data before you begin work, always clear the screen.

Result If the screen was already clear, you won't see any change. Whenever you start a new worksheet, however, it is wise to use this command to be sure the screen is clear of all previously entered data, some of which might be on the spreadsheet but not on the area covered by the screen.

To enter
a command to clear the screen

Select TC (for Transfer Clear) and type **Y** to confirm

STEP 3   **Set column widths.** Column widths on the worksheet must be wide enough to hold the largest numbers and labels. We need a column width of 30 characters for the labels in column 1; the other columns can be left at their default setting of 10 characters.

To enter
a command to widen column 1

Goto any cell in column 1

Select FW (for Format Width)
Type **30** in the "in chars or d(efault)" field (RET)

Result There should now be five columns visible on the screen. Column 1 should be three times wider than each of the adjacent columns.

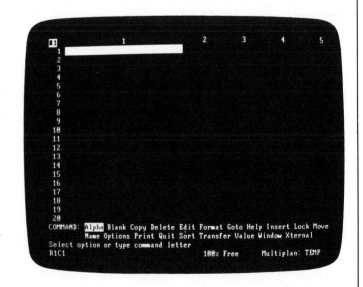

Entering the EOQ worksheet

Step One

Enter ruled lines and a heading for the EOQ worksheet

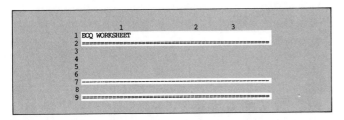

R O W
1　A heading identifies this as the Economic Order Quantity (EOQ) worksheet.

To enter
a heading for the EOQ worksheet

Goto R1C1

Select A (for Alpha)
　Type **EOQ WORKSHEET** (RET)

....

R O W S
2–9　Enter ruled lines to make the worksheet easier to read.

To enter
ruled lines to separate major sections of the worksheet

Select FC (for Format Cells)
　Type **R2C1:3,R7C1:3** in the "cells" field (TAB) (TAB)
　Type **C** (for Continuous) in the "format code" field (RET)

Goto R2C1

Select V (for Value)
　Type **REPT(" = ",50)** (RET)

Goto R7C1

Select V (for Value)
　Type **REPT("-",50)** (RET)

Goto R9C1

Select CF (for Copy From)
　Type **R2C1:3** in the "cells" field (RET)

Result　There should be three ruled lines visible on the screen, stretching across columns 1 through 3.

Step Two

Enter row labels

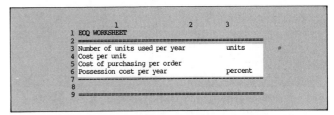

R O W S
3–6　Enter row labels to identify where trial values will be entered in the worksheet and to show that the *Possession cost* figure is expressed as a percent.

To enter
labels for the rows

Goto R3C1

Select A (for Alpha)
　Type **Number of units used per year** (→) (→)
　Type **units** (↓) (←) (←)
　Type **Cost per unit** (↓)
　Type **Cost of purchasing per order** (↓)
　Type **Possession cost per year** (→) (→)
　Type **percent** (RET)

Step Three

Enter a label and formula

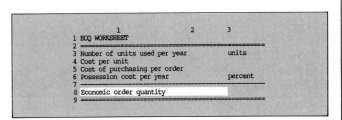

R O W
8　Enter a row label and formula for economic order quantity. This formula takes the product of the number of units sold times cost per unit times the cost per order, multiplies the product by two, divides the result by the possession cost, takes the square root of the resulting quotient, and finally divides the square root by the cost per unit.

To enter

a label to identify the economic order quantity
a formula to calculate that quantity

Goto R8C1

Select A (for Alpha)
 Type **Economic order quantity** (RET)

Goto R8C2

Select V (for Value)
 Type **IF(R4C2<>0,(SQRT(2*R3C2*R4C2*R5C2/
 (R6C2/100)))/R4C2,"")** (RET)

Step Four

Enter formats

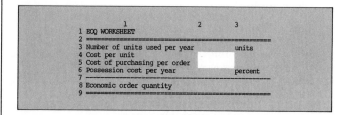

```
              1                2        3
1 EOQ WORKSHEET
2 ==================================================
3 Number of units used per year        units
4 Cost per unit
5 Cost of purchasing per order
6 Possession cost per year             percent
7 --------------------------------------------------
8 Economic order quantity
9 ==================================================
```

<u>C O L U M N</u>
2 **Format the data entry cells.** Since we are dealing with different quantities (units, dollars,
and percentages), using appropriate cell formats will
improve the usefulness of the worksheet.

To enter

a format for the cells in column 2

Select FDC (for Format Default Cells) (TAB)
 Type **I** (for Integer) in the "alignment" field (RET)

Select FC (for Format Cells)
 Type **R4:5C2** in the "cells" field (TAB) (TAB)
 Type **$** (for dollars) in the "format code" field
 (RET)

Step Five

Save your work. Before entering any data into the EOQ
worksheet, lock in the labels and formula, and save a
blank copy of the worksheet onto the data disk.

To save

the EOQ worksheet

Select LF (for Lock Formulas)
 Type **Y** (to confirm) (RET)

Select TS (for Transfer Save)
 Type **B:EOQ** in the "filename" field (RET)

Exploring "What Ifs"

Calculating economic order quantity. This "What If" will show Mr. Adams how the computer can be used to calculate economic order quantity (EOQ) — the lowest cost order size that will ensure adequate inventory levels to minimize stockouts. He will now use the worksheet to determine Acme's economic order quantity for the example calculated by hand in the introduction to Chapter 8. The basic information is:

# of hammers sold per year	1,200
Cost per hammer	$6.00
Cost of purchasing per order	$20.00
Inventory holding cost (possession cost) per year	30% of inventory value

To enter

> *the number* of units used per year, the cost per unit, the cost of issuing a purchase order, and the percentage inventory possession cost per year

> **Goto R3C2**
> Type **1200** (↓)
> Type **6** (↓)
> Type **20** (↓)
> Type **30** (RET)

Result The economic order quantity in cell R8C2 is 163 units.

ANALYSIS This problem merely requires the application of the EOQ formula to determine the ideal order quantity when only the inventory holding cost is balanced against the ordering cost for hammers. In the example given, the answer is 163 units at a time. There are clearly other costs and factors that must be considered. For example, volume discounts may well change the results. Similarly, transportation rates may vary with order size and may also change the results. As for other factors, the EOQ formula assumes a constant rate of demand and this is rarely the case. Thus, transit times and the potential for stockouts may require varying levels of safety stock.

"What If" 9

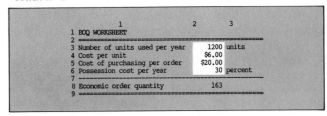

	1	2	3
1	EOQ WORKSHEET		
2			
3	Number of units used per year	1200	units
4	Cost per unit	$6.00	
5	Cost of purchasing per order	$20.00	
6	Possession cost per year	30	percent
7			
8	Economic order quantity	163	
9			

Entering the balance sheet ratios

Before we proceed with further "What Ifs," we are going to turn our attention to measuring or evaluating performance. One very helpful way to do this is to develop easily understood units of measurement appropriate for a business. These are commonly referred to as ratios. It is not the intent of this book to go into the subject of ratios fully, for that is often the subject of a complete text. However, there are several critical ratios appropriate to many businesses, such as the ones described in this book, that are commonly used to evaluate performance and efficiency.

Basically there are two types of ratio categories, financial and operating. The financial ratios are further subdivided into balance sheet or income statement ratios. Balance sheet ratios are described and entered here, and income statement ratios in Chapter 9. The financial ratios measure or evaluate the financial performance for a period or a point in time. An example of a balance sheet financial ratio is the average collection period, which calculates the average number of days it takes to collect receivables. A typical income statement financial ratio is the gross margin, or gross profit as a percentage of net sales. Operating ratios show the relationship between expense categories and functional activities within the firm. An example of an operating ratio may be wages per employee.

The ratios that will be used throughout this and the remaining chapters are primarily financial ratios. The balance sheet ratios described and entered in this section will be used to explore "What Ifs" in this and following chapters. The income statement ratios described and entered in Chapter 9 will deal with key expenses as a proportion of net sales. A truly variable expense, such as sales commissions, should be a constant percentage of sales revenues. A truly fixed expense, such as depreciation, should show a decreasing percentage in relation to net sales as sales increase.

Reload the DECISION worksheet

If you quit Multiplan after doing the "What If" exercises, or if you just saved the EOQ worksheet, you should now reload the DECISION worksheet. See the instructions on page 49 if you need a refresher. The values displayed in your version of the worksheet should match those in the illustration on page 136.

However, if you proceeded to this section directly after "What If" 8, be sure to restore the worksheet to its original values.

To restore
the worksheet

Goto R8C2 and type **336000** (RET)

Goto R94C3 and type **10000** (RET)

Goto R100C3 and type **4000** (RET)

If you wish to double-check the values on your worksheet, compare them with those in the illustration on page 136.

Step One

Enter section headings and ruled lines

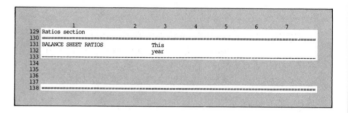

ROW 129   **Enter a heading** to identify the ratios section.

To enter
a label for the ratios section

Goto R129C1

Select A (for Alpha)
Type **Ratios section** (RET)

....

ROWS 130–138   **The ruled lines** in this section stretch across seven columns, like the ones in the income statement. So, we'll go back to using the *line1* and *line2* named ranges to make copies.

To enter
ruled lines to separate the ratios section

Select CF (for Copy From)
Type **line2** in the "cells" field (TAB)
Type **R130C1,R138C1** in the "to cells" field (RET)

Select CF (for Copy From)
Type **line1** in the "cells" field (TAB)
Type **R133C1** in the "to cells" field (RET)

<table>
<tr><td>R O W
131</td><td>Enter column headings for the balance sheet ratios. We can "recycle" the heading for column 2 from the balance sheet section, using the COPY FROM command.</td></tr>
</table>

To enter

labels for column heads

Goto R131C1

Select A (for Alpha)
 Type **BALANCE SHEET RATIOS** (RET)

Goto R131C2

Select CF (for Copy From)
 Type **R30:31C2** in the "cells" field (RET)

Step Two

Format the cells

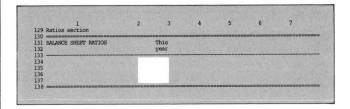

Set up cell formats for optimal display of the ratio values. The default cell format for the worksheet only displays integer values. In the ratios section, we need more accuracy in the results. The FORMAT CELLS command is used to specify a fixed point display of two decimal places.

To enter

a command to format column 2 entries

Select FC (for Format Cells)
 Type **R134:137C2** in the "cells" field (TAB) (TAB)
 Type **F** (for Fixed) in the "format code" field (TAB)
 Type **2** in the "# of decimals" field (RET)

Step Three

Enter labels and formulas

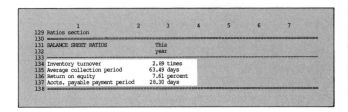

<table>
<tr><td>R O W
134</td><td>Inventory turnover refers to the number of times, on the average (at least in theory),</td></tr>
</table>

that a given item of inventory would be replaced on a shelf during the course of a year. This is an important measure of activity for many businesses since it helps in drawing up pro forma (projected) balance sheets and in projecting original start-up investments by determining what the required inventory level for the business should be relative to sales as compared to the inventory averages. It is also a measure of relative efficiency or effectiveness in inventory management once the business is underway. There may be some problems as well as benefits from having inventory ratios that are higher than the industry average. If our business is showing a higher than normal turnover, there may be a very real possibility that the business will experience stockouts or other deficiencies that may result in disappointed customers and lost sales. On the other hand, if the basic inventory is high relative to sales (lower than normal turnover), it may indicate that the business is maintaining the wrong types of inventory or has too much of its funds invested in inventory, all of which could lead to inventory obsolescence and/or shrinkage and generally lower the return on capital.

To enter

a label to identify the inventory turnover ratio line of the worksheet
a formula in cell R134C2 that will calculate inventory turnover. The formula calculates average inventory by adding opening and ending inventory and dividing the result by two. The average inventory is then divided into cost of goods.

Entering the balance sheet ratios Continued

Goto R134C1

Select A (for Alpha)
 Type **Inventory turnover** →
 Type **= R12C2/AVERAGE(R38C2,R38C4)** →
 Type **times** RET

Result Inventory turnover should be 2.89 times.

....

R O W 135 **The average collection period ratio** calculates the average number of days it takes to collect receivables or those sales that are made on credit. Its computation will sometimes lead to very shocking conclusions. Businesses may believe they're offering and maintaining terms, for example, of 30 days net, but when calculating the average collection period may discover that their receivables are 45 or 60 days old instead. This ratio both measures the relative liquidity of the receivables and suggests their relative safety. Generally speaking, the shorter the collection period, the more liquid the receivables and the safer the receivables; that is, the greater the likelihood that they will be paid. The longer the collection period, the more danger there is that the debtors may not pay. In many industries a collection period of over 90 days is seen as extremely dangerous. Calculating the average collection period from one operating period to the next will provide a quick indicator of trouble if the average collection period begins to get longer. This may suggest that the businesses or individuals owing money to the organization are having difficulty in making their payments or it may be symptomatic of some other trouble within the business or the industry. Especially for many smaller retail businesses, accounts receivable may not be necessary at all. Instead, the business may offer the same charge capabilities to its customers by utilizing VISA, MasterCard, or some other form of bank credit card, thus transferring the credit verification and collection activities to other organizations that have the professional staff capabilities to properly handle these functions.

To enter
 a label to identify the average collection period line of the worksheet
 a formula in cell R135C2 that will calculate the average collection period. The average collection period applies only to credit sales. In this example we assume 30 percent of net sales are made on credit.

Goto R135C1

Select A (for Alpha)
 Type **Average collection period** →
 Type **= R37C2/(R10C2*0.3/360)** →
 Type **days** RET

Result The average collection period should be 63.49 days.

....

R O W 136 **The return on equity ratio** tells the stockholders the profit that the company is producing through the use of stockholder investments. This ratio, also known as return on net worth, is the measure of the relative effectiveness of the owner's equity. The return on equity can be constructed either before or after taxes. The after-tax figure is the net figure of most interest to the stockholders. However, when comparing the results with industry standards, the before-tax figure is more commonly used because each firm has different tax alternatives, and consequently, different ways of treating tax. Therefore, the before-tax figures make for a more stable comparison.

To enter
 a label to identify the return on equity line of the worksheet
 a formula in cell R136C2 that will calculate the return on equity. The formula divides income before taxes by total owner equity minus net income. The results of the division are multiplied by 100 to display the percentage as a whole number.

Goto R136C1

Select A (for Alpha)
 Type **Return on equity** →
 Type **= R23C2/(R72C2-R26C2)%** →
 Type **percent** RET

Result The return on equity should be 7.61 percent.

A N A L Y S I S The return on equity for Acme is 8 percent before tax and 6 percent after tax. By today's standards, where interest rates are in excess of 15 percent, this is low. Thus, Mr. Adams's money in the store is not providing a very good return.

R O W
137 The accounts payable payment period tells a manager how fast, in terms of days, the trade creditors' invoices are being paid. In the case of Acme Hardware, the trade creditors are almost exclusively the suppliers of the purchases that are for inventory.

To enter

labels to identify this as the accounts payable payment period line of the worksheet

a formula in cell R137C2 to calculate the accounts payable payment period. This formula divides accounts payable (cell R57C2) by average daily inventory purchases. Daily inventory purchases are calculated by dividing inventory purchases in cell R107C4 by 360 days. (360 is an even number that is easily divisible by 12. In some cases 365 is used.)

Goto R137C1

Select A (for Alpha)

Type **Accts. payable payment period** (→)
Type **= R57C2/(R107C4/360)** (→)
Type **days** (RET)

Result The accounts payable payment period should be 28.30 days.

Step Four

Save your work. Again, it's advisable to lock in the formulas and to save a copy of the worksheet before you proceed. For detailed instructions on how to save, see page 31.

Exploring "What Ifs"

Inventory turnover is increased to 3.0 times.
Inventory turnover refers to how many times a company's base inventory has been sold and replaced during a given time period. Mr. Adams assumes that Acme Hardware's sales will increase 10 percent over the next year. Rather than tie up more money in added inventory to meet the increased sales, he may want to improve his inventory turnover so his gross profit remains at 34 percent. Acme's inventory turnover is now 2.89. Mr. Adams decides to try for a turnover of 3.0.

Inventory turnover is calculated by dividing the volume of goods sold by the average inventory held throughout that period. Since Acme Hardware records its inventory at cost, we use the following equations:

$$\text{Inventory turnover} = \frac{\text{Cost of goods sold}}{\text{Average inventory}}$$

$$\text{Average inventory}$$
$$= \frac{\text{Beginning inventory} + \text{Ending Inventory}}{2}$$

$$\text{Average inventory} = \frac{\text{Cost of goods sold}}{\text{Inventory turnover}}$$

Looking at the computer spreadsheet, we find cost of goods sold in cell R12C2, beginning inventory in cell R106C4, and ending inventory in cell R110C4. Thus, in the original worksheet:

$$\text{Average inventory} = \frac{\$70,000 + \$83,292}{2} = \$76,646$$

$$\text{Inventory turnover} = \frac{\$221,760}{\$76,646} = 2.89$$

In the new problem, we want turnover to be 3.0, but we don't know what the year's ending inventory will be. Therefore:

$$\text{Average inventory} = \frac{\$243,936}{3} = \$73,920$$

$$\$73,920 = \frac{\text{Beginning inventory} + \text{Ending inventory}}{2}$$

$$\$73,920 = \frac{\$70,000 + \text{Ending inventory}}{2}$$

$$\$73,920 = \frac{\$70,000}{2} + \frac{\text{Ending inventory}}{2}$$

$$\$73,920 = \$35,000 + \frac{\text{Ending inventory}}{2}$$

$$\$73,920 - \$35,000 = \frac{\text{Ending inventory}}{2}$$

$$2(\$38,920) = \text{Ending inventory}$$

$$\$77,840 = \text{Ending inventory}$$

Thus, the ending inventory is $7,840 higher than the beginning inventory. In the original example, the ending inventory ($83,292) was $13,292 higher than the beginning inventory. Inventory purchases will be reduced by the difference of $5,452 ($13,292 − $7,840).

Therefore, we will be entering the inventory change of $77,840 and the inventory purchases change of $229,600 ($235,052 − $5,452).

To enter
changes in inventory on the balance sheet and in inventory purchases on the cost of goods analysis of the worksheet

Goto **R38C2** and type **77840** (RET)
R107C4 and type **229600** (RET)

Result Inventory turnover in cell R134C2 is increased to 3.00 and cash is increased in cell R36C2 by $5,452 to $6,787.

The net reduction in the ending inventory in cell R38C2 due to the increase in inventory turnover is $5,452 ($83,292 − $77,840). In turn, this means that Acme will reduce purchases by this $5,452 amount. Thus, there is the same savings in cash.

There is no change in profit since the cost of goods sold and gross profit are the same before and after the change in inventory turnover.

The important lesson is that inventory takes cash to acquire. Excessive inventory ties up cash that may be better used elsewhere.

```
            1                  2      3        4       5      6        7
 1 DECISION worksheet
 2
 3 INCOME STATEMENT: January 1 through December 31, 19..
 4 ===========================================================================
 5                              This    % net    Last    % net  <----Deviation---->
 6                              year    sales    year    sales     $         %
 7 -------------------------------------------------------------------------------
 8 Gross sales                336,000   100    312,000-  100    24,000      8
 9 Sales discounts                  0     0          0     0         0
10 Net sales                  336,000   100    312,000   100    24,000      8
11 -------------------------------------------------------------------------------
12 Cost of goods sold         221,760    66    201,240    65    20,520     10
13 Gross profit               114,240    34    110,760    36     3,480      3
14 -------------------------------------------------------------------------------
15 General & administrative    49,600    15     52,000    17    -2,400     -5
16 Selling expenses            49,000    15     40,000    13     9,000     23
17 Depreciation                 6,000     2      5,500     2       500      9
18 -------------------------------------------------------------------------------
19 Operating income             9,640     3     13,260     4    -3,620    -27
20 Interest expense             6,000     2      6,750     2      -750    -11
21 Other income/expense             0     0       -800    -0       800   -100
22 -------------------------------------------------------------------------------
23 Income before taxes          3,640     1      7,310     2    -3,670    -50
24 Taxes                          728     0      1,462     0      -734    -50
25 -------------------------------------------------------------------------------
26 NET INCOME                   2,912     1      5,848     2    -2,936    -50
27 ===========================================================================
28 BALANCE SHEET: December 31, 19..
29 ===========================================================================
30                              This                 Last
31                              year                 year
32 -------------------------------------------------------------------------------
33 ASSETS:
34 -------------------------------------------------------------------------------
35 <Current assets>
36 Cash                         6,787                4,750
37 Accounts receivable         17,777               16,000
38 Inventory                   77,840               70,000
39 Prepaid expenses             3,400                3,400
40 -------------------------------------------------------------------------------
41 Total current assets       105,804               94,150
42 -------------------------------------------------------------------------------
43 <Fixed assets>
44 Buildings & equipment       33,000               38,950
45 Less accumulated depreciation -13,000            -7,000
46 Land                             0                    0
47 -------------------------------------------------------------------------------
48 Total fixed assets          20,000               31,950
49 -------------------------------------------------------------------------------
50 Other assets                 3,700                2,545
51 -------------------------------------------------------------------------------
52 TOTAL ASSETS               129,504              128,645
53 ===========================================================================
54 LIABILITIES:
55 -------------------------------------------------------------------------------
56 <Current liabilities>
57 Accounts payable            18,480               17,000
58 Accrued wages & taxes        6,357                6,000
59 Notes payable (current)      3,890                3,890
60 Other current liabilities    5,900                5,900
61 -------------------------------------------------------------------------------
62 Total current liabilities   34,627               32,790
63 -------------------------------------------------------------------------------
64 Long-term debt              44,110               48,000
65 -------------------------------------------------------------------------------
66 Total liabilities           78,737               80,790
67 -------------------------------------------------------------------------------
68 <Owner equity>
69 Common stock                37,000               37,000
70 Retained earnings           13,767               10,855
71 -------------------------------------------------------------------------------
72 Total owner equity          50,767               47,855
73 ===========================================================================
74 TOTAL LIABILITIES & EQUITY 129,504              128,645
75 ===========================================================================
```

```
             1                  2       3        4       5      6      7
 77 Analysis section
 78 ==========================================================================
 79 G&A EXPENSE BREAKDOWN            Fixed    Variable    Total
 80 --------------------------------------------------------------------------
 81 Rent                            12,000        0      12,000
 82 Officer salaries                20,000        0      20,000
 83 Clerical expenses                4,000    1,000       5,000
 84 Insurance                        3,600        0       3,600
 85 Utilities                        2,000      400       2,400
 86 Office supplies                    800      400       1,200
 87 Legal & accounting               3,000        0       3,000
 88 Miscellaneous                    1,200    1,200       2,400
 89 --------------------------------------------------------------------------
 90 Total G&A expenses              46,600    3,000      49,600
 91 ==========================================================================
 92 SELLING EXPENSE BREAKDOWN        Fixed    Variable    Total
 93 --------------------------------------------------------------------------
 94 Wages                           20,000   10,000      30,000
 95 Delivery                             0    1,800       1,800
 96 Operating supplies               4,000      800       4,800
 97 Advertising                      4,000    2,000       6,000
 98 Travel & entertainment             800      400       1,200
 99 Miscellaneous                      800      400       1,200
100 Credit card                          0    4,000       4,000
101 --------------------------------------------------------------------------
102 Total selling expenses          29,600   19,400      49,000
103 ==========================================================================
104 COST OF GOODS SOLD ANALYSIS
105 --------------------------------------------------------------------------
106 Beginning inventory                                  70,000
107 Inventory purchases                                 229,600
108 Less purchase discounts of           0 percent           0
109 Total goods available                               299,600
110 Less ending inventory                                77,840
111 --------------------------------------------------------------------------
112 Cost of goods sold                                  221,760
113 ==========================================================================
114 BREAKEVEN ANALYSIS
115 --------------------------------------------------------------------------
116 Sales revenue needed to break even                  322,683
117 --------------------------------------------------------------------------
118 Sales revenue needed to cover cash expenses         300,732
119 --------------------------------------------------------------------------
120 Sales revenue needed to cover cash expenses         314,963
121 and debt service
122 --------------------------------------------------------------------------
123 CASH FLOW ANALYSIS
124 --------------------------------------------------------------------------
125 Net cash throwoff from the income statement           8,912
126 --------------------------------------------------------------------------
127
128
129 Ratios section
130 ==========================================================================
131 BALANCE SHEET RATIOS                  This
132                                       year
133 --------------------------------------------------------------------------
134 Inventory turnover                  3.00 times
135 Average collection period          63.49 days
136 Return on equity                    7.61 percent
137 Accts. payable payment period      28.98 days
138 ==========================================================================
```

Introduction

Two individuals can take the same resources of time, money, and people; and one will develop a successful business venture, the other a failure. The difference between the two is management skill, and the application of that skill is control. Without control, the future of an organization is governed by pure chance. As we have said before, success can be a fortunate accident or the result of a systematic application of management techniques. Our arguments here, of course, are in favor of the latter.

Any business needs focus for its activities and the work efforts of its employees. Direction must be provided to make sure that it is headed toward a meaningful objective. The old cliché of the ship floundering without a rudder is appropriately applied to a business without direction. It too will flounder. But direction itself is not sufficient. Even the best of plans may not be effective or achieve their potential unless operations are carefully monitored to ensure that the actual activities and experiences are consistent with the plan. Control helps to make sure that the plans are working as expected and, if they are not, provides an opportunity to figure out why.

We have already described some planning tools, so the discussion here will provide an integrating framework for the effective use of these different techniques. All of these ideas can be brought together into a comprehensive management system. Any business should have an advertising plan, a marketing plan, a cash flow plan, and so forth. These separate plans are useful and important, but they will only work if they relate. The activities themselves must interact and overlap since they so thoroughly affect each other. Each of the subordinate plans must recognize these interrelationships and be seen as a component of a larger plan, a general plan designed to ensure both maximum control and flexibility for maximum effectiveness.

There is a framework for management. In general terms, management is getting things done with and through others. More specifically, management can be seen as a series of functional activities: planning, organizing, directing, and controlling.

Planning:

- Setting goals and objectives for the organization.
- Developing work maps showing how these goals and objectives should be attained.

Organizing:

- Bringing together resources — people, capital, and equipment.
- Determining the most effective way of attaining goals.
- Integrating resources.

Directing:

- Ensuring that the required work is performed.
- Identifying who will do a given task and making sure that it is done.

Controlling:

- Obtaining feedback on results.
- Following up to compare accomplishments with plans and making appropriate adjustments when outcomes deviate from expectations.

Management and leadership skills can be developed. Like any other skill, this development must occur in a series of stages for confidence to be gained. First, a conceptual or philosophical understanding must be reached, usually in the abstract, and then this conceptual understanding is applied. Finally, actual skills are developed and refined through conscious exercise and practice. An important difference between developing behavioral skills and physical skills is that, in the former, differences in personality require different approaches to achieve the same results. In other words, what may work for one individual may not work for another. So, in developing management strategies, it is important to remember that there is not a set pattern of behavior that will cure management problems or lead to effective management. Instead, there are ideas that different people must take and modify in the way that best suits them, their business situations, their own personalities, and the type of workers within the business.

What is management?

Management is a philosophy, an attitude toward a total business operation. Management is being in charge of your time use, your business, and your profits. Effective management does not provide any fail-safe rules or techniques. It does involve analyzing the techniques that work for others and using those that are most appropriate for you.

Management provides the needed focus for a business. It is the process of establishing goals and defining what must be done to achieve those targets. It recognizes how the different parts of a business contribute to these purposes. It is a framework for coordinating all of the different activities within the business to lead to two critical goals: survival and profitability.

Basically, defining management requires answering two questions: "What needs to be done?" and "Who will do it?" The first question can be described through a process of functional analysis; of looking at the business in terms of different activities that must be performed, both on a daily and a longer-term basis. The second question, "Who will do it?", leads to such issues as time planning, employment planning, delegation, management development, and of course, self-analysis. Here we will deal with the first question, "What needs to be done?", and then help you develop a methodology for implementation.

Functional analysis describes the different functions or activities within a business to make sure that all of the operations are performed completely. It is essential to determine all of the different functions that are required for your business to operate effectively, all the activities and specific tasks that must be accomplished for your business to function on a day-to-day basis. It is also important to identify the activities that must occur for your business to stay tuned to both internal and external changes and to respond to change in a creative and proactive manner.

Large corporations have many top-level officials who are assigned responsibility for different job functions within the organization. Looking at organizational charts for such corporations will show these areas of functional responsibility with the titles of the officials. Larger organizations typically have vice presidents of marketing, production, finance, personnel, planning, and various other relevant activities.

Smaller businesses are faced with exactly the same set of problems that larger firms must solve. While the problems may be relatively smaller, each functional area is still just as important to the total business operation. The special problem encountered in smaller firms, however, is that the business owner/managers generally cannot delegate the tasks of problem solving to others in the organization. Usually, these business operations are simply too small to be able to afford highly specialized staff experts. Since the owner/managers are unable to delegate these problems, they must solve them by themselves. This means that small business owner/managers must be able to control all of the separate and different areas represented in the large corporation's organizational chart.

Consequently, small business owner/managers must look at their businesses as being similar to larger organizations. Through this process, the different job functions can be placed in correct perspective. Through the functional organization represented by the organizational chart, a large corporation is able to place the correct emphasis on each of the problem areas within the company. A small firm must consciously perform this same division. However, it is a division that the owner/managers are making of their own time, attention, and skills, instead of delegating responsibility down through a complex support system.

One means of facilitating this planning, organizing, directing, and controlling is to establish profit-oriented goals or targets.

Profit-oriented goal setting

There is a five-step process for establishing profit-oriented goals. The steps are:

STEP 1: Establish profit goals.
STEP 2: Forecast expected sales and expense levels.
STEP 3: Compare the results of Step 2 with Step 1.
STEP 4: Reconcile differences revealed in Step 3.
STEP 5: Establish performance evaluation criteria.

STEP 1: Establish profit goals. A great many business owners do not have the faintest notion of what they should expect from their operations or of what is possible. Performing a methodical analysis of your personal and business needs and expectations will help to establish specific and rational targets. Essentially, the analysis has to do with what you expect from your business operation. There are basically three components to consider.

The first component is determining expected return on investment (ROI). You undoubtedly have invested your personal resources in the business operation. If this is the case, you should determine what kind of return you expect on these resources. The way to determine an appropriate yield is to compare the return possible if you were to take these same funds and invest them in other activities. Investment alternatives could include a bank (minimum risk), the stock market (medium risk), or somebody else's business (high risk).

The second profit component to consider is your own salary. After all, you are working for your business and there is probably an opportunity cost associated with that. The opportunity cost is the amount of money you would be able to earn if you were employed by someone else. You should ask yourself how much you could reasonably be paid for alternative employment.

The third part of the profitability issue to consider is risk. As with any other investment, a high-risk situation carries with it a premium or higher expected return. Certainly most small businesses carry high risk because the odds favor failure. If the risk is relatively high in your own situation, additional compensation should be included for that extra risk.

Once you have evaluated each of the profit components, you have three specific and quantifiable factors to use in determining an appropriate return from the operation. The result of this calculation becomes the profit objective. We asked Mr. Adams what his expectations were along these dimensions, and he said that he felt he could reasonably get 14 percent in safe outside investments, that he was worth probably $18,000 annually managing someone else's store, and that his operation, while relatively stable, was still "somewhat risky." This information can be organized using the following formula:

Profit objective = Salary + ROI + Risk factor
Salary = $18,000
ROI = 14% × Owner equity
Risk = 2% × Owner equity

Referring to his balance sheet for the owner equity value ($50,767), we can calculate his profit objective as follows:

$$Profit\ objective = \$18,000 + (.14 \times \$50,767)$$
$$+ (.02 \times \$50,767) = \$26,122$$

STEP 2: Forecast expected sales and expense levels.
There are a whole host of factors that come into play in developing legitimate forecasts for any business operation, and it is not our purpose here to present this methodology in detail. However, you should note that the key planning areas must be considered, including marketing and internal and external sales promotions, the position of the product or service relative to the market (whether it's at an introductory or a mature stage), market conditions themselves (in general and for your specific product or service), and of course, an assessment of what the competition is likely to do. By considering these factors, you will be able to develop at least a general understanding of how your business will probably behave.

For an established business, this process is greatly facilitated by an analysis of how the business has performed in the past. You then need to determine how the activities of the business in the future will differ from the past and how those differences will affect sales activity. You also need to consider how external forces will affect the business operation. Assessing the future is considerably more difficult for a brand-new business because this background of performance experience is not available.

A second part of forecasting is determining the expenses that will accompany the planned volume of sales. To do this you must differentiate between the fixed and variable costs, examine the capacity implications of the fixed costs, and analyze the variable costs, especially as they relate to volume. Again, if you have an established

business, this process may be facilitated by experience. The limitation of working with this experience base is that you may perceive yourself to be locked into given cost categories, which may or may not be true. In other words, just because you have experienced a given cost historically is not, in itself, a sufficient reason for you to necessarily continue to experience that cost in the future. For example, there may be a new machine available that would allow you to replace a variable cost, labor, with a fixed cost, that of the machine.

At this point, your analysis provides a good opportunity to take a functional view of the total operation. You can consider each activity as a separate component and evaluate the expenses that accompany that activity. This can help you to determine whether or not the activity and its related expenses are relevant to your overall operation. This is as much a thought process as an objective cost comparison, although there is cost data that can prove useful. For example, in most businesses, industry standards can be used as a comparison to historical performance or as the basis for forecasting costs for a totally new activity.

Back to Mr. Adams again for a forecasting example. Mr. Adams observed that his business has been experiencing a growth rate of between 6 and 12 percent per year for the last four years and that market conditions, while not good, have been stable throughout that time. He has also observed a counter-cyclical relationship between home handyman repair work and sales in the hardware industry. In other words, in times of an economic downturn, people are more prone to fix things themselves than they are to throw them away and buy replacements. This counter-cycle effect is beneficial to his business. Through his trade journals, he also has information available on trends within his industry and finds that his business is reasonably in line with industry growth. Further, he deflates his sales over the four-year period to remove the impact of inflation and observes that he is still showing an increase each year. Finally, he observes that the community is undergoing a steady rate of growth, so he expects to experience continued demand from his commercial business as well as his retail. Consequently, he is comfortable with forecasting a rate of growth of 6.0 percent per year.

Once Mr. Adams has projected a rate of sales growth he is comfortable with, he considers his expenses. He makes a careful analysis of the overall activities of his firm and considers whether he is likely to reduce his costs in any of his activities. Following this inspection, he then compares his operation to the industry standards. This comparative analysis is shown at the end of the chapter.

After Mr. Adams has completed his comparative analysis, he concludes that his expenses in the future will be similar to those in the past, except that he will have to add an additional sales clerk to deal with his increase in volume. He determines that his overall salary expense will increase by $12,000 if he adds this new employee. He now subtracts his total cost from his projected sales increase of 6 percent and finds a net profit after-tax figure of $9,438 ($26,160 increased sales − $12,000 increased wages = $8,160 increased pretax profit − $1,632 increased tax at 20% = $6,526 net income + $2,912 old net income = $9,438 new net income).

STEP 3: Compare the results of Step 2 with Step 1. This is a very simple and straightforward activity. It is merely a matter of comparing the expectations developed in Step 1 with the activities forecast in Step 2. For Mr. Adams, this was simple enough. In Step 1, he established a profit goal of $8,122 plus his salary, which is now $20,000 per year. In Step 2, he forecast a net profit of $9,438. Subtraction of Step 2 from Step 1 produces $1,316 excess. Therefore, he concludes that his plans are congruent with his goals and he can reasonably proceed.

STEP 4: Reconcile differences revealed in Step 3. We include this step because we expect that there will usually be differences between the targets established in Step 1 and the results anticipated in Step 2. This is a normal occurrence in virtually any planning activity. The problem is not that there are differences but what to do about them. Through Step 1, you have established what your expectations are in a rational and methodical manner. In Step 2 you have determined what the business is likely to yield if it proceeds as planned. Often, the results of Step 2 are inadequate to meet the expectations of Step 1.

The problem that emerges from the comparison is determining what changes could be made in the overall operation in order to narrow the differences or, even better, to eliminate them or to have the difference occur on the positive side. This analysis provides an opportunity to review the expectations and sets of assumptions that were made in the first two steps; to reevaluate their validity and determine where changes may be made. There are a series of options that may be available to the business at this point. These include increasing sales promotional activities, lowering prices and increasing volume, increasing prices and decreasing volume, broadening distribution, expanding markets (finding new uses and/or users for products), reducing overhead expenses, implementing better control systems, improving efficiency, finding better machines, redesigning products, adding new products, subcontracting work, bringing subcontracted work in-house, or any of many other alternatives. While evaluating this list may seem to be a hopeless task, we can actually quite easily consider the effects of these various decisions by playing the "What If" game with our computer program.

Mr. Adams, along with the rest of us, is interested in playing the "What If" game. He considers the possibility of increasing his sales promotional activity, thereby increasing his costs as well, and lowering his price, which he hopes will result in an increased volume. He considers this latter course of action to be particularly important as a response to a discount hardware operation that has recently opened in the same town. We advise him to be especially concerned with the impact of these decisions on his breakeven as well as his overall profitability.

STEP 5: Establish performance evaluation criteria. Once you have completed the analysis in Step 4, you will have established what appears to be a reasonable set of expectations for your business operation, balanced between what you would actually like to achieve and what you deem possible. You can now consolidate all of this information into a single forecast, which then becomes your budget. As soon as you have established your budget, you have the basis for controlling activities through your control system.

Control

Control is keeping the operation on the track to success. Control means being in charge of circumstances, at least to the greatest extent possible. This suggests, of course, that we know where we're going, and what we have to do to get there. This knowledge emerges from the planning process and is articulated in our plan. If the plan is not sufficiently specific to show what needs to be done in a given situation, it is simply not an adequate plan. Once plans are established, they can be communicated downward, along with the delegation of authority and responsibility, so that every employee will have a clear understanding of exactly what he or she should be doing and how activities contribute to the overall organizational action plan.

Planning is not a waste of time. It is a practical necessity. There are many benefits of organizational planning. First, all employees can understand what they are supposed to do. Second, ambiguities, redundancies, gaps, and overlaps in responsibilities are reduced or eliminated. Third, optimal use is made of organizational resources, reducing the need for internal competition. Finally, problems and opportunities are anticipated and contingency plans established accordingly, thus minimizing ineffective or even inappropriate decision making.

Once organizational planning has occurred, it provides a basis for organizational control. We have just described an outline for developing an organizational budget. The budget is the quantification of the organizational philosophy established earlier. Once we have established our budget, it becomes a target for our operations, and we can then compare our actual experience with our budget by way of budget deviation analysis.

Our computer can be a very valuable tool in the budget comparison process. The quantifiable budget data emerges in the form of both income (profit or loss) forecasts and cash flow projections. Together, these two statements become the traditional financial budget. Unfortunately, in many organizations this is the end of their usefulness. Projections are all too frequently seen as great planning tools but are then set aside in favor of other approaches in actually running the organization. However, once the time and money have been invested in the development of the budgets, they should be used to their full value.

To receive full benefit from the energy invested in this budgeting process, operating data must be compared to the budget and the differences between the two — the deviations — analyzed and evaluated. The process is called *budget deviation analysis* and is a process of comparing the operation's actual result, line by line, with the budget. We discuss it further in the next section. The budget is the plan of action. Comparing actual performance to the plan will show where the plan worked and where it did not. The important point is that when the budget was established, it made sense. We must now determine where reality deviated from the plan, the consequences of these deviations, and why they occurred. We must do this regularly. The recommended times are on a month-to-month and year-to-date basis.

There is a final step to this analytical/forecasting/budgeting process, which is also frequently ignored. It is the action implementation stage. More essential than a knowledge of analytic techniques is the willingness to use them and to make others within the organization treat them with the same respect. Knowing what should be done and how to do it are certainly prerequisites of success. They are, however, not sufficient. Also needed are the various organizational activities that will turn plans and ideas into reality and the management skill to keep them under control once they are established and under way.

Comparative analysis

In comparative analysis, we are interested in comparing our operation with other benchmarks. The two most commonly used reference points are prior periods of operation and the industry averages in general. Comparing our present operations with our prior years permits us to see changes that are occurring over time. Comparing our operation with the industry average shows us what we are doing that is similar to or different from the industry

standards. When our operation is different from the industry standards, particularly if our expense categories are higher, it means that we are probably going to make less money in the long run, thus indicating areas where further analysis could provide future savings. Another term, which is also sometimes used here for these comparative purposes, is *deviation analysis*. Deviation analysis, however, has a particular meaning; it specifically refers to a comparison between the present operating results and the budget for the same period. In any event, all of these comparisons are most appropriately made by evaluating expenses as percentages of sales. To calculate any percentage of sales, we divide that expense by the net sales. This gives us a common base for comparing different operating periods with significantly different sales levels, and it facilitates the comparison between different businesses within the same industry, which may have extremely different sales levels. The following analysis will call for the recalculation of all major expense categories as a percentage of sales.

Reload the DECISION Worksheet

Before continuing, start up Multiplan again and load the original version of the DECISION worksheet. Be sure that the values visible on your worksheet match those in the illustration on page 136.

If you are starting this chapter immediately after completing the last "What If" scenario, make sure that inventory (cell R38C2) and inventory purchases (cell R107C4) have been returned to their original values. Cell R38C2 should be equal to $83,292, and cell R107C4 should contain a value of $235,052. Recalculate the worksheet once to carry out any uncompleted calculations.

Entering the income statement ratios

Step One

Enter headings and ruled lines

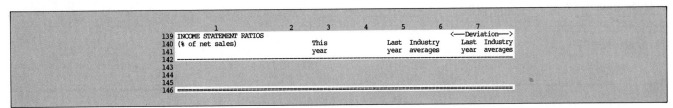

```
                     1          2      3       4       5      6        7
139  INCOME STATEMENT RATIOS                                    <——Deviation——>
140  (% of net sales)                This        Last  Industry   Last  Industry
141                                  year        year  averages   year  averages
142  ════════════════════════════════════════════════════════════════════════
143
144
145
146  ════════════════════════════════════════════════════════════════════════
```

ROWS 142 & 146 **Copy the single and double ruled lines** down from the balance sheet ratios section.

To enter
ruled lines to separate sections of the worksheet

  Select CF (for Copy From)
    Type **line2** (TAB)
    Type **R146C1** in the "to cells" field (RET)

  Select CF (for Copy From)
    Type **line1** (TAB)
    Type **R142C1** in the "to cells" field (RET)

....

COLUMN 1 **Enter a heading** to identify the income statement ratios. All three ratios are expressed as a percentage of net sales.

To enter
a label for this section of the worksheet

  Goto R139C1

  Select A (for Alpha)
    Type **INCOME STATEMENT RATIOS** (RET)

  Goto R140C1

  Select A (for Alpha)
    Type **(% of net sales)** (RET)

COLUMNS 2 and 4 **Enter headings** to identify the "this year" and "last year" columns. Since the same column headings were used in the financial statements, we can "recycle" them from rows 30 and 31.

To enter
labels for the column heads

  Goto R140C2

  Select CF (for Copy From)
    Type **R30C2:R31C4** in the "cells" field (RET)

....

COLUMN 5 **Label and name the "industry averages" column.** The formulas in this section will refer to this column by the name *industry*.

To enter
a label for column 5

  Select FC (for Format Cells)
    Type **R140:141C5** in the "cells" field (TAB)
    Type **R** (for Right) in the "alignment" field (RET)

  Goto R140C5

  Select A (for Alpha)
    Type **Industry** (↓)
    Type **averages** (RET)

  Select N (for Name)
    Type **industry** in the "define name" field (TAB)
    Type **R142:160C5** in the "to refer to" field (RET)

COLUMNS 6 and 7   **Enter headings** to identify the "deviation" columns. We can "cut and paste" with headings from elsewhere, using the COPY FROM command.

To enter
  a label for the deviation columns
    Goto R139C6

Select CF (for Copy From)
  Type **R5C6:7** in the "cells" field ⟨RET⟩

Goto R140C6

Select CF (for Copy From)
  Type **R140C4:R141C5** in the "cells" field ⟨RET⟩

Step Two

Set cell formats for screen display

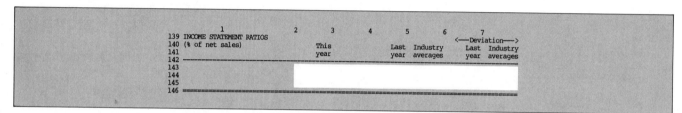

```
         1                    2      3       4       5       6          7
139 INCOME STATEMENT RATIOS                                    <---Deviation--->
140 (% of net sales)               This          Last Industry    Last Industry
141                                 year          year averages    year averages
142 -----------------------------------------------------------------------------
143
144
145
146 =============================================================================
```

ROWS 143–145   **Change display format** to show ratio figures to an accuracy of two decimal places.

To enter
  a command to format ratios

Select FC (for Format Cells)
  Type **R143C2:R145C7** in the "cells" field ⟨TAB⟩ ⟨TAB⟩
  Type **F** (for Fixed) in the "format code" field ⟨TAB⟩
  Type **2** in the "# of decimals" field ⟨RET⟩

Step Three

Enter labels and formulas for the ratios

```
           1                  2      3       4       5       6          7
139 INCOME STATEMENT RATIOS                                    <---Deviation--->
140 (% of net sales)                This          Last Industry    Last Industry
141                                 year          year averages    year averages
142 -----------------------------------------------------------------------------
143 Gross profit                   34.00
144 Profit (before taxes)           1.08
145 Profit (after taxes)            0.87
146 =============================================================================
```

ROW 143   **Gross profit,** shown as a percentage of sales, is a common means of evaluating direct operating activities and provides the common basis for comparison just noted.

To enter
  a label to identify this line of the worksheet as gross profit as a percentage of sales
  a formula in cell R143C2 that will divide gross profit by net sales

Goto R143C1

Select A (for Alpha)
Type **Gross profit** (→)
Type **=R13C2/R10C2%** (RET)

Result The value 34.00 should appear as the gross profit as a percentage of net sales figure (called *gross margin*).

· ·

R O W
144 **Profit before taxes** is shown as a percentage of sales. Net profit before and after taxes is another common percentage relationship used to describe "how well we are doing" and, again, facilitates comparative analysis.

To enter
a label to identify this line of the worksheet as profit before taxes as a percentage of net sales
a formula in cell R144C2 that will divide income before taxes by net sales

Goto R144C1

Select A (for Alpha)
Type **Profit (before taxes)** (→)
Type **=R23C2/R10C2%** (RET)

Result Profit before taxes as percentage of net sales should be 1.08.

· ·

R O W
145 **Profit after taxes** is also expressed as a percentage of net sales.

To enter
a label to identify this line as profit after taxes as a percentage of net sales
a formula in cell R145C2 that will divide net income by net sales

Goto R145C1

Select A (for Alpha)
Type **Profit (after taxes)** (→)
Type **=R26C2/R10C2%** (RET)

Result After-tax profit should display as 0.87.

Step Four

Enter data for last year and industry averages

	1	2	3	4	5	6	7	
							←—Deviation—→	
139	INCOME STATEMENT RATIOS				Last	Industry	Last	Industry
140	(% of net sales)		This		year	averages	year	averages
141			year					
142								
143	Gross profit		34.00		35.50	34.00		
144	Profit (before taxes)		1.08		2.34	3.00		
145	Profit (after taxes)		0.87		1.87	3.00		
146	==========							

C O L U M N
4 **Enter data** in the "last year" column, for comparison with current values.

To enter
values for "last year's" income statement ratios

Goto R143C4
Type **35.5** (↓)
Type **2.34** (↓)
Type **1.87** (RET)

C O L U M N
5 **Enter data** in the "industry" column, which will also provide a basis for comparison.

To enter
values for industry averages

Goto R143C5
Type **34** (↓)
Type **3** (↓)
Type **3** (RET)

Entering the income statement ratios Continued

Step Five

Enter formulas in the deviation columns

	1	2	3	4	5	6	7 Deviation	
							Last	Industry
139	INCOME STATEMENT RATIOS							
140	(% of net sales)		This		Last	Industry	Last	Industry
141			year		year	averages	year	averages
142								
143	Gross profit		34.00		35.50	34.00	-1.50	0.00
144	Profit (before taxes)		1.08		2.34	3.00	-1.26	-1.92
145	Profit (after taxes)		0.87		1.87	3.00	-1.00	-2.13
146								

COLUMN 6 **Enter formulas** to calculate the deviation between this year's and last year's ratios. This column will help us to spot trends. Positive trends should be reinforced, negative trends reversed.

To enter
formulas for the deviation column

Goto R143C6

Select V (for Value)
Type **thisyear-lastyear** (RET)

Select CD (for Copy Down)
Type **2** in the "number of cells" field (RET)

Recalculate the worksheet

Result Your worksheet should display figures identical to those in the illustration.

COLUMN 7 **Enter formulas** to calculate deviation from industry averages.

To enter
formulas for industry deviation

Goto R143C7

Select V (for Value)
Type **thisyear-industry** (RET)

Select CD (for Copy Down)
Type **2** in the "number of cells" field (RET)

Recalculate the worksheet

Result Your "deviation from industry averages" column should match the one in the illustration.

Entering the operating expense ratios

Enter headings and ruled lines

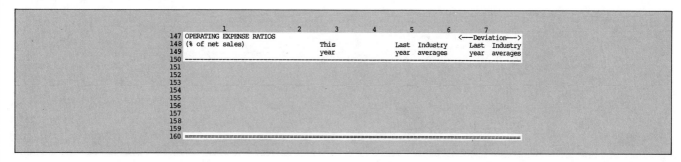

```
                    1           2     3     4     5     6         7
147 OPERATING EXPENSE RATIOS                              <----Deviation---->
148 (% of net sales)              This          Last  Industry    Last  Industry
149                               year          year  averages    year  averages
150 -----------------------------------------------------------------------------
151
152
153
154
155
156
157
158
159
160 =============================================================================
```

ROWS 150 & 160   **Copy the single and double ruled lines** down from the income statement ratios section.

To enter
   ruled lines to separate sections of the worksheet

     Select CF (for Copy From)
       Type **line1** (TAB)
       Type **R150C1** in the "to cells" field (RET)

     Select CF (for Copy From)
       Type **line2** (TAB)
       Type **R160C1** in the "to cells" field (RET)

· ·

ROW 147   **Operating expense ratios** show various line items on the income statement and worksheet as a percentage of net sales.

To enter
   a label to identify this as the operating expense ratios section of the worksheet

     Goto R147C1

     Select A (for Alpha)
       Type **OPERATING EXPENSE RATIOS** (RET)

     Goto R148C1

     Select CF (for Copy From)
       Type **R140C1** in the "cells" field (RET)

COLUMNS 2–7   **Enter headings** to identify the "this year," "last year," industry averages, deviation from last year, and deviation from industry averages columns. Since the same column headings were used in the previous section, we can copy them from rows 139–141.

To enter
   labels for columns 2–7

     Goto R147C2

     Select CF (for Copy From)
       Type **R139C2:R141C7** in the "cells" field (RET)

Step Two

Set cell formats for screen display

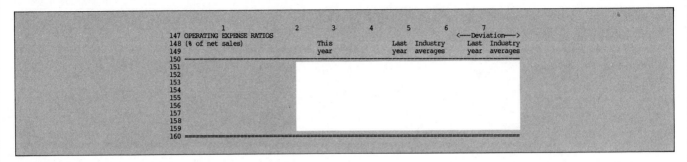

```
             1                  2    3        4    5        6       7
147 OPERATING EXPENSE RATIOS                               <———Deviation———>
148 (% of net sales)                This          Last Industry  Last Industry
149                                 year          year averages  year averages
150 ————————————————————————————————————————————————————————————————————————
151
152
153
154
155
156
157
158
159
160 ════════════════════════════════════════════════════════════════════════
```

ROWS 151–159 **Change the display format** to show ratio figures to an accuracy of two decimal places.

To enter
formats for rows 151–159

Select FC (for Format Cells)
 Type **R151C2:R159C7** in the "cells" field (TAB) (TAB)
 Type **F** (for Fixed) in the "format code" field (TAB)
 Type **2** in the " # of decimals" field (RET)

Step Three

Enter line item labels and formulas

```
             1                  2    3        4    5        6       7
147 OPERATING EXPENSE RATIOS                               <———Deviation———>
148 (% of net sales)                This          Last Industry  Last Industry
149                                 year          year averages  year averages
150 ————————————————————————————————————————————————————————————————————————
151 Officer salaries               5.95
152 Rent                           3.57
153 Utilities                      0.71
154 Insurance                      1.07
155 Interest                       1.79
156 Depreciation                   1.79
157 Advertising                    1.79
158 Employee wages                 8.93
159 Delivery                       0.54
160 ════════════════════════════════════════════════════════════════════════
```

ROW 151 **Officer salaries,** from the G&A expenses breakdown, are expressed as a percentage of net sales.

To enter
a label to identify this line as officer salaries as a percentage of net sales
a formula in cell R151C2 that will divide officer salaries by net sales

Goto R151C1

Select A (for Alpha)
 Type **Officer salaries** (→)
 Type **=R82C4/R10C2%** (RET)

Result The officer salaries figure should be 5.95.

ROW 152

Rent, from the G&A expenses breakdown, is expressed as a percentage of net sales.

To enter

a label to identify this line as rent as a percentage of net sales

a formula in cell R152C2 that will divide rent by net sales

Goto R152C1

Select A (for Alpha)
Type **Rent** $\rightarrow$
Type **=R81C4/R10C2%** (RET)

Result The value of this item should be 3.57.

. . . .

ROW 153

Utilities, from the G&A expenses breakdown, is expressed as a percentage of net sales.

To enter

a label to identify this line as utilities as a percentage of net sales

a formula in cell R153C2 that will divide utilities by net sales

Goto R153C1

Select A (for Alpha)
Type **Utilities** $\rightarrow$
Type **=R85C4/R10C2%** (RET)

Result The value of this item should be 0.71.

. . . .

ROW 154

Insurance, from the G&A expenses breakdown, is expressed as a percentage of net sales.

To enter

a label to identify this line as insurance as a percentage of net sales

a formula in cell R154C2 that will divide insurance by net sales

Goto R154C1

Select A (for Alpha)
Type **Insurance** $\rightarrow$
Type **=R84C4/R10C2%** (RET)

Result The value of this item should be 1.07.

. . . .

ROW 155

Interest, from the income statement, is expressed as a percentage of net sales.

To enter

a label to identify this line as interest as a percentage of net sales

a formula in cell R155C2 that will divide interest by net sales

Goto R155C1

Select A (for Alpha)
Type **Interest** $\rightarrow$
Type **=R20C2/R10C2%** (RET)

Result The value of this item should be 1.79.

. . . .

ROW 156

Depreciation, from the income statement, is expressed as a percentage of net sales.

To enter

a label to identify this line as depreciation as a percentage of net sales

a formula in cell R156C2 that will divide depreciation by net sales

Goto R156C1

Select A (for Alpha)
Type **Depreciation** $\rightarrow$
Type **=R17C2/R10C2%** (RET)

Result The value of this item should be 1.79.

. . . .

ROW 157

Advertising, from the selling expense breakdown, is expressed as a percentage of net sales.

To enter

a label to identify this line as advertising as a percentage of net sales

a formula in cell R157C2 that will divide advertising by net sales

Goto R157C1

Select A (for Alpha)
Type **Advertising** →
Type **=R97C4/R10C2%** RET

Result The value of this item should be 1.79.

....

ROW
158 Employee wages, from the selling expense breakdown, is expressed as a percentage of net sales.

To enter
a label to identify this line as employee wages as a percentage of net sales
a formula in cell R158C2 that will divide employee wages by net sales

Goto R158C1

Select A (for Alpha)
Type **Employee wages** →
Type **=R94C4/R10C2%** RET

Result The value of this item should be 8.93.

....

ROW
159 Delivery, from the selling expense breakdown, is expressed as a percentage of net sales.

To enter
a label to identify this line as delivery as a percentage of net sales
a formula in cell R159C2 that will divide delivery by net sales

Goto R159C1

Select A (for Alpha)
Type **Delivery** →
Type **=R95C4/R10C2%** RET

Result The value of this item should be 0.54.

Step Four

Enter data for last year and industry averages

	1	2	3	4	5	6	7	
							<—Deviation—>	
147	OPERATING EXPENSE RATIOS				Last	Industry	Last	Industry
148	(% of net sales)		This		year	averages	year	averages
149			year					
150								
151	Officer salaries		5.95		5.80	5.30		
152	Rent		3.57		3.20	2.70		
153	Utilities		0.71		1.00	1.00		
154	Insurance		1.07		1.00	0.80		
155	Interest		1.79		2.16	1.90		
156	Depreciation		1.79		1.76	1.00		
157	Advertising		1.79		2.10	0.90		
158	Employee wages		8.93		8.00	9.30		
159	Delivery		0.54		0.58	0.80		
160								

COLUMN
4 Enter data in the "last year" column, for comparison with current values.

To enter
values in column 4

Goto R151C4
Type **5.8** ↓
Type **3.2** ↓
Type **1** ↓

Type **1** ↓
Type **2.16** ↓
Type **1.76** ↓
Type **2.1** ↓
Type **8** ↓
Type **.58** RET

Enter data in the "industry averages" column. This will also provide a basis for comparison. Industry averages are very important benchmarks for just about any business. They represent the average operating relationships for similar firms that are successful. Differences or deviations from these norms are not necessarily bad, but they do call for analysis, examination, and justification to see if the differences are warranted and desired.

To enter

values in column 5

Goto R151C5

Type **5.3** ⊥

Type **2.7** ⊥

Type **1** ⊥

Type **.8** ⊥

Type **1.9** ⊥

Type **1** ⊥

Type **.9** ⊥

Type **9.3** ⊥

Type **.8** (RET)

Step Five

Enter formulas in the deviation columns

	1	2	3	4	5	6	7	
							<—Deviation—>	
147	OPERATING EXPENSE RATIOS							
148	(% of net sales)		This		Last	Industry	Last	Industry
149			year		year	averages	year	averages
150								
151	Officer salaries		5.95		5.80	5.30	0.15	0.65
152	Rent		3.57		3.20	2.70	0.37	0.87
153	Utilities		0.71		1.00	1.00	−0.29	−0.29
154	Insurance		1.07		1.00	0.80	0.07	0.27
155	Interest		1.79		2.16	1.90	−0.37	−0.11
156	Depreciation		1.79		1.76	1.00	0.03	0.79
157	Advertising		1.79		2.10	0.90	−0.31	0.89
158	Employee wages		8.93		8.00	9.30	0.93	−0.37
159	Delivery		0.54		0.58	0.80	−0.04	−0.26
160								

Deviation from last year is entered next. Once we have compared our operation to the industry, it is also of interest to see how we are doing from one operating period to the next. A comparison here will help us to spot trends. Positive trends should be reinforced, negative trends reversed. Both are important tools for management control as they help us to better understand "what is happening."

To enter

formulas to calculate the deviation between this year's and last year's ratios (We will use the same formula that we used in the income statement ratios section.)

Goto R151C6

Select CF (for Copy From)

Type **R145C6** in the "cells" field (RET)

Select CD (for Copy Down)

Type **8** in the "number of cells" field (RET)

Recalculate the worksheet

Result Your worksheet should display figures identical to those in the illustration.

· ·

Deviation from industry averages is entered next.

To enter

formulas to calculate deviation from industry averages (Again, the formula will be copied from the income statement ratios section.)

Goto **R151C7**

Select CF (for Copy From)
Type **R145C7** in the "cells" field (RET)

Select CD (for Copy Down)
Type **8** in the "number of cells" field (RET)

Recalculate the worksheet

Result Your deviation industry column should match the one in the illustration.

Step Six

Lock cells and save your work

Since you won't be directly entering any new data in the ratios section when we work through the next "What If" scenarios, you should use the LOCK CELLS command to protect the entire section from inadvertent change. This is a better choice than LOCK FORMULAS, since it affects the data entries in columns 2 and 3, not just the columns containing headings and formulas.

To enter
a command to lock your formulas and data

Select LC (for Lock Cells)
Type **R129C1:R160C7** in the "cells" field (TAB)
Type **L** (for Locked) in the "status" field (RET)

Result The entire ratios section should now be protected. Test it by going to any cell in this section and trying the ALPHA, BLANK, or EDIT commands.

Save your work. Again, it's advisable to save your work before you proceed.

Analysis of the ratios

The year-to-year internal deviation analysis, obtained by reviewing the income statement, balance sheet, and the various ratios, points out the following:

1 Net sales have increased 8 percent over the prior year (cell R10C7). In an industry where growth tends to be slow, this appears to be a healthy growth rate. However, if the inflation rate is 8 percent or higher, it means that the company is actually declining in sales when measured by constant dollars.

2 A bad sign is the 10-percent increase in the cost of goods sold (cell R12C7). This is 2 percent more than the sales increase, and the ever-important gross profit has increased only 3 percent (cell R13C7). Collectively, these figures suggest a pricing problem. If prices were reduced, net sales should have increased more than 8 percent. If prices were increased, the growth in sales should have been greater as well. Thus, the cost of goods has increased faster than sales. Accordingly, the entire cost/price relationship requires further probing.

3 The total reduction of 5 percent in G&A expense (cell R15C7) is a positive sign. However, the G&A as a percentage of sales should decrease with a sales increase because most of these expenses are fixed. The 15 percent of sales (cell R15C3) for this item seems to be high.

4 Selling expense increased $9,000, or 23 percent (cell R16C7). At the same time, sales increased only 8 percent. It suggests that the marketing mix is not producing the desired results. Selling expense, at worst, should only increase in proportion to sales.

5 The bottom line, net income, shows a 50-percent reduction (cell R26C7) on a sales increase of 8 percent. This is a bad trend. In the final analysis, this profit shows the need to obtain an improved return on equity. This year the return was only 7.61 percent after taxes (cell R136C2).

6 The creditors' investment, total liabilities, in the company was reduced from $1.69 to $1.55 for each dollar of owner's equity investment. To calculate these for each year, divide total liabilities on row 65 by total owner equity on row 71. This is slight progress.

The deviation analysis comparing Acme Hardware's performance with its industry shows the following:

1 The gross profit for Acme (cell R143C2) is the same as the industry (cell R143C4) at 34.0 percent. However, the net profit before taxes, 1.08 percent (cell R144C2), is significantly below industry average (3 percent) (cell R144C4).

2 The return on equity (before taxes) was only 7.61 percent for Acme, while industry averages in published surveys might show 17 percent. When combined with the previous item, this suggests a reasonable cost of goods and pricing balance, but the poor bottom line and the poor return on equity suggests that the costs after the gross profit are out of line with the sales level.

3 Viewing the operating expense ratios, officer salaries (row 151), rent (row 152), insurance (row 154), depreciation (row 156), and advertising (row 157), it is apparent that Acme has costs above industry averages. All the other items evaluated are smaller. All the items where industry expense data is available indicate that many Acme Hardware expense items are above industry averages. It suggests that these items are too high considering the volume of sales.

4 The average collection (accounts receivable collection) period, when using total net sales, is only 19 days (daily sales at $933.33 ($366,000 divided by 360) divided into accounts receivable at $17,777 equals 19 days) and appears to be very effective compared to industry averages in published surveys of 33 days. However, a probe of the computation suggests that the 19-day computation assumes all sales are for credit. Unfortunately, only 30 percent, or $100,000, are credit sales. This means that the real collection period is 63 to 64 days (cell R135C2). This is deplorable, because it ties up approximately $8,000 more than required for a collection period close to industry average. The final concern in this area is the collectibility of the accounts with this lengthy collection period.

5 The inventory turnover (cell R134C2) of 2.9 times is 20 percent better than industry averages as revealed in published industry surveys. This frees approximately $20,000 in cash compared to having an industry average turnover. In part, it is an offset for slow accounts receivable collection.

10 The cash flow game

Introduction

Cash management is a problem for almost any firm, large or small. The worst symptom of the problem is your business running out of cash. For most small firms, cash flow is more important than profits, particularly if the firms are new and growing. Analysis of small business successes and failures shows that the small company that focuses on cash flow rather than profit lasts longer and is actually more profitable in the long run. In addition to improving profits, cash flow analysis is particularly useful in helping to cope with seasonal fluctuation and in avoiding the cash crunches caused by rapid growth.

For financing purposes, cash flow analysis is more important than any other single form of financial management. Banks and other outside financing sources will almost always look for a cash flow analysis in preference to any other financial statement. Consequently, this is our final topic, not because it is the least important but because it is the most important. Further, it involves the use of tools and techniques described in earlier chapters.

We are calling the management of cash flow a game, not because it is fun or entertaining to play (although some do find a reward in the challenge) but because it is more of an art than a science. If it were a science, our solutions would be simple. We would show you how to program your computer so that you would always know the exact answer. Science falls short, however, because of the very subjective nature of many of the decisions that must be made. You have many variables at your disposal; the question is how to use them to the best advantage. Your answer should be subjective and based on your own good judgment once the computer has pointed out the real and immediate or the potential problem areas.

The heart of the cash flow game is cash management, and its secret is the effective control of the working capital accounts. This raises further questions:

- What is working capital?

- Where is cash in the business?

- Which cash categories or accounts do you in fact have control over?

The underlying question, of course, is:

- What is cash flow?

In answering these questions, we will describe an analytical process that will help you to understand your own business better. For many users, this approach provides a somewhat different view of their business than they have had before. The underlying objective is to make your business planning and management more profitable and enjoyable. The approach is simple and direct. The results, however, depend entirely upon your thoughtful appreciation.

What is cash flow?

Think in terms of cash, dollar bills flowing into and out of your business. Aside from operating profits (net income), there are a relatively limited number of sources of cash. The external or end-result sources of cash include new investments, new debt, and the sale of fixed assets. These external sources are the logical options that occur to people when they need additional cash in their business. Unfortunately, however, they tend to ignore the internal sources of cash, the other forms that cash takes in the business as it proceeds about its duties as working capital.

In order to understand the internal sources of cash and working capital, it is important to go back to the discussion on current assets and current liabilities. By definition, working capital is the difference between current assets and current liabilities. Thus, increases in current assets and/or decreases in current liabilities will increase working capital. The difference here, however, is that just the opposite will increase the available cash within the business. If you can't collect your receivables, then you probably can't pay your payables. The *contrasources* of cash are the uses of cash, the expenses found on your income statement. Spending less is just as important an option in improving cash flow as getting more revenue.

The external sources of cash are limited and can only be used infrequently, but the internal sources can be managed and controlled as part of an ongoing operations strategy. It is this management process that we are calling the cash flow game. We have been using cash flow statements in evaluating the effect of decision-making tools on the cash flow. Now it is time to go a step further and bring cash flow itself under control.

Why is cash flow so important? Simple — if the cash inflows exceed the cash outflows, the business can continue operations. On the other hand, if the cash outflows exceed cash inflows, the business runs out of cash and grinds to a halt. Even if the imbalance is only for a short period, it can still spell disaster. Cash management, controlling the cash flow, is vital to businesses of all sizes. Smaller businesses are especially vulnerable to cash flow problems as they tend to operate with inadequate or no cash reserves and, worse, often miss the implications of a negative cash flow until it is too late.

Timing and cash flow are inseparable companions. Payments to your suppliers are often expected before your customers pay you for the goods you have produced. As a result, you can often have a negative cash flow when your business grows dramatically. Periods of change are always reflected in an altered cash flow: If sales fall off, the cash flow slows down; if sales increase, cash flow may increase but could stop completely or even become negative, particularly if you produce goods that you supply to your customers on credit terms. Seasonal fluctuations in your business may pose cash flow problems as well. It is also possible that you could be faced with a one-time event, such as a population shift or new competition, which could cause a disruption in your business operation and a negative cash flow. Whatever the cause, the underlying message is simple: If you run out of cash, you are in trouble. Even if you can locate additional funds to plug the deficit, sooner or later you must match the timing of cash inflows with outflows if you want to remain in operation.

How do you get your cash flow under control? It's not easy. Some businesses never achieve cash flow control. These businesses are always in trouble. They are chronically overdue on bills, often overdrawn at the bank, and eventually fold. They fold, though, only after their owners have spent a great deal of time worrying and have probably exhausted their personal resources trying to cover the operating deficits. Rather than worry, plan and schedule so that the cash flow for your business is positive.

Where is your cash?

The first step in playing the cash flow game is to identify all of the possible sources of cash for your business. As noted earlier, there are both external and internal sources of cash. External sources are the easiest to identify and so tend to be the sources that are most often used and abused. New investment is a limited option; there is only so much of your business that you can sell to others and still have enough to maintain the level of control that is necessary for your own purposes and satisfaction. Long-term debt is a means of leveraging your business's ability to make payments over time. Too high a reliance on this source of cash, however, and your business will not be able to meet its debt service obligations. Short-term debt, if inappropriately used for longer-term purposes, generally cannot be repaid in the time available. Further, short-term debt, unless managed properly, may only help create a flurry of activity for the business without leaving any residual benefit. In fact, in times of high interest costs, it may well be possible that short-term debt carries a price far beyond its benefits.

The sale of fixed assets is certainly a limited option. They can only be sold once. If they are clearly not needed to support business activity, fine. However, if they continue to remain useful to the organization, their sale may well compromise the business's ability to perform, and so such a sale would represent a problem rather than a cure.

Operating profits could also be called an external source of cash. They are to the extent that net profit and cash balances are equal. Unfortunately, this is all too often not the case. In fact, if you use an accrual-accounting system, much of operating profits may well reside in accounts receivable and so represent a use of cash rather than a source. A further limitation on operating profits as a source of funds is the owner's inclination to leave them in the business. If the owner withdraws these profits as dividends or salary, then clearly they are not available as a source of funds at all.

Once these major external and/or end-result sources of cash flow have been considered, and they usually are the first to be given attention in a crisis, you can look inside the business operation for other sources. It has often been said there are two basic ways of getting more cash into a business. One is to sell more goods, and the other is to spend less. Therefore, the first thing to consider is the possibility of increasing sales. We've discussed this in Chapter 6, so we will not repeat ourselves here. The second thing to consider, then, is the other side of the equation, spending less. There may be expenses that can be reduced without impairing the operating ability of the firm. There are two ways to determine this: using a *zero-based budgeting approach* or using a *comparative analysis approach*.

In the zero-based budgeting approach, every expense category would be considered without regard to its historical performance. Zero-based budgeting provides us with an opportunity to completely reevaluate our spending patterns on a regular basis without being biased by what we have grown accustomed to. The trouble with historically based budgeting is that we become comfortable with a given level of expenditures and do not force ourselves to evaluate carefully the real necessity of these expenditures. This is not to suggest that we should ignore historical analysis, one of our more useful tools. Rather, we must be careful not to be blindly guided by events in the past without a continual serious reevaluation as to their appropriateness.

Comparative analysis means comparing your operation with similar businesses by the use of industry standards. The approach may show you areas where your spending differs significantly from other firms in your industry. If your costs are higher, ask yourself if this higher cost is really necessary for your business. If not, it may represent an opportunity for savings. Our computer can certainly help us in the evaluation process, both by performing historical analysis and by helping us to quickly compare ourselves with industry standards.

The limitation of using the income statement as the exclusive means of identifying the potential sources of cash is that while the statement reports on the amounts of revenues and costs, it does not show their timing. The problem is that timing is an additional dimension of both revenue and expense that can dramatically change the impact of a given category on the cash position of the firm. For example, let's say your rent expense doubles. While this would suggest an increase of the use of cash, let us assume that for some reasons better known to you, you don't pay it. The benefit, of course, is that you have more cash rather than less at the end of the operating period.

What has happened, and where we can trace the impact of this decision of yours not to pay that particular expense, is that the balance sheet liability account, rent payable, increased. This simple example leads us to the useful observation that an increase in liability accounts acts as a source of cash. This also leads us to one of the most popular sources of working capital for those firms fortunate enough to have access to it. This is known as *leaning on the trade*, which means delaying payment to trade suppliers. The process starts by your developing a credit relationship with trade suppliers and, after the relationship is secure, stretching out your payments. (Of course, this is a delicate balance to maintain — abuse this goodwill too much and you may be cut off altogether.) Particularly in times of high interest rates, leaning on the trade has become increasingly popular, not only because it is a readily available source of cash but because it is interest-free in most cases as well.

Another expense category that belies its impact on the business operation is cost of goods sold. Inventories are by implication represented in this cost category. It is generally assumed in accrual accounting that when an item is sold, it is replaced on the shelf. This is not necessarily true. We can sell the goods that we have in the business, and *if* we choose not to replace them, we will have the funds that their sale generated to use for other purposes. Thus, we can see that a decrease in an asset account can also act as a source of funds.

Now we can move from using the income statement for expense control over to the balance sheet and begin to consider which of the asset and liability accounts we actually have the ability to change and, when we do, the effect of this change on our total operation. Our computer can be a particularly valuable tool here because it allows us to play the "What If" game. What if, for example, we shorten our accounts receivable period? Let's look at a specific example: Mr. Adams decides that his accounts receivable, while they have not changed much

in recent years, are still somewhat older (higher) than the industry averages. He decides to institute a program to shorten the life of these receivables. How is he going to do this? He can call his customers up and tell them he would like to have them pay him sooner. Of course, they may not be particularly interested in doing so, since his accounts receivable are their accounts payable. They also know that if they don't pay their accounts payable any sooner than they have to, this represents a source of funds for their own business operations. Consequently, Mr. Adams may decide that he can provide his customers with an additional incentive if they will pay their accounts sooner than they have in the past, so he offers them a quick-pay discount of 2 percent if they pay their account within fifteen days (2/15, N/30), figuring that this will speed up the flow of funds into his business. We inspect the actual impact of this change of the business operation in the "What If" section at the end of this chapter.

As we mentioned earlier, another account where we may have some flexibility is inventory. Inventory clearly uses a significant amount of capital in any business. For many smaller businesses, it represents the major asset investment. If we were able to reduce our inventory investment, we would certainly have more cash available for other purposes. The question here, however, is whether reducing the investment in our inventory is a wise decision. In order to make this decision, we would have to reconsider the impact of varying inventory levels, discussed earlier. Reducing our investment in inventory is clearly going to have a benefit as far as our cash balance is concerned. However, there are some important downside risks that are associated with this reduction. Possible dangers are stockouts and a higher cost of goods. The latter will occur as our order quantities become smaller than our suppliers' economic shipment quantities and/or as we order more frequently and through more expensive channels. Consequently, we would have additional costs in order preparation and transportation that we might not otherwise incur, so a higher cost of goods results.

Depreciation is the last important item that we must include in this discussion of the cash flow game. It has often been said that depreciation is a source of funds. In fact, a banker looking at an income statement will immediately add back depreciation as a quick means of testing the fund flow within the operation. What does this mean? How is depreciation a source of funds? It doesn't actually add any cash to the business, but it does have two effects. First, when a banker adds back depreciation to see the flow of funds, he is acknowledging the difference between the income statement and the cash flow. Depreciation is a noncash expense and therefore, even though it reduced net profits, it did not use up cash. Consequently, it is appropriate to add it back to see the true cash result.

The second way in which depreciation is a source of funds is through its after-tax effect. Of course, to have an after-tax effect, you must have a profitable operation. Assuming a corporate tax rate of 50 percent (close enough for our purposes here), one dollar in expense is equal to fifty cents saved after tax because the expense reduces the tax liability by that amount. It is through this latter means that depreciation becomes a tax shelter. By using the maximum accelerated rate of depreciation permitted under the IRS code, it is sometimes possible to create a substantial paper loss when, in fact, the actual operation is profitable. The benefit of the tax shelter comes into play as this substantial loss is passed through to the stockholders, normally through the use of the subchapter S corporation. Of course, in a hardware business, as in many other small retail operations, depreciation is not a very large expense and therefore not a very significant consideration. If you think some of these ideas may be appropriate for your business, it would be wise to discuss them in detail with your tax lawyer and accountant.

The conclusion of the cash flow game rests in your hands. We have given you some tools. We hope you understand how the computer can help you make decisions in selecting alternatives, and that you have the confidence to begin experimenting with the use of these tools on your own. We will now show you the impact of some of these choices on Mr. Adams's business.

What is the aggregate effect of the changes discussed earlier on the total business operation? First, let's consider the impact of the quick-pay discount. We assumed that Mr. Adams would change his terms from N/30 to 2/15, N/30. However, probably not all customers will take advantage of the quick-pay discount, so let's assume that half his customers do take advantage of the quick-pay discount and the other half pay in the normal thirty-day period. This will give us an average age of receivables of twenty-two days.

As we will see, clearly cash flow has improved. But what is the cost of this improvement? To determine this, we will have to look at the effect of the 2-percent quick-pay discount on the overall profitability of the operation in "What If" 12.

To inspect the other side of this quick-pay equation, let's say that one of Mr. Adams's suppliers offers him an opportunity to take a quick-pay discount of 2/10, N/30. What might be the effect on Mr. Adams's business? Mr. Adams elects to take the discount, pays the bill in ten days rather than thirty days, and shortens the average life of his payables. Unfortunately, he uses up his precious cash in the process. Consequently, the cash balances deteriorate; but profitability improves because Mr. Adams

has also reduced his cost of goods sold by the amount of the quick-pay discount that he is taking.

To determine whether the quick-pay discount program has been a wise choice for Mr. Adams, we would have to consider the cost of alternative sources of cash. Perhaps he has an opportunity to borrow an equivalent amount of funds (a short-term debt) for a similar period of time. To evaluate this choice, he would have to compare the actual cost of borrowing these funds with the cost of the quick-pay discount he has taken. Similarly, if he were evaluating the desirability of instituting his own discount to encourage his customers to pay their accounts more quickly, he would have to consider the cost of this program against the cost of other sources of credit (if any) that may be available to him. The reality, of course, for many small businesses is that there are no alternative sources of credit, so this exercise becomes worse than academic. It is irrelevant, and even discouraging.

Now we will proceed with these cash flow "What Ifs" and look more closely at the results of Mr. Adams's options in reducing his accounts payable and speeding the return on his accounts receivable. If you have turned off the computer, you will need to reload the example (see page 49).

Exploring "What Ifs"

WHAT IF 11 **Materials purchased are paid for in 10 days instead of 30 days in order to obtain a 2 percent purchase discount.** The operations management chapter indicated that the net income for Acme this year is unsatisfactory. Mr. Adams thinks that borrowing money in sufficient amounts to reduce his payables and obtain a 2-percent discount on Acme purchases might improve both profits and cash flow.

To see the results of the proposed action, the steps are:

1 Calculate the accounts payable level for paying materials invoices in ten days. (Assume purchases are made equally over 360 days a year.)

Daily purchases of materials

$$= \frac{\text{Annual inventory purchases}}{360} = \frac{\$235,052}{360} = \$653$$

Accounts payable for payment in 10 days

$$= \text{Annual daily purchases} \times 10 \text{ days}$$

$$= \$653 \times 10 = \$6,530$$

(Annual inventory purchases comes from cell R107C4.)

2 Calculate the increased payment necessary to reduce accounts payable to 10 days. (Assume all accounts payable are for materials purchased.)

Old accounts payable level	$18,480
New accounts payable level	6,530
Increased payment	$11,950

In other words, Acme will have to pay an additional $11,950 in accounts payable in order to reduce the annual level on the balance sheet to $6,530. (Accounts payable level comes from cell R57C2.)

3 Estimate the added interest cost of borrowing funds to reduce accounts payable (assume 12 percent interest).

Extra cash required × interest rate =

$$\$11,950 \times 12\% = \$1,434$$

(This amount will be added to the original interest expense in cell R20C2.)

4 Compute the effect of obtaining a 2-percent discount on all purchases.

Purchases × percent discount =

$$\$235,052 \times .02 = \$4,701$$

(This discount is recorded in cell R108C4.)

5 Estimate the approximate impact on the income statement.

		Amount	%
Net sales		$336,000	100.0
Old cost of goods sold	$221,760		
Less purchase discounts	4,701		
New cost of goods sold		217,059	64.6
Gross profit		118,941	35.4
General & admin. exp.	49,600		
Selling expense	49,000		
Depreciation	6,000	104,600	
Operating income		14,341	
Old interest	6,000		
Added interest—1st year	1,434		
New interest		7,434	
Income before taxes		6,907	
Taxes		1,381	
Net income		$5,526	

6 Estimate the impact on cash flow.

Old net income	$2,912
New net income	5,526
Net increase (decrease) in cash from income	2,614

To restore
the worksheet

Goto **R38C2** and type **83292** (RET)
    R107C4 and type **235052** (RET)

To enter
changes in interest expense, accounts payable, long-term debt, and inventory purchase discounts

Goto **R20C2** and type **7434** (RET)
    R57C2 and type **6530** (RET)
    R64C2 and type **56060** (RET)
    R108C2 and type **2** (RET)

Recalculate the worksheet

Result On the income statement, cost of goods sold (cell R12C2) decreases by $4,701 to $217,059 because of the $4,701 obtained in purchase discounts (cell

	1	2	3	4	5	6	7
1	DECISION worksheet						
2							
3	INCOME STATEMENT: January 1 through December 31, 19..						
4	========						
5		This	% net	Last	% net	<----Deviation---->	
6		year	sales	year	sales	$	%
7							
8	Gross sales	336,000	100	312,000	100	24,000	8
9	Sales discounts	0	0	0	0	0	
10	Net sales	336,000	100	312,000	100	24,000	8
11							
12	Cost of goods sold	217,059	65	201,240	65	15,819	8
13	Gross profit	118,941	35	110,760	36	8,181	7
14							
15	General & administrative	49,600	15	52,000	17	-2,400	-5
16	Selling expenses	49,000	15	40,000	13	9,000	23
17	Depreciation	6,000	2	5,500	2	500	9
18							
19	Operating income	14,341	4	13,260	4	1,081	8
20	Interest expense	7,434	2	6,750	2	684	10
21	Other income/expense	0	0	-800	-0	800	-100
22							
23	Income before taxes	6,907	2	7,310	2	-403	-6
24	Taxes	1,381	0	1,462	0	-81	-6
25							
26	NET INCOME	5,526	2	5,848	2	-322	-6
27	========						
28	BALANCE SHEET: December 31, 19..						
29	========						
30		This		Last			
31		year		year			
32							
33	ASSETS:						
34							
35	<Current assets>						
36	Cash	3,949		4,750			
37	Accounts receivable	17,777		16,000			
38	Inventory	83,292		70,000			
39	Prepaid expenses	3,400		3,400			
40							
41	Total current assets	108,418		94,150			
42							
43	<Fixed assets>						
44	Buildings & equipment	33,000		38,950			
45	Less accumulated depreciation	-13,000		-7,000			
46	Land	0		0			
47							
48	Total fixed assets	20,000		31,950			
49							
50	Other assets	3,700		2,545			
51							
52	TOTAL ASSETS	132,118		128,645			
53							
54	LIABILITIES:						
55							
56	<Current liabilities>						
57	Accounts payable	6,530		17,000			
58	Accrued wages & taxes	6,357		6,000			
59	Notes payable (current)	3,890		3,890			
60	Other current liabilities	5,900		5,900			
61							
62	Total current liabilities	22,677		32,790			
63							
64	Long-term debt	56,060		48,000			
65							
66	Total liabilities	78,737		80,790			
67							
68	<Owner equity>						
69	Common stock	37,000		37,000			
70	Retained earnings	16,381		10,855			
71							
72	Total owner equity	53,381		47,855			
73							
74	TOTAL LIABILITIES & EQUITY	132,118		128,645			
75	========						

	1	2	3	4	5	6	7
77	Analysis section						
78	========						
79	G&A EXPENSE BREAKDOWN		Fixed	Variable	Total		
80	========						
81	Rent		12,000	0	12,000		
82	Officer salaries		20,000	0	20,000		
83	Clerical expenses		4,000	1,000	5,000		
84	Insurance		3,600	0	3,600		
85	Utilities		2,000	400	2,400		
86	Office supplies		800	400	1,200		
87	Legal & accounting		3,000	0	3,000		
88	Miscellaneous		1,200	1,200	2,400		
89							
90	Total G&A expenses		46,600	3,000	49,600		
91							
92	SELLING EXPENSE BREAKDOWN		Fixed	Variable	Total		
93	========						
94	Wages		20,000	10,000	30,000		
95	Delivery		0	1,800	1,800		
96	Operating supplies		4,000	800	4,800		
97	Advertising		4,000	2,000	6,000		
98	Travel & entertainment		800	400	1,200		
99	Miscellaneous		800	400	1,200		
100	Credit card		0	4,000	4,000		
101							
102	Total selling expenses		29,600	19,400	49,000		
103	========						
104	COST OF GOODS SOLD ANALYSIS						
105	========						
106	Beginning inventory				70,000		
107	Inventory purchases				235,052		
108	Less purchase discounts of		2	percent	-4,701		
109	Total goods available				300,351		
110	Less ending inventory				83,292		
111							
112	Cost of goods sold				217,059		
113	========						
114	BREAKEVEN ANALYSIS						
115	========						
116	Sales revenue needed to break even				311,961		
117							
118	Sales revenue needed to cover cash expenses				291,079		
119							
120	Sales revenue needed to cover cash expenses				304,617		
121	and debt service						
122	========						
123	CASH FLOW ANALYSIS						
124	========						
125	Net cash throwoff from the income statement				11,526		
126	========						
127							
128							
129	Ratios section						
130	========						
131	BALANCE SHEET RATIOS		This				
132			year				
133	========						
134	Inventory turnover		2.83 times				
135	Average collection period		63.49 days				
136	Return on equity		14.43 percent				
137	Accts. payable payment period		10.00 days				
138	========						
139	INCOME STATEMENT RATIOS					<----Deviation---->	
140	(% of net sales)		This		Last	Industry	Last	Industry
141			year		year	averages	year	averages
142	========						
143	Gross profit		35.40		35.50	34.00	-0.10	1.40
144	Profit (before taxes)		2.06		2.34	3.00	-0.28	-0.94
145	Profit (after taxes)		1.64		1.87	3.00	-0.23	-1.36
146	========						
147	OPERATING EXPENSE RATIOS					<----Deviation---->	
148	(% of net sales)		This		Last	Industry	Last	Industry
149			year		year	averages	year	averages
150	========						
151	Officer salaries		5.95		5.80	5.30	0.15	0.65
152	Rent		3.57		3.20	2.70	0.37	0.87
153	Utilities		0.71		1.00	1.00	-0.29	-0.29
154	Insurance		1.07		1.00	0.80	0.07	0.27
155	Interest		2.21		2.16	1.90	0.05	0.31
156	Depreciation		1.79		1.76	1.00	0.03	0.79
157	Advertising		1.79		2.10	0.90	-0.31	0.89
158	Employee wages		8.93		8.00	9.30	0.93	-0.37
159	Delivery		0.54		0.58	0.80	-0.04	-0.26
160	========						

Exploring "What Ifs" Continued

R108C4). This directly increases the gross profit by $4,701 to $118,941 (cell R13C2). Because interest expense has increased by $1,434 ($7,434 in cell R20C2) and taxes have increased by $653 ($1,381 in cell R24C2), the net income only increases by $2,614 ($4,701 − $1,434 − $653 = $2,614). Net income totals $5,526 in cell R26C2.

On the balance sheet, cash increases by the same amount as net income to $3,949 ($1,335 + $2,614 in cell R36C2). In order to reduce accounts payable (cell R57C2) by $11,950, a loan for the same amount increases the long-term debt to $56,060 in cell R64C2.

ANALYSIS The results of this change in payment of accounts payable are:

1 Faster payment of accounts payable will require $11,950 in cash.

2 Borrowing this amount would mean an annual increase in interest of $1,434.

3 Purchase discounts would decrease cost of goods sold by $4,701. This in turn would improve the gross profit margin to 35.4 percent. This would be 1.4 percent above industry.

4 The revised net income after tax is $5,526 or a 90-percent increase over the old $2,912 income. This improves the return on equity after tax by 90 percent to a more respectable 14.43 percent (previously 7.61 percent, in cell R136C2).

5 Cash is seen to increase $2,614 as a result of this program. Remember that $11,950 was borrowed to make the extra payment to obtain the discount.

Overall, taking advantage of the 2-percent purchase discount for a 10-day payment appears to be a desirable program. This is true even though it may require borrowing additional funds.

WHAT IF 12 **The accounts receivable collection period is reduced by offering a 2-percent discount for payment in 15 days (2/15 net 30).** Assume credit sales equal 30 percent of sales and 50 percent of credit sales will take advantage of the discount. These customers now pay in 15 days, while the remainder pay in an average of 84 days. Funds collected will be used to pay long-term debt. The steps in this process are:

1 Calculate the original accounts receivable collection period. Accounts receivable are in cell R37C2 on the original worksheet. Credit sales equal gross sales (cell R8C2) times the assumed percent.

$$\frac{\text{Accounts receivable}}{\text{Credit sales/360 days}} = \frac{\$17,777}{\$336,000 \times .30/360}$$

$$= \frac{\$17,777}{\$100,800/360} = \frac{\$17,777}{280}$$

$$= 63 \text{ day A/R collection period}$$

2 Calculate the cost of discounts with 50 percent of credit sales being paid in 15 days.

$$\begin{array}{c}\text{Credit} \\ \text{sales}\end{array} \times \begin{array}{c}\text{percent} \\ \text{taking discount}\end{array} \times \begin{array}{c}\text{percent} \\ \text{discount}\end{array}$$

$$= \$100,800 \times .50 \times .02 = \$1,008$$

3 Estimate the extra cash available due to accelerated credit payments by 50 percent of credit sales. (Assume 50 percent of customers take advantage of the discount and pay in 15 days; the remaining 50 percent of customers pay in 84 days.)

Breakdown of former daily credit sales (credit sales/360 days = $100,800/360 = $280):

50 percent who now pay in 15 days	$140.00
50 percent who now pay in 84 days	140.00
Total	$280.00

Revised accounts receivable balance:

A/R for credit customers

taking discount = $140 × 15 days = $2,100

A/R for credit customers

not taking discount = $140 × 84 days = $11,760

Revised A/R balance $13,860

(Note: Because the computer uses six decimal places in its computations, we will actually enter $13,857 as the A/R balance from now on.)

New A/R collection period:

$$\frac{\$13,857}{280} = 49.5 \text{ days}$$

Left panel

	1	2	3	4	5	6	7
1	DECISION worksheet						
2							
3	INCOME STATEMENT: January 1 through December 31, 19..						
4	===						
5		This	% net	Last	% net	<----Deviation---->	
6		year	sales	year	sales	$	%
7	---						
8	Gross sales	336,000	100	312,000	100	24,000	8
9	Sales discounts	1,008	0	0	0	1,008	
10	Net sales	334,992	100	312,000	100	22,992	7
11	---						
12	Cost of goods sold	221,760	66	201,240	65	20,520	10
13	Gross profit	113,232	34	110,760	36	2,472	2
14	---						
15	General & administrative	49,600	15	52,000	17	-2,400	-5
16	Selling expenses	49,000	15	40,000	13	9,000	23
17	Depreciation	6,000	2	5,500	2	500	9
18	---						
19	Operating income	8,632	3	13,260	4	-4,628	-35
20	Interest expense	5,530	2	6,750	2	-1,220	-18
21	Other income/expense	0	0	-800	-0	800	-100
22	---						
23	Income before taxes	3,102	1	7,310	2	-4,208	-58
24	Taxes	620	0	1,462	0	-842	-58
25	===						
26	NET INCOME	2,482	1	5,848	2	-3,366	-58
27	===						
28	BALANCE SHEET: December 31, 19..						
29	===						
30		This		Last			
31		year		year			
32	---						
33	ASSETS:						
34	---						
35	<Current assets>						
36	Cash	905		4,750			
37	Accounts receivable	13,857		16,000			
38	Inventory	83,292		70,000			
39	Prepaid expenses	3,400		3,400			
40	---						
41	Total current assets	101,454		94,150			
42	---						
43	<Fixed assets>						
44	Buildings & equipment	33,000		38,950			
45	Less accumulated depreciation	-13,000		-7,000			
46	Land	0		0			
47	---						
48	Total fixed assets	20,000		31,950			
49	---						
50	Other assets	3,700		2,545			
51	===						
52	TOTAL ASSETS	125,154		128,645			
53	===						
54	LIABILITIES:						
55	---						
56	<Current liabilities>						
57	Accounts payable	18,480		17,000			
58	Accrued wages & taxes	6,357		6,000			
59	Notes payable (current)	3,890		3,890			
60	Other current liabilities	5,900		5,900			
61	---						
62	Total current liabilities	34,627		32,790			
63	---						
64	Long-term debt	40,190		48,000			
65	---						
66	Total liabilities	74,817		80,790			
67	---						
68	<Owner equity>						
69	Common stock	37,000		37,000			
70	Retained earnings	13,337		10,855			
71	---						
72	Total owner equity	50,337		47,855			
73	---						
74	TOTAL LIABILITIES & EQUITY	125,154		128,645			
75	===						

Right panel

	1	2	3	4	5	6	7
77	Analysis section						
78	===						
79	G&A EXPENSE BREAKDOWN	Fixed	Variable	Total			
80	---						
81	Rent	12,000	0	12,000			
82	Officer salaries	20,000	0	20,000			
83	Clerical expenses	4,000	1,000	5,000			
84	Insurance	3,600	0	3,600			
85	Utilities	2,000	400	2,400			
86	Office supplies	800	400	1,200			
87	Legal & accounting	3,000	0	3,000			
88	Miscellaneous	1,200	1,200	2,400			
89	---						
90	Total G&A expenses	46,600	3,000	49,600			
91	===						
92	SELLING EXPENSE BREAKDOWN	Fixed	Variable	Total			
93	---						
94	Wages	20,000	10,000	30,000			
95	Delivery	0	1,800	1,800			
96	Operating supplies	4,000	800	4,800			
97	Advertising	4,000	2,000	6,000			
98	Travel & entertainment	800	400	1,200			
99	Miscellaneous	800	400	1,200			
100	Credit card	0	4,000	4,000			
101	---						
102	Total selling expenses	29,600	19,400	49,000			
103	===						
104	COST OF GOODS SOLD ANALYSIS						
105	---						
106	Beginning inventory			70,000			
107	Inventory purchases			235,052			
108	Less purchase discounts of	0 percent		0			
109	Total goods available			305,052			
110	Less ending inventory			83,292			
111	---						
112	Cost of goods sold			221,760			
113	===						
114	BREAKEVEN ANALYSIS						
115	---						
116	Sales revenue needed to break even			323,552			
117							
118	Sales revenue needed to cover cash expenses			301,423			
119							
120	Sales revenue needed to cover cash expenses			315,770			
121	and debt service						
122	===						
123	CASH FLOW ANALYSIS						
124	---						
125	Net cash throwoff from the income statement			8,482			
126	===						
127							
128							
129	Ratios section						
130	===						
131	BALANCE SHEET RATIOS	This					
132		year					
133	---						
134	Inventory turnover	2.89 times					
135	Average collection period	49.64 days					
136	Return on equity	6.48 percent					
137	Accts. payable payment period	28.30 days					
138	===						
139	INCOME STATEMENT RATIOS					<----Deviation---->	
140	(% of net sales)	This		Last	Industry	Last	Industry
141		year		year	averages	year	averages
142	---						
143	Gross profit	33.80		35.50	34.00	-1.70	-0.20
144	Profit (before taxes)	0.93		2.34	3.00	-1.41	-2.07
145	Profit (after taxes)	0.74		1.87	3.00	-1.13	-2.26
146	---						
147	OPERATING EXPENSE RATIOS					<----Deviation---->	
148	(% of net sales)	This		Last	Industry	Last	Industry
149		year		year	averages	year	averages
150	---						
151	Officer salaries	5.97		5.80	5.30	0.17	0.67
152	Rent	3.58		3.20	2.70	0.38	0.88
153	Utilities	0.72		1.00	1.00	-0.28	-0.28
154	Insurance	1.07		1.00	0.80	0.07	0.27
155	Interest	1.65		2.16	1.90	-0.51	-0.25
156	Depreciation	1.79		1.76	1.00	0.03	0.79
157	Advertising	1.79		2.10	0.90	-0.31	0.89
158	Employee wages	8.96		8.00	9.30	0.96	-0.34
159	Delivery	0.54		0.58	0.80	-0.04	-0.26
160	===						

Exploring "What Ifs" Continued

Increased cash available:

Old accounts receivable balance	$17,777
New accounts receivable balance	13,857
Additional cash available	$3,920

4 Estimate the approximate reduction in interest if Acme reduces its long-term debt by the additional cash available due to the accelerated accounts receivable collection. (Assume the rate of interest is 12 percent per year.)

Extra cash available × interest rate =

$3,920 × 12% = $470 interest saved the first year

The new interest in cell R20C2 will be $5,530 ($6,000 − $470).

5 Estimate the approximate impact on the income statement.

		Amount	%
Old net sales		$336,000	
Less: Sales discounts		1,008	
New net sales		$334,992	100.0
Cost of goods sold		221,760	66.2
Gross profit		113,232	33.8
General & admin. exp.	49,600		
Selling expense	49,000		
Depreciation	6,000	104,600	
Operating income		8,632	
Old interest	6,000		
Interest saved	470		
New Interest		5,530	
Net income before taxes		3,102	
Taxes		620	
Net income		$2,482	
Increase (decrease) in income		−430	
		($2,912 − $2,482)	

6 Estimate the change in annual long-term debt.

Old long-term debt balance (cell R64C2)	$44,110
Reduction in long-term debt due to acceleration in A/R collection	3,920
New long-term debt balance	$40,190

To restore
the worksheet to its original values

Goto R57C2 and type **18480** (RET)
    R108C2 and type **0** (RET)

To enter
changes in sales discounts, interest, accounts receivable, and long-term debt

Goto R9C2 and type **1008** (RET)
    R20C2 and type **5530** (RET)
    R37C2 and type **13857** (RET)
    R64C2 and type **40190** (RET)

Recalculate the worksheet

Result Net income ($2,482 in cell R26C2) and cash ($905 in cell R36C2) are each reduced by $430.

ANALYSIS The original accounts receivable collection period, applied to the 30 percent of sales that are on credit, is a horrendous 64 days (see above). This requires some action. Offering a 2-percent discount for payment in 15 days is an attempted solution.

The results of this change are:

1 A decrease in net income of $430. This reduces cash by $430 to $905.

2 A one-time reduction of $3,920 in long-term debt due to the accelerated accounts receivable collection.

3 The average collection period (cell R135C2) is only reduced to 50 days.

These indicate that, over the long term, the 2-percent discount ($1,008) will not produce sufficient savings in interest ($470) and taxes ($108, for a total of $578) to generate an annual improved cash position. Also, the discount only brings the collection period down to a still unacceptable 50 days. Thus, the 2/15 net 30 program won't do the job.

Perhaps a 2/10 net 30 with a 1-percent monthly charge for balances due beyond 30 days might be evaluated. Whatever is tried, it is clear that a significant internal effort should be made to screen and collect accounts receivable. A collection of 30 days would generate nearly $9,500 in cash and save over $1,100 in annual interest charges on borrowed money. After tax, this would be $880 of improved cash flow if no discounts were necessary.

Epilogue: Planning management strategy

The epilogue generally provides us with an opportunity to find out what the consequences were of foregoing action. In a murder mystery, we usually get to find out "who done it," and in an historical novel, we find out what happened to the long-lost brother/sister, lovers, business partners, enemies, and so forth . . . 20 years later. Here, in Mr. Adams's case, we have described a series of tools and have shown their application and impact on the business. However, although we are certainly interested in the results of changes in each of the subproblem areas, we are more concerned with the total, cumulative impact of these problem-solving activities. Much earlier we talked about using a systems view and how a system was composed of interrelated and interdependent parts. That is the most appropriate way of looking at our activities here. Problem solving in one area affects other areas. We have already considered these cross-implications to a limited extent. Now we are interested in looking at how the total system is affected by all of the decision options we have been exploring on an individual basis.

Up to this point, Mr. Adams has had an opportunity to explore different choices with each of the "What Ifs." By now (we hope), he has developed enough of an understanding of how his business operation works so that he is able to select the best of these "What If" options and bundle them together into a total business strategy. In reality, this process is quite complex, involving the interaction of a whole range of variables. However, our computer makes light work of this complexity and, as you have seen in the individual cases, is able to instantly show us the results of these different choices. We can now use our computer to integrate these choices into a single comprehensive strategy. The methodology here is simple and straightforward: We need to look back through each of our "What If" explorations and select the single alternatives that seem to have the most favorable implications for the total business operation. We will then incorporate all of these changes into an overall management strategy and be able to observe the aggregate impact on the total operation. We hope, especially if you have been following along with us in the earlier examples, that you will apply the same logic to your own operation. It may be helpful here, as we develop our comprehensive business strategy model, to turn back and inspect each of the subproblem areas if you don't remember quite how they worked or what the implications were of those subproblem-solving activities.

Following our good advice, Mr. Adams went back and reviewed the results of the "What If" problems that we explored in this chapter. Fortunately for all of us, Mr. Adams now feels that he has a much better idea of the things he can do to improve the performance of Acme Hardware. Accordingly, Mr. Adams has selected those alternatives that he feels will have the most favorable impact on the operation.

As with each of the earlier "What If" considerations, the way to determine the desirability of any of these choices is to measure the impact of the decisions on Acme Hardware's income statement and the breakeven levels. We can then see how the business stacks up under the same type of comparative analysis performed earlier.

Mr. Adams's choices follow:

1 Increase prices by 5 percent with a consequent 2 percent loss of customers. (Chapter 7, "What If" 5.)

2 Increase inventory turnover to 3.0 times through improved inventory control and more efficient purchasing by using EOQ. (Chapter 8, "What Ifs" 9 and 10.)

3 Aim for credit purchases in ten days in order to obtain a 2-percent purchase discount. (Chapter 10, "What If" 11.)

4 Borrow funds at 12 percent, adding to the present long-term debt, in order to take advantage of the purchase discounts. (Chapter 10, "What If" 11.)

5 Reduce the variable sales commission to 2.5 percent of gross sales. At the same time, eliminate the part-time salesperson who is paid $4,800 a year plus commission. (Chapter 6, "What If" 4.)

6 Offer a 2-percent discount for payments in ten days to credit customers. (Chapter 10, "What If" 12.)

7 Reduce long-term debt by the amount of the reduction in accounts receivable. (Chapter 10, "What If" 12.)

With further thought, Mr. Adams decided to add:

8 Increase gross profits to 38 percent through improved purchasing and by emphasizing higher-margin items in the marketing program; increase the fixed component of advertising by $2,000 to stimulate sales.

9 Reduce officer salaries to $18,000 until profit and return on equity improve.

Mr. Adams would like to determine:

1 The estimated impact of these decisions on Acme's income statement.

2 The impact on the various breakeven levels: sales revenue needed to break even, cover cash expense, and cover cash expense plus debt service.

3 The impact on the deviation analysis.

The complexity of this problem set and its compound results reflect the reality of the business world. However, Mr. Adams, or you, the user, would have to enter one change at a time to allow for the ramifications of each step upon the next. To save time, simply enter the following precalculated changes.

To enter

changes in gross sales, sales discounts, interest, accounts receivable, inventory, accounts payable, long-term debt, officer salaries, wages, advertising, inventory purchases, and supplier discounts

Goto **R8C2** and type **346080** (RET)
R9C2 and type **1038** (RET)
R20C2 and type **6927** (RET)
R37C2 and type **13163** (RET)
R38C2 and type **72624** (RET)
R57C2 and type **6140** (RET)
R64C2 and type **51836** (RET)
R82C2 and type **18000** (RET)
R94C2 and type **15200** (RET)
R94C3 and type **8652** (RET)
R97C2 and type **6000** (RET)
R107C4 and type **220979** (RET)
R108C2 and type **2** (RET)

Recalculate the worksheet

Result Net income has increased by $17,670 to $20,582 in cell R26C2. Cash has increased by $28,338 to $29,673 in cell R36C2. The three breakeven levels have decreased as follows: cell R116C4, from $322,683 to $264,381; cell R118C4, from $300,732 to $245,570; and cell R120C4, from $314,963 to $257,766.

ANALYSIS Mr. Adams's decisions, if implemented, could improve the store's position and financial statements considerably. The net income has improved 3.5 times over that of last year (cells R26C2 and R26C3). The return on equity before tax in cell R136C2 is a nifty 54 percent. All the income statement ratios are better than industry average and show considerable improvement over last year (columns 5 and 6). Debt interest payments of $6,927 in cell R20C2 are now well covered by the tripled operating income (cell R19C2). The only exception to industry data is the still slow collection of the accounts receivable: the average collection period is 46 days vs. 33 days for the industry as shown in published surveys. (Accounts receivable/

Daily credit sales = $13,163/$288 = 46. See "What If" 12, Step 1.) Industry averages can be found in reference books such as *Annual Statement Studies*, published annually by Robert Morris Associates.

The expense ratio analysis in relation to industry shows improvement in most areas (columns 5 and 6). However, the distribution of the expense is still troublesome. Advertising is approximately 150 percent higher than that of comparable stores (cells R157C2 and R157C4). Depreciation and rent are also above industry averages (cells R152C2 and R156C2 and R152C4 and R156C4).

The breakeven sales required are now significantly lower as a result of these decisions:

	Old annual breakeven levels	Revised annual breakeven levels	Reduction in breakeven sales needed
Sales to break even	$322,683	$264,381	$58,302
Sales to cover cash expenses	330,732	245,570	55,162
Sales to cover cash expenses & debt service	314,963	257,766	57,197

This is not only a reduction in breakeven sales requirements but also a great increase in the margin for error:

	Projected net sales	Revised breakeven levels	Margin for error amount	%
Sales to break even	$345,042	$264,381	$80,661	23.4
Sales to cover cash expenses	345,042	245,570	99,472	28.8
Sales to cover cash expenses & debt service	345,042	257,766	87,276	25.3

This shows that Acme can miscalculate sales by 23 to 28 percent and still cover the various categories of expense.

Mr. Adams's remaining concerns are these:

1 His ability to obtain 38.0 percent gross profit in an industry that averages 34 percent. If gross profit were 34 percent, operating income would be reduced approximately $14,000. After tax, this would reduce the net income to approximately $9,500, or a reduction of $11,000.

Epilogue

```
1 DECISION worksheet
2
3 INCOME STATEMENT: January 1 through December 31, 19..
```

	This year	% net sales	Last year	% net sales	Deviation $	Deviation %
8 Gross sales	346,080	100	312,000	100	34,080	11
9 Sales discounts	1,038	0	0	0	1,038	
10 Net sales	345,042	100	312,000	100	33,042	11
12 Cost of goods sold	213,935	62	201,240	65	12,695	6
13 Gross profit	131,107	38	110,760	36	20,347	18
15 General & administrative	47,600	14	52,000	17	-4,400	-8
16 Selling expenses	44,852	13	40,000	13	4,852	12
17 Depreciation	6,000	2	5,500	2	500	9
19 Operating income	32,655	9	13,260	4	19,395	146
20 Interest expense	6,927	2	6,750	2	177	3
21 Other income/expense	0	0	-800	-0	800	-100
23 Income before taxes	25,728	7	7,310	2	18,418	252
24 Taxes	5,146	1	1,462	0	3,684	252
26 NET INCOME	20,582	6	5,848	2	14,734	252

```
28 BALANCE SHEET: December 31, 19..
```

	This year	Last year
33 ASSETS:		
35 <Current assets>		
36 Cash	29,673	4,750
37 Accounts receivable	13,163	16,000
38 Inventory	72,624	70,000
39 Prepaid expenses	3,400	3,400
41 Total current assets	118,860	94,150
43 <Fixed assets>		
44 Buildings & equipment	33,000	38,950
45 Less accumulated depreciation	-13,000	-7,000
46 Land	0	0
48 Total fixed assets	20,000	31,950
50 Other assets	3,700	2,545
52 TOTAL ASSETS	142,560	128,645
54 LIABILITIES:		
56 <Current liabilities>		
57 Accounts payable	6,140	17,000
58 Accrued wages & taxes	6,357	6,000
59 Notes payable (current)	3,890	3,890
60 Other current liabilities	5,900	5,900
62 Total current liabilities	22,287	32,790
64 Long-term debt	51,836	48,000
66 Total liabilities	74,123	80,790
68 <Owner equity>		
69 Common stock	37,000	37,000
70 Retained earnings	31,437	10,855
72 Total owner equity	68,437	47,855
74 TOTAL LIABILITIES & EQUITY	142,560	128,645

```
77 Analysis section
```

79 G&A EXPENSE BREAKDOWN	Fixed	Variable	Total
81 Rent	12,000	0	12,000
82 Officer salaries	18,000	0	18,000
83 Clerical expenses	4,000	1,000	5,000
84 Insurance	3,600	0	3,600
85 Utilities	2,000	400	2,400
86 Office supplies	800	400	1,200
87 Legal & accounting	3,000	0	3,000
88 Miscellaneous	1,200	1,200	2,400
90 Total G&A expenses	44,600	3,000	47,600

92 SELLING EXPENSE BREAKDOWN	Fixed	Variable	Total
94 Wages	15,200	8,652	23,852
95 Delivery	0	1,800	1,800
96 Operating supplies	4,000	800	4,800
97 Advertising	6,000	2,000	8,000
98 Travel & entertainment	800	400	1,200
99 Miscellaneous	800	400	1,200
100 Credit card	0	4,000	4,000
102 Total selling expenses	26,800	18,052	44,852

```
104 COST OF GOODS SOLD ANALYSIS
106 Beginning inventory                      70,000
107 Inventory purchases                     220,979
108 Less purchase discounts of   2 percent   -4,420
109 Total goods available                   286,559
110 Less ending inventory                    72,624
112 Cost of goods sold                      213,935

114 BREAKEVEN ANALYSIS
116 Sales revenue needed to break even               264,381
118 Sales revenue needed to cover cash expenses      245,570
120 Sales revenue needed to cover cash expenses      257,766
121 and debt service

123 CASH FLOW ANALYSIS
125 Net cash throwoff from the income statement        26,582

129 Ratios section
131 BALANCE SHEET RATIOS           This year
134 Inventory turnover              3.00 times
135 Average collection period      45.78 days
136 Return on equity               53.76 percent
137 Accts. payable payment period  10.00 days
```

139 INCOME STATEMENT RATIOS (% of net sales)	This year	Last year	Industry averages	Deviation Last year	Deviation Industry averages
143 Gross profit	38.00	35.50	34.00	2.50	4.00
144 Profit (before taxes)	7.46	2.34	3.00	5.12	4.46
145 Profit (after taxes)	5.97	1.87	3.00	4.10	2.97

147 OPERATING EXPENSE RATIOS (% of net sales)	This year	Last year	Industry averages	Deviation Last year	Deviation Industry averages
151 Officer salaries	5.22	5.80	5.30	-0.58	-0.08
152 Rent	3.48	3.20	2.70	0.28	0.78
153 Utilities	0.70	1.00	1.00	-0.30	-0.30
154 Insurance	1.04	1.00	0.80	0.04	0.24
155 Interest	2.01	2.16	1.90	-0.15	0.11
156 Depreciation	1.74	1.76	1.00	-0.02	0.74
157 Advertising	2.32	2.10	0.90	0.22	1.42
158 Employee wages	6.91	8.00	9.30	-1.09	-2.39
159 Delivery	0.52	0.58	0.80	-0.06	-0.28

2 His ability to achieve an inventory turnover of 3.0. A turnover of 2.3 (the industry average) would increase cash needs for inventory by approximately $20,000 (cost of goods sold divided by 2.3 = $93,000 average inventory).

3 The reduction in the sales staff may make it difficult to achieve the increased sales. On the other hand, perhaps the increase in advertising will compensate for this reduction.

If these results are achieved, the business will, happily, have excess cash of $20,000 or more. The next decision is how to use this cash. Perhaps the long-term debt can be reduced or the funds can be invested.

The successful implementation of the proposed decisions clearly shows how the dramatic impact of changes can put a firm above industry averages. The financial rewards are comforting and make future decision making, even in a competitive business, much easier.

✓ Troubleshooting

If you encounter any problems with your worksheet, either when entering it or when using it to explore the "What Ifs," here are some suggestions on how to identify the problem.

If your worksheet doesn't give results identical to those described in the book, there are several possible causes. Listed in order of their likelihood they include:

1 The worksheet wasn't recalculated with the ! or recalculation function key.

2 Values or formulas were not entered correctly into the worksheet.

3 After changing some numbers in a "What If," you neglected to restore the worksheet to its original values before proceeding with the next step.

4 When entering changes in the worksheet, you inadvertently typed a value into a cell containing a formula, erasing the formula.

5 After making changes in a "What If," you saved the changed file on top of the original example by mistake. You should never save a "What If" file, and you should write-protect the disk containing the original worksheet when it's finished so this can't happen. See "Protecting your worksheets" on page 42.

The first step is to identify the cause of the problem:

Step 1. If you noticed the problem when you explored "What Ifs," clear the screen and reload the original worksheet. See if that cleared the problem up. If so, it was probably caused by 2 or 3 above. If the problem still exists, go on to the next step.

Step 2. Check the basics. When you follow the troubleshooting steps below, first set recalculation to automatic by using the Option command and always check the worksheet from the top down. If you follow both of these suggestions, any error you correct will automatically recalculate all values in the entire worksheet. This will prevent you from exploring figures that appear to be incorrect because they haven't been recalculated.

Step 3. Check the totals against the printout on page 136. Begin by checking the totals in columns 2 and 4 to see if they are correct; if one of them isn't, you have located the general area of the problem. The key total lines should read as follows:

Row #	Item	Column 2	Column 4
26	Net income	2,912	5,848
52	Total assets	129,504	128,645
66	Total liabilities	78,737	80,790
72	Total owner equity	50,767	47,855

Step 4. If in Step 3 above you isolated the problem on a specific statement, begin checking the columns of that statement against the printout on page 136 row by row. If none of the totals were incorrect in Step 3, you will have to check both columns from row 8 to row 74. Values can be checked against the printout on page 136, but formulas will have to be checked by finding the section in the book where they were entered, and comparing them against the "type" instructions for the appropriate row.

■ If you have to check the entire column, begin at row 8 and use the ⬇ key to scroll down the column, comparing each entry with the printout on page 136.

■ If you find a figure that doesn't match, put the cursor in that space and read the cell contents line to see if the cell contains a formula or value. If it contains a formula, check it against the formula that you entered earlier in this book.

■ If the cell contains a value, check to see if it should. You may have inadvertently typed a value on top of a formula. Check the cell contents against the entry you should have made.

Note: If the figures that are wrong are in column 4, and are either cost of goods sold, general and administrative expenses, or selling expenses, then the problem might be caused by values or formulas on one of the breakdowns in the analysis section. See the appropriate chapter, and compare the cell contents against the step-by-step instructions.

Step 5. If any of the numbers in the columns are different from the figures in the book, change them, making sure not to type over formulas. You can always tell what is in a cell by looking at the cell contents line on the top of the Multiplan screen display when your cursor is positioned in that cell.

Printout of original worksheet

```
         1              2      3      4      5      6      7
 1 DECISION worksheet
 2
 3 INCOME STATEMENT: January 1 through December 31, 19..
 4 =========================================================
 5                      This   % net  Last   % net  <----Deviation---->
 6                      year   sales  year   sales    $      %
 7 -------------------------------------------------------
 8 Gross sales          336,000  100  312,000  100  24,000    8
 9 Sales discounts            0    0        0    0       0    0
10 Net sales            336,000  100  312,000  100  24,000    8
11 -------------------------------------------------------
12 Cost of goods sold   221,760   66  201,240   65  20,520   10
13 Gross profit         114,240   34  110,760   36   3,480    3
14 -------------------------------------------------------
15 General & administrative 49,600  15  52,000   17  -2,400   -5
16 Selling expense      49,000    15  40,000    13   9,000   23
17 Depreciation          6,000     2   5,500     2     500    9
18 -------------------------------------------------------
19 Operating income      9,640     3  13,260     4  -3,620  -27
20 Interest expense      6,000     2   6,750     2    -750  -11
21 Other income/expense      0     0    -800    -0     800 -100
22 -------------------------------------------------------
23 Income before taxes   3,640     1   7,310     2  -3,670  -50
24 Taxes                   728     0   1,462     0    -734  -50
25 -------------------------------------------------------
26 NET INCOME            2,912     1   5,848     2  -2,936  -50
27 =========================================================
28 BALANCE SHEET: December 31, 19..
29 =========================================================
30                      This          Last
31                      year          year
32 -------------------------------------------------------
33 ASSETS:
34 -------------------------------------------------------
35 <Current assets>
36 Cash                  1,335         4,750
37 Accounts receivable  17,777        16,000
38 Inventory            83,292        70,000
39 Prepaid expenses      3,400         3,400
40 -------------------------------------------------------
41 Total current assets 105,804       94,150
42 -------------------------------------------------------
43 <Fixed assets>
44 Buildings & equipment 33,000       38,950
45 Less accumulated depreciation -13,000  -7,000
46 Land                      0             0
47 -------------------------------------------------------
48 Total fixed assets   20,000        31,950
49 -------------------------------------------------------
50 Other assets          3,700         2,545
51 -------------------------------------------------------
52 TOTAL ASSETS         129,504      128,645
53 =========================================================
54 LIABILITIES:
55 -------------------------------------------------------
56 <Current liabilities>
57 Accounts payable     18,480        17,000
58 Accrued wages & taxes 6,357         6,000
59 Notes payable (current) 3,890        3,890
60 Other current liabilities 5,900     5,900
61 -------------------------------------------------------
62 Total current liabilities 34,627   32,790
63 -------------------------------------------------------
64 Long-term debt       44,110        48,000
65 -------------------------------------------------------
66 Total liabilities    78,737        80,790
67 -------------------------------------------------------
68 <Owner equity>
69 Common stock         37,000        37,000
70 Retained earnings    13,767        10,855
71 -------------------------------------------------------
72 Total owner equity   50,767        47,855
73 -------------------------------------------------------
74 TOTAL LIABILITIES & EQUITY 129,504 128,645
75 =========================================================
```

```
         1              2      3      4      5      6      7
77 Analysis section
78 =========================================================
79 G&A EXPENSE BREAKDOWN    Fixed  Variable  Total
80 -------------------------------------------------------
81 Rent                    12,000      0    12,000
82 Officer salaries        20,000      0    20,000
83 Clerical expense         4,000  1,000     5,000
84 Insurance                3,600      0     3,600
85 Utilities                2,000    400     2,400
86 Office supplies            800    400     1,200
87 Legal & accounting       3,000      0     3,000
88 Miscellaneous            1,200  1,200     2,400
89 -------------------------------------------------------
90 Total G&A expenses      46,600  3,000    49,600
91 =========================================================
92 SELLING EXPENSE BREAKDOWN  Fixed Variable Total
93 -------------------------------------------------------
94 Wages                   20,000 10,000    30,000
95 Delivery                     0  1,800     1,800
96 Operating supplies       4,000    800     4,800
97 Advertising              4,000  2,000     6,000
98 Travel & entertainment     800    400     1,200
99 Miscellaneous              800    400     1,200
100 Credit card                 0  4,000     4,000
101 -------------------------------------------------------
102 Total selling expenses  29,600 19,400    49,000
103 =========================================================
104 COST OF GOODS ANALYSIS
105 -------------------------------------------------------
106 Beginning inventory                     70,000
107 Inventory purchases                    235,052
108 Less purchase discounts of  0 percent        0
109 Total goods available                  305,052
110 Less ending inventory                   83,292
111 -------------------------------------------------------
112 Cost of goods sold                     221,760
113 =========================================================
114 BREAKEVEN ANALYSIS
115 -------------------------------------------------------
116 Sales revenue needed to break even     322,683
117 -------------------------------------------------------
118 Sales revenue needed to cover cash expenses  300,732
119 -------------------------------------------------------
120 Sales revenue needed to cover cash expenses  314,963
121 and debt service
122 =========================================================
123 CASH FLOW ANALYSIS
124 -------------------------------------------------------
125 Net cash throwoff from the income statement   8,912
126 =========================================================
127
128
129 Ratios section
130 =========================================================
131 BALANCE SHEET RATIOS          This
132                               year
133 -------------------------------------------------------
134 Inventory turnover       2.89 times
135 Average collection period 63.49 days
136 Return on equity          7.61 percent
137 Accts. payable payment period 28.30 days
138 =========================================================
139 INCOME STATEMENT RATIOS                     <----Deviation---->
140 (% of net sales)         This    Last  Industry  Last  Industry
141                          year    year  averages  year  averages
142 -------------------------------------------------------
143 Gross profit            34.00   35.50   34.00   -1.50    0.00
144 Profit (before taxes)    1.08    2.34    3.00   -1.26   -1.92
145 Profit (after taxes)     0.87    1.87    3.00   -1.00   -2.13
146 =========================================================
147 OPERATING EXPENSE RATIOS                    <----Deviation---->
148 (% of net sales)         This    Last  Industry  Last  Industry
149                          year    year  averages  year  averages
150 -------------------------------------------------------
151 Officer salaries         5.95    5.80    5.30    0.15    0.65
152 Rent                     3.57    3.20    2.70    0.37    0.87
153 Utilities                0.71    1.00    1.00   -0.29   -0.29
154 Insurance                1.07    1.00    0.80    0.07    0.27
155 Interest                 1.79    2.16    1.90   -0.37   -0.11
156 Depreciation             1.79    1.76    1.00    0.03    0.79
157 Advertising              1.79    2.10    0.90   -0.31    0.89
158 Employee wages           8.93    8.00    9.30    0.93   -0.37
159 Delivery                 0.54    0.58    0.80   -0.04   -0.26
160 =========================================================
```

Step 6. Check your corrections. Check to make sure all totals and ratios match the illustration on page 136. If the ratios don't match those in the illustration, you still have a problem. Look up the ratio formula in this book, and check to see if the values in each cell are correct. Find out what contributes to the incorrect cell: for instance, a total is the sum of the rows above it, so perhaps one of those rows is wrong.

Things to look for: A troubleshooter's checklist

Format errors. Do you show too many or too few digits for ease of readability or the required precision? To know that your profit is 10.1001345% doesn't tell you much more than knowing that your profit is 10%. In this case, formatting the screen with the Format Cells command makes it easier to read and compare figures.

Formula errors. These can frequently be found by displaying your formulas with the Format Options command, and then checking them against the row descriptions in this book. Scan the step illustrations to find the section in which the row or column involved was entered, and check that section to see if the illustration and your cell contents match. If you still don't get the right answer, it is wise to assume some independent judgment. Although the authors have tried to be painfully accurate, mistakes do happen.

Recalculation errors. When troubleshooting the example, be sure your recalculation mode is set to automatic. This will ensure that once an error is corrected, the sheet will be recalculated and any rows to which the cell referred will be corrected as well. If the worksheet is recalculating manually, any data entered or changes made won't be carried throughout the worksheet. There are many forward references in this example, so in some cases the ! or recalculation key has to be pressed as many as three times. You should always hit the ! key at least once before printing or examining a report.

Copying errors. If you have a serious problem, such as an entire section that isn't functioning properly, the problem was probably caused when you copied an incorrect formula to a row or column or cells. Fortunately, errors caused in this way are frequently so bizarre that the problem is immediately obvious.

Error messages. These are usually caused by incorrect formulas, such as #DIV0! (division by zero), #REF! (nonexistent cell reference) or "unresolved circular references." Cells which refer to the incorrect cell will also display the same error message, so you should track back to the first error and correct it.

Index

Disk order form

SAVE TIME AND ENERGY . . . A special disk is available that contains the completed example and worksheets used throughout this book. Although this disk isn't essential, it will save you time and energy because you don't have to enter the example and worksheets yourself and it eliminates the possibility of introducing errors. You can begin immediately to explore the principles and problems of business. Since Curtin & London disks are not write-protected, you can adapt or customize the templates and make copies for use on more than one computer.

As this book goes to press, disks are available for Apple and IBM Personal Computers and IBM PC compatibles. However, disks for other personal computers will be available in the future, so please inquire about other formats.

If you did not purchase the Disk Edition of this book, write directly to the publisher at the address on the order form. The disk will be shipped via UPS within two days of receipt of your order and complete payment. For a small additional fee (see order form), we will ship the disk via UPS Second Day Air. To assure prompt delivery of the correct disk, please be sure to enclose correct payment together with your completely filled out order form and mail to:

Curtin & London, Inc.
6 Vernon Street
Somerville, MA 02145